THE UNSETTLED ACCOUNT

THE UNSETTLED ACCOUNT

AN AUTOBIOGRAPHY
by
EUGENIA HUNTINGDON

This title first published in the U.S.A. 1988 by
SEVERN HOUSE PUBLISHERS INC.
First World edition published in Great Britain 1986 by
SEVERN HOUSE PUBLISHERS LTD. of
40–42 William IV Street, London WC2N 4DF.

Reprinted 1988

British Library Cataloguing in Publication Data
Huntingdon, Eugenia
The unsettled account.
1. Poles—Russian S.F.S.R.—Siberia
—Social life and customs   2. Siberia
(R.S.F.S.R.)—Social life and customs
I. Title
957'.0842'0924   DK759.P6
ISBN 0-7278-2085-0

Back cover photograph by Ray Marwood

Typeset by The Word Factory, Lancashire.

Printed in Great Britain
at the University Printing House, Oxford

To my granddaughters Zofia and Wanda

CONTENTS

Prologue

Yet another day of travelling and our mobile prison takes us further and further away from our country and from everybody and everything that is familiar and dear to us. We have no idea how long the journey is going to last and where our jailers are taking us. Each day we feel more and more acutely the cold, hunger and, most of all, the extreme deprivation and misery of our children. The cattle wagon into which fifty or so of us are crammed is bitterly cold as it has no heating at all and the icy wind and the snow are blowing through the many cracks in the walls. In the middle of April, when we were forced to leave our homes in the south of Poland, spring was well advanced but now we are passing through countryside still in the grip of severe winter.

We are hungry because, unlike ordinary prisoners, we are not issued with daily meals, but only with some hot water for tea and, from time to time, with loaves of heavy dark bread. Since we boarded the train a week ago we have not been allowed out of our car and do not have any water for even a superficial wash. The results are repellent.

As long as the train moves people are reasonably quiet. The monotonous rattle of the wheels and the vibrations seem to mesmerise everyone into a state of apathy. There is also a feeling that we are progressing towards the end of our journey and that whatever awaits us should be better than this. Unfortunately there are frequent interruptions to this journey which

ix

almost always happen at night, probably to avoid even the most surreptitious contact with the local population, which would confirm the sinister meaning of our journey east. Inside the car most people take such interruptions to be the end of the journey, which gives rise to panic as everybody tries to sort out and collect their belongings in a hurry. This is far from easy, especially in the dark, and hence there is confusion and even quarrels. We, on our bunk, try to remain calm and only the pounding of our hearts betrays our inner state. Outside there is the usual commotion; sounds of running feet, loud and crude exchanges between the soldiers escorting our train, flashes of light from lamps carried by the railway staff. Finally, when the unnerving and now familiar tapping of the wheels begins, we know that this is just another of those frustrating delays we had experienced before. For me personally the physical hardships, however bad, are easier to bear than the feelings of outrage at the thought of the great injustice being done to us. During the sleepless nights, in the car, I relive the nightmarish experience of Soviet soldiers, with guns at the ready, bursting into our bedroom in Poland in the middle of the night, and I try in vain to get over the shock. I still remember the bewildered look on the faces of the uncouth Soviet soldiers at the sight of my body clad in a flimsy silk nightgown, and can still hear the plaintive cry of my child brutally aroused out of his sleep and ordered to dress. I cannot get over the humiliation of being pushed about and herded into that smelly cattlewagon. I cannot suppress my anger and despair at the thought of my gallant husband imprisoned by the inhuman rulers of the country against which he did not commit any crime, and with which we are not at war.

During the sleepless nights I also try to seek escape from my impotent, bottled-up anger against that inhuman regime, by thinking of my recent and very happy life in Poland.

THE UNSETTLED ACCOUNT

Early Days in Russia

My father's ancestors came from the South-West of Poland, with the beautiful and scholarly city of Cracow as its capital. The family name, Drozdowski, was closely associated with the region, and one of its members Alexsander Drozdowski, bearing the title of Margrave, became, around 1700, the Governor of Cracow and its domain.

In 1795, following the third Partition of Poland, the whole region became part of the Austro-Hungarian Empire.

My mother's family originated from the North-East with Wilno as its main city. At the time of my birth, in September 1910, my parents lived in Wilno, which was under Russian rule. Here the life of the Polish inhabitants was harsh, as the Russians tried to destroy anything connected with Polish tradition and culture. Use of the Polish language was banned in public and could only be taught secretly. Punishment for such activity was very severe – imprisonment or, more often, confiscation of property and deportation to Siberia. In spite of that, a secret school existed in my grandmother's house in Wilno.

Persecution of the population for real or alleged anti-Russian activities was commonplace and my father became one of its victims. However, for some unknown reason, instead of being sent to Siberia he was sentenced to so-called free exile. He had to leave his native land, but was allowed to settle in Russia itself, anywhere except in St. Petersburg. He chose a suburb of Moscow, Petrovski Park, so called because a

1

castle named after Peter the Great, former Tsar of Russia, was situated there. It was only natural that my mother should follow him into exile and thus, at the age of six months, I started my life of long travels.

My parents rented a house in Petrovski Park not far from the castle. It faced a natural park in the centre of which was a café in the form of a rotunda. This was surrounded by cultivated lawns and colourful flowerbeds. As these were designed to follow the circular shape of the café the whole area was called *kruzok*, which means circle in Russian. The café was open only in summer and a band played there every day, attracting the local society – mostly ladies who arrived in open carriages either to meet friends for a chat or just to go for a ride.

I have vivid memories of life in Moscow from my earliest years there, partly because all four seasons of the year differed dramatically from each other. Each had its charm, but, oddly enough, I seem to remember the winters most of all. Long, frosty white winters. For me they meant rides in a horse-drawn sledge. It was such a delight to get under the furry apron which the coachman fastened to the sides of the sledge, carefully tucking it round my legs. Frost pinched our noses and cheeks, painted our eyelashes and hair white and turned the ends of the coachman's moustache into two icicles. Little bells jingled at every movement of the horse's head and snow crunched crisply under its hooves. And after such a ride how pleasant it was to come into a warm house, jump up and down in the hallway to shake the snow from one's felt boots and coat and watch it turn rapidly into drops of water!

In the summer there were picnics in the huge Petrovsko-Razumovski forest where we competed with each other to collect the most wild strawberries, blueberries or mushrooms. Usually we went there by *britzka*, a light open carriage drawn by two horses, and the journey caused lots of excitement and laughter, or cries of anguish when the *britzka* jolted unexpectedly on the protruding roots of trees, or leaned dangerously to one side.

There was not much to do in the spring, but it was a remarkable season in its way. It was so unpredictable. The winter snow melted, sometimes rapidly, sometimes agonisingly slowly. One day water was running from the gutters and roofs; the next, icicles were hanging down again. Sometimes spring came in March, only to retreat quickly and wait until May, before returning.

Although my father was not allowed to visit his native land, my mother was able to visit Wilno every year to see her parents. She once took me with her and I remember a toy which my grandmother gave me – a cow almost as tall as me, covered with real hide. It had a hidden container in its back into which milk could be poured, so that its udders produced milk. It was an object of great envy among the other children and I was very proud of it, although, for some reason unknown to me, my mother did not approve of it. I also remember an illuminated religious volume. It lay on a little table in the drawing-room and I had some difficulty in pulling it on to my knees as it was thick and heavy. I used to close my eyes, put my hand inside the book and open it at random. Holding my breath, I would open my eyes to see what fate had in store for me. I sighed with relief if I saw scenes from the lives of the Saints, with a benevolent-looking God sitting on His throne on top of frothy clouds and surrounded by floating angels. These were very nice to look at, but did not hold my attention for long. What really fascinated me were pages depicting hairy demons with huge forks in their claws, and all kinds of repulsive monsters dancing round a seething cauldron, filled with distorted human bodies. If I happened to open the book on such a page, I closed it quickly, only to open and close it again and again until I was paralysed with fear. Apart from the angels and demons, the book contained scenes from the lives of ordinary mortals. Sometimes there were beautifully dressed ladies with elaborate hair-styles and at other times, very plain-looking women with plastered down hair and shabbily dressed. What puzzled me was that those beautiful ladies were depicted with hearts filled with demons

3

and monsters, while the plain women's hearts housed angels and saints. When I asked my grandmother for an explanation, she told me about the pitfalls of vanity and of attaching too much importance to clothes. I was shattered. Apparently, at an early age I was betraying a considerable degree of vanity and an excessive interest in clothes and now I was in a real dilemma about which way of life to choose. Being cooked alive in a cauldron or roasted on a spit did not seem to me much worse than spending the rest of my life with plastered-down hair and ugly clothes.

During that same trip to Wilno I also visited my godmother, who was a very eccentric lady and the subject of amusing anecdotes even many years after her death. She lived in a large house which surrounded a courtyard on three sides. On the fourth there was an imposing gate in the middle of a tall wall. The front door faced the gate and the path between was of marble, lined with palm trees in huge pots. I imagine that these must have been brought indoors during the winter. Overhead along the path were large coloured balls suspended from wires. From the hall you went straight into the drawing-room, the windows of which faced the gate. Opposite one of the windows my godmother sat on a podium in a large arm-chair covered with red plush and gold trimmings, watching everyone who crossed the gate. Her fingers were covered in rings and her chest with gold chains. She seemed tall and majestic-looking then. When my mother and I returned to Poland some years later, I was surprised to see how tiny she was. At that time she was contemplating her fourth marriage and her fiancé was complaining that when he proposed to her, not only did he have to kneel and kiss her hand, but her feet as well. I think that the prospect of inheriting her wealth must have made it much easier for him. He was much younger than she, but as far as I know, she outlived him.

At the rear of my godmother's house, facing the narrow back street (which, I think, belonged to her as well) were the stables. Unusually they had large windows adorned with net curtains and plants, behind which stunned passers-by could

4

see horses' faces peering at them. My godmother maintained that her horses were as sensitive to their surroundings as humans.

The war unleashed in 1914 gradually brought changes to our lives in Moscow. New people began to appear in our house. Distant relatives, escaping from the advancing Germans, friends of the family and the friends of friends, all came seeking temporary shelter. Quite often men in military uniform arrived, some in bandages and leaning on sticks or crutches. At times all beds and divans were occupied, and people lay on floors all over the house. Having undergone Red Cross training, for which she volunteered, my mother was helping to nurse wounded soldiers in the castle, now turned into a hospital, and I very seldom saw her at home. My father kissed me one day and then disappeared for ever. When I was older I learned that, after the collapse of the Tsar's army at the start of the Revolution, he joined the White Guards fighting the Bolsheviks in Russia. At first my parents' absence did not affect my life very much as they had never devoted very much time to me. My upbringing and later my education was entrusted to Mme Marie, a Polish widow of a doctor, who lived with us and acted as my governess. I was passionately attached to her.

Drastic changes came with the Bolshevik Revolution of 1917. Even a child as young as I then was could not fail to notice them. Sweets and fruit disappeared from our table. The cook and maid left. Their duties were taken over by a distant relative, a refugee from the west, who stopped with us 'temporarily' with her little daughter who was about my age. Carriage horses vanished from the stable and were replaced by a cow, which was much more useful because the milk delivery had stopped. Finally, when it was no longer possible to get fodder for the cow, she was replaced by a nanny-goat who could live on boiled potato peelings. For me the most painful parting was from my dear Mme Marie who found a job in the household of an important Bolshevik.

My mother, by now an experienced nurse, found a job and

thanks to that we were allowed to stay in our old home, although we had to share it with two other families. A few years later we all had to move out because the house was requisitioned by the state and turned into a kind of people's recreation home. We moved into a much more modest part of Petrovski Park, where we were given one room in a flat occupied by the family of a professor from Moscow University. The family consisted of his wife, two children and a servant girl who was passed off as a relative because no one was allowed to have servants. Being next to the kitchen, the room was warm, so we did not have to worry about getting fuel which was difficult to obtain.

The professor was probably someone quite important in the Party hierarchy because, while other people starved, his family never seemed to be in want of anything. We seldom saw him and I became quite friendly with his children, a boy of nine and a girl in her teens, although their mother always tried to keep a distance between us. I think that my mother was even less keen on that friendship, fearing that the girl might have a bad influence on me. I have never seen such shocking behaviour of children towards their mother. If she refused any of their demands the food would be pushed from the table to the floor, and on a few occasions I saw buttered bread thrown straight into her face. I could never understand how she could have tolerated such manners or why. In fact, the boy was quite gentle, but was made to follow his sister's example. She could be a real fiend in other ways as well. In the hall of the flat was my mother's large trunk on which the servant girl usually slept. Often, when passing through the hall, I would see the daughter playing sex games with the girl. Luckily neither my mother nor I were often at home. Lessons and other occupations took most of my time. I was unable to attend school although my parents did enter my name as a boarder for the Convent of St Catherine (situated in Milutinski Street in the centre of Moscow) to which I was supposed to go when I was seven. But things changed with the war and the Revolution and St Catherine's was turned into a day school, and the daily journey was impossible. There was no suitable school in Petrovski Park and other families had similar difficulties. The new masters busied themselves in other parts of Moscow, not paying much attention to the educational problems of this 'nest of bourgoisie', from which by now most males had been removed, and the women and children could be left alone for the moment. A solution had to be found within the parents' own resources, and someone discovered a retired schoolmistress who agreed to start classes so long as at least four girls of the same age would attend. This was not difficult to arrange and very soon our own little group was formed. Apart from myself there was a doctor's daughter, Shoura, (the lucky one who still had both parents at home), and Katia, the daughter of an ex-millionaire, owner of a famous biscuit factory, who had been arrested and executed at the start of the Revolution. Katia and her beautiful mother still lived in their old home. The mother now acted as house-keeper to a high Party official who was mostly away, but when he did come back he often brought other dignitaries, and large parties were held there. We could never learn from Katia what life was like in that house as she seemed reluctant to discuss it. We felt a great sympathy for her, even though we knew that, unlike us, she had no problems about food and other everyday necessities, which, in those days, could make people envious. Even at that early age we understood that there were things of more value than food and we suspected that she greatly missed her father and hated the man who now ruled her home, and was probably ashamed of her mother. There was an aura of unhappiness about her. By contrast the fourth girl, Nura, was always cheerful, though God knows why. Her mother, a widow with three other children pre-viously earned her living as a high-class dressmaker and con-tinued to work even now, although there was little demand for smart clothes. Her services were mostly needed for altering clothes for the fast-growing children of her former clients. Nura never complained but we knew that the family was often short of food and that the flat in which they lived was very

7

cold in winter. Officially, there was no recognised job for Nura's mother in Petrovski Park and she had to rely entirely on her clients. We all used to bring our 'second breakfast' to class, all that is, except Nura with whom we used to share our food, which she accepted quite naturally and cheerfully. At times Katia brought enough food for all of us and then Nura could even take some home.

We took our lessons seriously and tried to work hard. We started at nine o'clock each day except Sunday and finished about two. We were taught arithmetic, Russian language and grammar, history (for some reason with an accent on Greek mythology, which we enjoyed most of all) and geography. I was the only Polish girl in the group so it was left to my mother to teach me my native tongue. In addition, two afternoons a week were devoted to French conversation, and the lady who taught us was something of a mystery. She always wore a very thick veil over her face which, we understood, was disfigured. As compensation she had the sweetest voice and manner one could imagine. Her teenage son sometimes took part in reciting Russian poetry with us and he and I became good friends. His mother encouraged this friendship saying that I exercised a good influence over him. We went skiing together and he often met me on my way to lessons offering to carry my books. I suppose he was my first boyfriend.

Much to my disappointment I had to resume piano practice, which had been interrupted when we were turned out of our house as the piano, together with other furniture, had to be left behind. Now one of my mother's friends offered the use of her piano because she thought it would encourage her daughter to compete with me and that we would play duets together. In my opinion the daughter needed no challenge and I thought the whole idea preposterous, but my mother insisted that I spend at least an hour three times a week at the piano. Personally I preferred to spend it on skis while the winter lasted. Skiing was a very popular sport for the young people in Petrovski Park. There were no hills but conditions for ski runs on the level were excellent. We often used skis as a means of transport and I invariably went to my lessons on skis in winter, carrying books in a satchel on my back. This, however, I considered rather as a necessity; the real skiing was in the afternoons with a lot of young people racing, and piano practice was too great an interference.

Petrovski Park had two main parallel thoroughfares, one was a commercial area with modest dwellings, shops, tearooms and small workshops, while the other was a long tree-lined boulevard. In summer the boulevard swarmed with people either passing through or just promenading, but in winter it was covered in deep snow, and because no one bothered to clear it away, it was ideal for ski-racing. Between the commercial section and the boulevard ran streets forming residential quarters with beautiful villas in large gardens. At the outbreak of the Revolution many of the villas were looted, often by the servants who had been left in charge. Later on these houses, emptied of their contents and stripped of brocade wall coverings and other lavish trimmings, were either requisitioned as homes for Party officials or used as public buildings. I can still remember the looting and the wild cries of the mob as they made bonfires of antique furniture, works of art and rare books.

Pre-war Petrovski Park was famous not only for its beautiful setting, but also for its restaurants and night clubs, where gypsy orchestras and graceful, fiery gypsy girls entertained the guests. In the centre of the Park was the fabulous 'Strelna' restaurant with its Winter Garden and, not far away, no less a renowned restaurant 'Yar'. Both these places had been frequented by the notorious Grigori Rasputin, whenever he visited Moscow. Nearby was Khodynka Fields where in 1896 3,000 people were trampled to death in a stampede to get free food and drink during the celebrations of Tsar Nicholas II's coronation. Now Khodynka Fields were used as an aerodrome, and one of the pilots was given a villa in Petrovski Park.

To our great delight his wife, who had been a ballerina, decided to open a ballet school. I immediately wanted to join and my mother, who doubtless thought that the busier I was the better it would be for everyone, gave her consent. While I was busy with my lessons and all the other activities, my mother's work kept her out most of the time. She now worked as an assistant to the local doctor, helping him in his surgery and sometimes accompanying him on his visits to patients. She also had her own small practice when someone needed an injection or cupping. The latter was in great demand when people had coughs or colds. Her previous work for the Red Cross enabled her to register as a nurse. This gave her the status of a useful citizen of the new Bolshevik regime instead of the stigma of being so-called parasitical bourgoisie which she would doubtless have carried, together with all the unpleasant consequences. Now she was entitled to food rations for the two of us at government prices instead of having to pay black market rates. Private patients were asked to pay in kind instead of cash, which meant we could live without starving and did not have to trade jewellery and other valuables for food.

By 1922 I was quite used to our new way of life, living in one room, queuing for bread, drinking substitute tea and acorn coffee sweetened with saccharine, and eating horse meat which was often stale and smelt badly. I had many friends among the local boys and girls. Friendships in those difficult times were far more intense and meaningful than they would ever again be for me, so that when my mother began to mention the prospect of our returning to Poland, I was torn between the desire to go back to the land of my ancestors and the pain at the thought of parting from my very dear friends.

With Poland's independence there was now a possibility that we would be able to leave Russia and return to our homeland. Our relative and her little daughter had returned to Poland a few years previously. However it was difficult for my mother to get permission to leave because strictly speaking we were not refugees having lived in Russia, albeit involuntarily, for many years. We were lucky because one of our close relatives had arrived from Poland as the Head of the

Repatriation Commission, and thanks to him, things went reasonably smoothly. My mother, who had been trying to get news of my father for a long time, was finally told that he had been executed for being an officer of the White Guards fighting against the Red Army. Our repatriation came in 1924 and, after a long and tiring train journey, we reached Wilno, where many unpleasant surprises awaited us.

My mother was entitled to a considerable inheritance, but on arrival we did not find even a small corner to live in. Our relatives had taken everything, establishing their rights by claiming that both my parents were executed, and that I had died of typhoid fever in Russia. My mother had to employ a solicitor to claim back her inheritance and in the meantime we had to live in a hotel. Luckily she still had some valuable pieces of jewellery and gold coins, which she had succeeded in smuggling from Russia, some in a false-bottomed saucepan, and some sewn into clothes. The man who had hidden them for us in Moscow had done so in great secrecy and at odd moments when no one else was present. He knew that we were leaving Russia for good and might have taken advantage of the situation so our relief, joy and gratitude to that good man, when we once again saw our treasures, can well be imagined. The sale of the jewellery and coins enabled us to live in comfort for a while and I was able to restart my music lessons, for which I enrolled in the Wilno Conservatoire as well as to continue my general education. This, out of necessity, had to be private, because although I was strong in languages and art subjects, I did not have much knowledge of mathematics, physics and chemistry, as my tutor in Russia could not teach science. However with the help of an excellent teacher I was able to overcome the difficulty and in due course received my matriculation certificate from Eliza Orzeszkowa school.

My Marriage to Nik

We did not meet at a ball nor in the house of friends or relations which would have been the usual way. No inquisitive eyes watched our bewilderment at the sudden discovery of each other, no whispered comments were exchanged by those who witnessed the scene of our first meeting, as our only witness was discreet and mute.

It happened when one afternoon I took my mother's Pomeranian dog for a walk along a short avenue, not far from our house. The dog was on a lead, but although small it was strong and, in his impatience to get ahead quickly, managed to pull the lead out of my hand. I was petrified because it ran towards the grassy bank at the bottom of which was a railway line. I called it to come back, but being definitely and solely my mother's dog, never showing me any respect or loyalty, it ignored my cries completely. While I was contemplating whether or not to risk running after it into the steep and slippery grass, a nice looking man suddenly appeared, dived under the rail dividing the avenue from the slope, and in no time had the naughty dog in his arms. I recognised in him a man whom I had passed once or twice in the street, and whom I rather liked although on those occasions he did not take any notice of me. He was tall and slim, had slightly wavy, ash-blond hair and a characteristic quick and bouncing walk. He now stood before me with the dog under his left arm, saying nothing, just looking at me intensely. I stretched my hand to take the lead from him, but before I could do that he took my fingers into his and said with a charming smile,

'Allow me to introduce myself – I am Henryk Duszynski – I live across the road. From my window I saw your dog run away.'

Before releasing my hand, he bent down low and kissed it as in a formal act of introduction. I was taken aback and at the same time charmed and impressed by being treated with such reverence by this stranger. He seemed to me very mature and sophisticated, and when finally he handed the dog to me, our eyes met and that was the start of our great love. My unorthodox meeting with Nik was frowned upon by my mother, especially as at the time I was considered to be engaged, albeit unofficially to another young man, the son of my mother's friend. Everyone, including myself, thought that I had been in love with him and I felt like a traitor to my mother and to my ex-beau, but as I spent more time with Nik, I discovered the difference between real and imaginary love. Nik, as I learnt later from his sister, had also had his emotional problems. Before meeting me he was involved with a well known married society lady. But that was a Romance and here was Love. He ended the romance by returning his lady-friend's letters and photos in a box filled with roses.

Nik's past in some ways resembled mine as part of his youth was also spent in Russia. He was born and grew up in the family property (Lazy) in central Poland, which at that time was part of the Russian Empire. During the 1914–1918 war this territory had been subjected to particularly fierce battles between the German and Russian Armies, which forced many families to seek safety in parts of Russia unaffected by war. For this reason his mother with her three children (Nik's younger brother and sister) travelled as far as possible from the scene of the conflict, finally settling in Taganrog in Southern Russia on the Sea of Azov, to await the end of the war. Meanwhile Nik's father, who was a government official, remained in his native land. The three young people received their schooling in Taganrog and Nik obtained his

13

matriculation certificate there in 1918 with distinction. Their peaceful and comparatively comfortable life in the beautiful climate of the area ended with the Bolshevik Revolution of October 1917 which brought with it upheavals and deprivations with severe shortages of food, fuel and other commodities. With peace returning to Europe they were able to go back to a liberated Poland where the whole family was reunited. While for the rest of Europe the war ended with the Treaty of Versailles in 1918, Poland had to wage yet another war in 1920 against the Bolshevik troops advancing on her Eastern frontiers. This war fought by the Polish legions under their creator, Joseph Pilsudski, ended with a Polish victory in the decisive battle known as 'The Miracle over the Vistula', followed by the peace treaty of Riga in 1921, which established Poland's independence.

After his return to Poland, Nik joined the Legions as a young volunteer soldier, was wounded, received his commission as a First Lieutenant, and was awarded the Cross for Gallantry. When the war was over, Nik left the Army and continued his education. For two years he studied Architecture at Warsaw University but later switched to Law in Wilno, where the rest of his family had settled. He obtained his degree in Law at the Stefan Batory University there.

At this point Nik and I met and married. Our wedding took place on the 27th of June 1928 in the famous Church of the Madonna of Ostrobrama in Wilno. I was 17 and Nik 27 years old.

After our marriage Nik decided to re-enter the Army and his application was favourably received by his old regiment, then stationed in Rowne, the main city of the province of Wolyn. Before we could move there, Nik had to do his military duty as a reserve officer as it was his turn to take part in Army manoeuvres in Wolyn. Such manoeuvres normally lasted about six weeks and we were very sad at having to part so soon after our wedding and honeymoon. However, only a few days after Nik's departure, I received a telegram: 'You must come, I feel like a fish out of water without you'. A fish out of

14

water? It sounded very dramatic. I did not want my husband to suffer, and I dearly wanted to go to him but my mother, with whom I was staying at the time, was very critical of the idea, and somehow it did not seem quite right to follow one's husband on military exercises. I kept receiving letters from Nik and answering as many, with him insisting on my coming and me hesitating, until one day the tickets for the trip arrived and so the decision was made for me. Everything, down to the smallest detail concerning the itinerary, the clothes I was to take, the names of the stations at which the train was stopping long enough for me to have a meal or refreshments as the journey was lengthy and slow and there was no restaurant car, had been taken care of. All this was necessary at the time as I was young and had no experience of travelling on my own, but the same care and attention was given to me on similar occasions in all the years of our life together.

The situation in which I found myself on arrival had its piquancy as my presence had to be kept secret. I lived in an enchanting cottage looked after by a caretaker and his wife, and Nik spent all his free time with me. On his free Sundays he used to bring a horse for me and we both used to ride to the neighbouring apiary and gorge ourselves on honeycombs, sour cream and dark, pungent bread. For me it was an idyllic existence like being a Snow White but with one knight instead of seven dwarfs.

To celebrate the end of the manoeuvres, there was a regimental dance to which the ladies of the neighbourhood were invited, so Nik could at last bring me into the open to be introduced to his superiors and colleagues. There was general surprise at discovering that Nik had his wife with him.

One of the officers during a dance with me said, 'We all thought that he had a girl-friend nearby, but we never imagined that anyone would bring his wife to the manoeuvres.'

Perhaps nobody except Nik would but he was not like anybody else. Someone who did not know Nik well might have considered this particular incident as a manifestation of a possessive, masculine nature, but in all the years of our life

15

together I had innumerable proofs of his completely selfless, deep love for me.

The main event of our life in Rowne was the birth on the 1st of November 1929 of our son. He was christened Henryk-Andrzej but we called him by an affectionate nickname Nooka, from the Polish word Synuka, meaning son. I had a very hard time during the delivery and poor Nik had to face the possibility of either me, or our baby, or both of us dying. This was a terrible experience and although we came out of it alive, our son being delivered by forceps, Nik was determined not to allow a similar ordeal to happen again. As no doctor could safely say that the next childbirth would be any easier, to protect me from another pregnancy, Nik offered to be sterilised. I rejected such a suggestion outright, but we had to make a decision not to have any more children, and so our son was to remain our only child.

Nik's next posting was connected with his transfer to the Army Judiciary Corps and his subsequent appointment was in the Military Court in Wilno in the capacity of Defending Counsel.

Wilno was one of the most important and beautiful cities in Poland and our social life there was full and glamorous. Nik, as a lawyer and an officer, belonged to two different spheres of society, military and civilian. Also being a graduate of the local University, he had strong connections with it as an ex-member of one of the Students' Associations of that University. We had invitations to so many functions that answering them alone took a lot of my time, as it was mostly up to me to decide which to accept or refuse. In any case to accept them all would have been a physical impossibility. Polish people on the whole, know how to enjoy themselves, and there were many reasons at that particular time to feel happy. We had at last achieved freedom after more than a century of subjugation to three foreign powers. We had never given up hope that one day that freedom would come, and this feeling of hope expressed itself in generation after generation of Poles fighting for it in our own and other lands. In spite of all sorts of administrative and other difficulties connected with the devastations of war together with the problems of unifying one State out of three former partitioned sectors, the mood was buoyant as there were expectations of better things to come and plenty of challenge for everybody. With Poland's resurgence, literature, fine art and science blossomed. We were building the new town and port of Gdynia; our writer Wladyslaw Reymont received the Nobel Prize for his novel *Chlopi* (Peasants), we were happy, we were proud and full of hope for the future.

For me, brought up in the gloom and deprivations of the Soviet Union, everything was new and exciting. The shops full of beautiful clothes and marvellous food in unlimited quantities, cafés and restaurants brimming with life, free access to books in our own language and theatres with plays written and acted by talented Polish people, my own people. I loved my new life and plunged into it with all my heart. I was young, pretty, (no false modesty here), I had just the figure that Polish men liked (full bust and small waist), very good skin and sparkling eyes, which made my rivals say that I used special drops, and my admirers read in them messages that were not there. I liked nice clothes (I still do) and knew how to wear them to the best advantage. My ball gowns were apparently stunning, and for years afterwards I used to meet women who remembered dresses I had totally forgotten. Nik seemed to enjoy my social success too and, far from criticising me for my weaknesses, shared my interest in clothes, was often present at my fittings at the dressmaker, knew by heart the sizes of my shoes, gloves and underwear, and whenever he made trips to Warsaw returned loaded with beautiful things for me. Would there be any woman who could honestly say that she would not have enjoyed such a life?

As a mother I did not have much to do. There was always a nanny to look after our son. My maternal instincts came to the fore only if he was ill when I would give him my full love and attention spending all day and often night by his bedside. In any case he was developing well, was very bright but was

17

inclined to suffer from colds which brought the threat of pneumonia, always very worrying. Nik proved to be a good father, much more aware of his duties than I was. Young, well-off mothers of that period did not, on the whole, appreciate the importance of the part they could personally play in the development of their children. If a child was well looked after, was clean, warm and well fed, by whoever was in charge, that was enough. A baby was only a baby, not a person in its own right. We, the grown-ups, had our lives and the children had theirs. I am sad and ashamed to admit it, but that seemed to have been the general pattern.

Nik and I attended many balls. We were both good dancers, but were never allowed to have more than one dance together. As soon as the music stopped after the first dance and Nik put his arm round my waist to start another, someone came with the words,

'No more than one dance with one's own wife is allowed.'

It was a sort of 'excuse me dance' and nothing short of a duel would have succeeded in shaking off the intruder. Anyhow there was usually more than one such challenger. While I was dancing with other partners Nik performed his 'duty' dances and occasionally allowed himself the pleasure of dancing with some beautiful woman if, by any chance, she was free. Later he would spend some time in the bar drinking and talking to his male acquaintances and finally would join those men who preferred watching the dancing couples from the doorway to being in the ballroom. Nik's and my eyes often met but that was all we could do.

Normally I was not very willing to go home before the morning. In Poland balls started mostly about ten or eleven o'clock in the evening and went on for the whole night. Nik, who was ready to go home much sooner, had his own gentle ways of persuading me to go. I remember one such occasion. I had been dancing a third consecutive dance with a dashing and very persistent officer which, I am sure, did not escape Nik's notice. In the next break he approached me.

'You look very tired, little one, (that was how he used to call me) aren't you feeling well?'

That made me reach for my little mirror, only to find that there were indeed ugly blue circles under my eyes and that I looked older and much less attractive than at the beginning of the evening. As I could not possibly allow everybody to see any further deterioration in my looks, I was anxious to leave at once. Only after arriving home and making a careful examination of my appearance could I see that there was no change in it. Nevertheless I was glad to be back home with Nik and was full of appreciation for his tact or cunning, or whatever one would like to call it. Nik did not waste his time watching the dancing couples either, as often, on reaching home and before going to bed, he would take a piece of paper and pencil and draw for me a detail of a ball-dress, such as an interesting decolleté or unusual sleeve which he noticed and which he thought would look nice on me and could be used in my next creation.

Although I still enjoyed it, my life, divided between visits to dressmakers and hairdressers and meeting other women at Sztrall and Rudnicki cafés in Wilno, stopped satisfying me and made me look for other more rewarding ways of spending my free time. By now I was much more involved with my son's upbringing, but that still left me enough time and energy to do other things. So when I learnt of the plans put forward by the Military Families' Association to create open-air kindergartens, I volunteered, with Nik's wholehearted approval, to go on a month's course to Warsaw to learn what I could about starting and running such kindergartens.

I came back full of enthusiasm for the project and joined the newly formed organisation devoted to popularising it and raising the necessary funds. The Chairman of the Organisation was the wife of the Commander-in-Chief of the Wilno garrison, who was also a close friend of Marshal Pilsudski's wife, and I was made the Secretary. My duty, among the usual ones, was to write to the local papers about the activities of the organisation and to talk on the radio. The organisation received recognition and support from the Town authorities who allocated us suitable sites and some funds. I put all my heart into my work and, before I knew what was happening, I came to be considered an authority on open-air kindergartens so much so that when in 1934 an order came for Nik's transfer to another post, there were cries of protest and intervention at the highest level in the capital, asking for the postponement of our departure. They did not succeed as the reply from Warsaw, said to have been from Marshal Pilsudski himself, was: 'An officer's career will not be influenced by what his wife does.' Thus my love affair with open-air kindergartens was ended.

Our next destination was Grudziadz in Western Poland where Nik was posted as prosecutor in a Military Court. With the lack of other outlets my life in Grudziadz reverted to social rounds, but this time relying more on private entertainments. We gave parties and were, in turn, invited to a lot. Apart from starting some good long lasting friendships, my memories of that year in Grudziadz were rather sad. First of all there was my mother's early death, at 51. On the way back from her funeral in Wilno, Nik suffered bad burns on the train. The two of us occupied a sleeping compartment. Before settling down for the night I went into the bathroom to have a wash. Soon afterwards Nik noticed a lot of steam in the corridor. When he inquired he was told that a hot water pipe had burst in one of the bathrooms. He immediately assumed that it was the bathroom I had gone to. He threw a coat over his head and rushed into the bathroom, but not being able to see at all because of the dense steam, he crawled on the floor feeling for me, thinking that I might have fainted. Someone realising what was happening, pulled him out almost unconscious. In the meantime, completely unaware of what was happening, I returned from the other bathroom to find a crowd of people round our door and Nik completely unrecognisable, his face terribly swollen and discoloured, lying on the seat.

It was a most horrible experience. There was no doctor on the train, nobody knew what had to be done and he received first aid only after our arrival at the next station. His face and hands in the meantime were getting worse with blisters appearing all over them. I could hardly see his eyes and his lips were cracking but I could still see that he tried to say something to reassure me. It must have been terribly painful, but he did not utter a sound to indicate his suffering. Did I deserve to be married to such a man?

Nik had to spend a considerable time in hospital and I stayed there with him. It was a slow and painful process and it was the first time in our life together that I had a chance to show fully my love for him. The treatment and his own resilience led to his complete recovery and in the end he came out unscathed without the necessity for a skin graft.

The climate of Grudziadz, humid and with frequent strong winds, did not agree with our son. He suffered more often than before from colds, had a poor appetite and became thin. We felt that he needed a change of climate and sent him to Rabka, a famous health resort for children. He spent several months there and came back plump, if not completely immune from colds.

We left Grudziadz in 1935 and our next four very happy years were spent in Stanislavov, a medium size town, south of Lvov, where Nik now a Captain, was appointed Head of the Military Court. This was a freshly created post with the Court occupying part of a brand new building, and Nik, given a free hand in planning the lay-out of the premises, was able to use his talent and skills acquired during his studies of Architecture. The results were greatly admired. He also started writing to law magazines and established his name as a respected writer on legal matters. Nooka back from Rabka started his new school and we all were very happy to be together again. I got down to organising our new household, a job in which I became quite skilled. Although unsettling I nevertheless liked our way of life which, at every move, presented us with a new challenge and opportunities. So now I was looking forward to finding out what this new phase would bring us. In spite of our frequent moves we did not lose contact with our friends. On the contrary some friendships seemed to deepen with the passing of time as we continued to

21

correspond and meet in the intervening years. As in other places, so now in Stanislavov, the pattern of our social life was gradually emerging with many invitations from the military circles of the large garrison in Stanislavov. There was also a civilian Club (Klub Polski) of which Nik became a member.

In Stanislavov I tried my hand at writing by taking part in a competition run by a Warsaw Literary Weekly. The theme was 'Folklore in a holiday Region' and I received the second prize. It was a great encouragement to me and a cause of pride for my two men. My chosen subject was 'The Hutzuls' Country' of which more later. From then on, as a freelance journalist, I wrote for several dailies and periodicals in Lvov and Cracow, finally becoming official reporter for the prestigious Warsaw daily 'Polska Zbrojna' writing feature articles on many different subjects. As my reputation as a journalist became established I was invited to use the Klub Polski's facilities such as library and reading room and later co-opted as the first and only woman member of the Club, which caused quite a stir.

We took a very active part in sports especially canoeing and skiing for which the region, with its rivers and mountains, was particularly suitable. The first two summer holidays (1936, 1937) out of Stanislavov we spent in the foothills of the Carpathian Mountains renting a chalet from a Hutzul, the name for a local mountain dweller, hence the Hutzuls' Country. The chalet was in a small but fashionable resort called Yaremche Waterfall, easily accessible from Stanislavov by train or car. It was also a place renowned for its scenic beauty, lying in a gorge of the River Prut, which came down in rapids and formed a powerful waterfall. Nooka and I usually stayed there for the whole summer, as we believed that the climate was good for our son, but Nik, who had only a month's holiday, commuted from Stanislavov which meant that he had to get up at 5 in the morning, because of an awkward timetable, to be in his office by 8 o'clock. He could have stayed comfortably in Stanislavov, coming only at the week-ends, but he wanted us to be together as much as possible.

I liked our rented chalet mostly for its position on a hill from which we had a magnificent view of the valley below and the mountains on the opposite side, across the river Prut. There was one mountain in particular, called Malava, which I never tired of watching, as it seemed to trap the passing delicate clouds, which kept changing their shape and hues continuously. So when in 1938 we were not able to have our usual chalet, I was very disappointed. But I did not reckon with having a husband who could bring magic into any situation.

One day he suddenly produced an offical looking paper and said, 'Now, you will always be able to look at your Malava.' He had bought a plot of land in Yaremche Waterfall, offering the best view in the whole place. I had not had the slightest suspicion of what he was doing and that was the greatest surprise of my life.

The building of our house started the same year. Nik designed it himself, needing only the approval of a qualified architect. He also designed the furniture and during his week-end visits from Stanislavov to check the progress of the work, searched for the most unusual and beautiful pieces of ceramics and textiles for which the neighbourhood was famous. He did not want me to see the house until it was almost finished, and I did not insist, knowing of his impeccable taste. The house was finished in May of 1939 and in June of that year we celebrated our 11th wedding anniversary there with pomp and a lot of noise provided by the local amateur band.

The house was ingeniously planned and stylishly furnished. Only local building material was used for its construction. The walls were made of half logs, with the bark removed, and resting on foundations of light grey stone. It had a very large terrace with its roof supported by massive square columns of the same stone, wide at the base and gradually tapering towards the top thus creating an impression of lightness. The roof was made from a special kind of red tile. The large terrace and open fireplace, which was built with the idea of spending our Christmas and Easter holidays there, distinguished our house from the others in the neighbourhood.

Fireplaces were rare in Poland because houses were gener-

23

ally heated by iron or tiled stoves so the construction of ours caused great problems. No builder in the district had ever seen or heard of such a thing. The supply of wood for its use, however, was easy to come by. Huge logs were pulled down from the dense forest which started behind the house and stretched up the hill. We were helped by the frequent storms when lightning struck trees sending them crashing down with a terrific noise. Our fireplace, built in the manner of an old English hearth, had an enormous capacity and our reliance on storms, to satisfy its appetite, was one of the reasons why we were able to enjoy these terrific outbursts of nature. We stood on the terrace spellbound unable to tear ourselves away from the beauty and majesty of that incomparable spectacle. We also relied on our lightning conductor.

Apart from its beautiful location with the river and mountain walks offering healthy pastimes, Yaremche Waterfall had other attractions for the holiday-maker. In the valley, near the waterfall, was a very pleasant café restaurant (Lankoshovka) where every Sunday afternoon people met at a thé-dansant with music by a good professional band, and where we saw each other smartly dressed instead of in our usual swim-suits or beach wear. A short journey from Yaremche Waterfall was a much larger spa – Yaremche – very popular because of its pine forests and health establishments, but most of all because of its restaurant (*Skrzynski*) with cuisine fit for Lucullus. This attracted gourmets from as far away as Stanislavov, who came just for dinner. No wonder that our holidays, always very enjoyable, became even more so during the few months spent in our own house. It was surrounded by a large garden, which, because of its newness resembled a jungle, with bushes due for clearing and trees for felling. It gave us complete privacy so Nik's sister who believed in nudism, could roam freely within its confines when she stayed with us.

It was difficult to believe that it was about five minutes' walk down the hill from our house to find ourselves at the lively *Lankoshovka*, dancing. On Sunday mornings we had an invasion of friends from Stanislavov who, after changing into swimming suits, rushed to the small rocky beach, plunging into the chilly waters of the Prut and recklessly sliding on the slippery stones of the river, often coming back with their swim-suits in shreds. They were ravenously hungry by then and usually several additional chickens had to be slaughtered and cleaned in haste, our maid being helped by the local Hutzul women. Afterwards they used to stretch for a siesta, often two or more people, together on a bed or divan. About five o'clock, rested and changed, we all used to go to *Lankoshovka* for coffee and a dance and, to finish the day most of the company repaired to *Skrzynski* for the last dance of the day and a wonderful meal. I must confess that after such excesses I greatly appreciated the peace and isolation of our house with just Nik and Nooka for company and, on occasions, a staid house guest.

There are no words that could adequately express our happiness at that time. Everything seemed to go right for us. Our new home was a delight and we were looking forward to spending there many more summers in the future.

After this holiday in Yaremche Nik was not returning to his post in Stanislavov, as he was appointed Deputy Head of the Department of Justice at the War Ministry in Warsaw. It was a great distinction with which went also a promotion to a higher military rank. We were all very excited with the prospect of a new life in our beautiful capital, where we were allotted an apartment in one of the most elegant districts. Nik's brilliant future seemed assured and Nooka and I basked in his glory.

The Outbreak of War – Soviet Invasion

In connection with Nik's transfer to his new job and the preparations for our move to Warsaw, we had shortened our holiday and returned to Stanislavov at the beginning of August 1939. The closing down of our house in Yaremche Waterfall did not involve much work as we left the house as it was in readiness for our future holidays there. All we had to do was to pack some of our clothing and a few personal items. We locked the house and gave instructions to our caretaker, Hutzul asking him to look well after the house until our return. We did not then suspect that we were never to see it again.

It was a different story in Stanislavov. Nik had to hand over to his successor the Court and also to advise and help me in planning and organising the removal of our possessions to Warsaw. We also had many farewell visits to pay and receive. On the whole although we seemed to be pressed for time, everything was proceeding smoothly and to our entire satisfaction when, like a bolt from the blue, came a summons for Nik to report at once to the Headquarters of the X.N. Division in Czortkov, which he knew was his assignment in case of war. This was shattering news. Poland did not expect and did not want war. In an endeavour to insure peace our Government had recently concluded non-aggression pacts with our powerful neighbours: Germany and Russia. Although during the summer of 1939 we heard rumours about incidents on our

26

frontier with Germany and we knew that there was some tension over Danzig, war did not seem likely. But if war was to come we had no alternative but to defend our country to the last. Not for nothing had Howard Kennard, British Ambassador to Poland, said in his telegram to London on 30th August 1939: 'They would certainly sooner fight and perish rather than submit to humiliation especially after examples of Czechoslovakia, Lithuania and Austria'. That was the general mood, but we still hoped, together with our British and French Allies, that a war could be avoided.

On receiving his orders Nik left immediately and I, suddenly deprived of his comforting presence and support, surveyed in dismay our partly dismantled home and seeing the bewilderment on my small boy's face, wondered what would happen to both of us now. But, of course, we were not alone in our distress. There were other military families who were going through the same experience. Our building, apart from the Army Headquarters and Military Court, provided accommodation for families of men connected with these institutions. Very soon all the men I knew personally or by sight disappeared to be replaced by reservists who had been recalled and had to report to the registration centres set up in our building. We, the wives of military personnel, who lived in the building organised a sort of canteen for the men working at the centres, as well as for those who had been recalled. People came and went making room for new arrivals. Lifts never stopped their up and down movement. Orders from higher authorities arrived constantly. We were fortunate to have something to keep us busy during this stressful time and to be useful to others.

As late as the 31st August 1939 talks were going on in Berlin between our Ambassador Lipski and the German Foreign Minister von Ribbentrov. In view of this how could anyone have expected that on the 1st September at five o'clock in the morning, without any warning or formal declaration of war, the Germans would start bombing Poland and that their tanks would invade our country in their thousands?

27

The German advance was rapid and merciless. Despite heroic fighting, the Polish Army was unable to stop the onslaught of German tanks on land, while the unexpected attacks of the Luftwaffe, carried out with an unheard-of fury, paralysed Polish airfields almost immediately. This was not a war – it was a massacre. Refugees arriving from the West of Poland had frightening stories to tell. On the 3rd September Great Britain and France declared war on Germany, which created enormous enthusiasm in Poland. Unfortunately, this did not change the situation as neither of these countries actively came to Poland's help, who was left alone to fight the enemy.

I had no news of Nik since we had parted in Yaremche and my worry about him increased daily. He was never out of my thoughts. It seemed to me that in this way I could protect him from evil. I saw him constantly in my dreams, not always the way I wanted, which increased my anxiety. But when he appeared as I knew him, smiling and loving I felt his presence almost tangibly. I snuggled closer to him only to wake up in the middle of the night hugging a dummy. Like a silly little girl, to relieve my loneliness, I made a dummy out of his blanket and put it in bed next to me every night.

I shall never forget the 15th September. Not because of the intense bombardment we received in Stanislavov that day from the German planes but because I heard the sound of the lift stopping on our floor and, if driven by some irresistible force, I rushed out of our flat and saw my dearest husband coming towards me. He looked much thinner and weary but was otherwise unharmed. We fell into each other's arms and I suddenly felt so weak from emotion, that he almost had to carry me inside. Just then another air-raid alarm sounded so we told our maid to fetch Nooka and go with him to the nearest shelter. As for us we decided not to waste the opportunity to be together, and the memory of those last precious moments in his arms I carry with me to this day.

During his brief visit Nik told me that his division had been virtually annihilated, and it was a miracle that anyone had survived. Those that had were ordered to try and reach, by any means available to them, their respective headquarters in order to be reorganised into new fighting units. Thus Nik with three other officers, from the same unit, had had to work their way down to Czortkov, a small town near the Romanian border. They travelled by car until they were forced to abandon it when German pilots, flying their planes very low, showered them with bullets from their machine guns. By various means they finally approached their destination, but while the other three men continued on their way to Czortkov, Nik had to go to Lvov as he had a special mission to perform delivering a secret message to the Supreme Command there. His mission completed, he continued his journey to Czortkov by rail, but the necessity of changing trains in Stanislavov gave him a chance to see me. I saw him off at the station and as the train started to move away, I thought my heart would break. If it had not been for the thought of our child I would have jumped on the train after him. We had agreed then that, whatever happened, I would wait for him in Stanislavov.

If we had known then that the Soviet forces were gathering on our Eastern frontier we wouldn't have made such a decision and all our lives would have taken quite a different course.

There were no more German air-raids in the eastern territories of Poland after the 15th September. On that day they also stopped the advance of their Army to the east. We were puzzled. Why had the Germans stopped their attacks so suddenly? We knew from the radio broadcasts that some Polish units were still fighting desperately in the pocket near Brest Litovsk, which meant that the war was continuing. Why were we spared?

The answer came two days later on 17th September, when the Soviet Army crossed our eastern border. Their tanks, heavy artillery and infantry flooded our land, moving westwards in an unbroken line. They were followed by the powerful apparatus of the civilian administration, composed chiefly of the officers of the NKVD (the Soviet secret police, now the KGB). The sudden appearance of the Soviet troops deceived many. At first it was thought that our Slavonic neighbour was coming to our aid and that was the reason why the German advance had stopped. Having survived the German onslaught, Polish soliders who were retreating towards the east, had similar illusions when they came face to face with the Russians. However they soon realised that here was an enemy no less cruel and ruthless than the Germans. Although no war existed between Russia and Poland, the Russians disarmed Polish officers and NCOs and declared them prisoners of war. Later on they were crammed into the waiting trains and deported to Russia where they were dispersed between three POW camps: Kozelsk, Starobelsk and Ostashkov. Those who refused to hand over their arms were shot on the spot. Thus on 22nd September one of our gallant generals, Olszyna-Wilczynski was executed. Altogether 15,000 Polish officers and NCOs were captured in this way. The Russians' task was easy, not only because there was an element of surprise and confusion about their intentions, but also because by then these men, whose regiments were shattered, moved in small disorganised groups unable to offer any effective resistance.

A heinous crime was perpetrated against the Polish, anti-Nazi guerilla groups, whose members were in hiding. A message had been sent to them proposing a meeting between their representatives and high NKVD officers in order to discuss ways of fighting the Germans. At the meeting the representatives were promised safe conduct for all guerilla fighters as well as the right to form their own fighting units, on condition that they would reveal themselves. When, relying on such assurances, the guerillas came into the open, they were surrounded by the Russian soldiers, forced to surrender their arms and put under arrest. All their leaders were executed.

Having got rid of practically all trained army men, the Russians concentrated on dealing with the civilian population. All prominent members of the local

30

administration were put in jail and replaced by Russians. Their next move was to seize and arrest members of the Bund, a Jewish Socialist Workers' Party, which had officially existed in Poland since 1921, as well as eminent members of the Polish Socialist Party. In spite of being communist sympathisers they did not escape arrest and deportation to the labour camps in northern Siberia.

In all these tasks the Russians were assisted by members of the newly formed red militia squads, made up of the dregs of society. When their services were no longer required, they too were arrested and sent to the same terrible places.

The full historical facts came to light years after these events took place. The world learned that the Soviet invasion of Poland was a prearranged act, agreed between the German and Russian Foreign Ministers, Ribbentrop and Molotov, on 23rd August 1939, only a week before the German attack on Poland. On the strength of that agreement the Soviet Union had guranteed non-intervention during the German attack on Poland in return for which the German advance was to stop on the line of the rivers Bug and San. The Germans were to take Polish lands to the west of that line leaving to the Russians the territories to the east of it. But even so the Russians waited on the border until the Polish Army was crushed before invading. That despicable Russian act, that cowardly stab in the back of a nation fighting for its life, put an end to any further open resistance by the Polish Army. From then on our two enemies were to collaborate in the destruction of the Polish nation. Also, from that moment, the influx of refugees ceased – there was little sense in running from one enemy only to fall into the hands of the other. Our only source of reliable information were the Polish radio broadcasts from London, and we listened to them greedily and illegally.

The occupation of the eastern territories of Poland presented no difficulty to the Russians. The bewildered population watched helplessly as regiment after regiment of shabbily dressed soldiers marched past. Their food rations must have been inadequate as, whenever they stopped they fell like vultures on shops and private households, confiscating any food they could lay their hands on, often eating it straight away by the roadside.

There was no army to fight them. The empty military barracks vacated by Polish soldiers fighting in the west of the country, were now filled up with Russian soldiers. For those officers and NCOs for whom there was not enough accommodation in the barracks, Russians requisitioned rooms in private houses. In this way they also placed a spy in every household.

The building in which we lived in Stanislavov was requisitioned by the NKVD and used as their headquarters. Nooka and I, together with the other Polish officers' families had to move out immediately. We were allowed to take with us only as much as was necessary for our immediate use. This we had packed into a few suitcases and a large wicker basket into which I had managed to put some bulkier articles of clothing and bedding and a few extras, when the man supervising our packing was not looking. These now represented our entire fortune, while the contents of our spacious and comfortable home, acquired gradually during our married life, went to the Russians. I, who (according to my friends) had the reputation of being one of the most elegant women in town, had to sacrifice vanity to practicality and praised myself later for choosing the warmest and most useful clothes, succumbing to temptation only once when, after a momentary struggle, I threw into the basket my latest black ball gown.

We had no home and only little money, with no access to any more since all bank accounts had been frozen. If it had not been for the kindness of a friend, Nella Polanska, who offered us a room in her apartment, we would have had to sleep on a bench in a park. She lived in a block of flats in the centre of Stanislavov, and we thankfully accepted her generous offer.

Nella was one of the lucky few who still kept their homes, but she was far from free of personal worries. Her husband, who because of his age had not been called-up at the beginning of the war, had recently gone into hiding and she had had no news of him. Their very successful business was in ruins after the imposition of the Soviet regime. Her brother who had been mobilised, was missing, probably killed in the September campaign.

The Russians seemed to bring decay to everything: streets grew dirtier, shops emptier, good restaurants changed rapidly into third-rate chop-houses where service was slow and apathetic. As the Polish *zloty* had been declared invalid and there was not much one could buy for Russian roubles, there was no incentive to work well. Those few who remained in their jobs because they were needed to show their new masters the local customs and practices, were under great stress. Daily more and more people deserted, most of them escaping across the border to Romania and Hungary. During the daytime, detachments of Russian soldiers passed through the street, leaving behind them a strong, sickly smell of unwashed bodies and dirty clothes. At night the streets were shunned by the native population which preferred the comparative safety of its homes, and only the Russians could be seen, more and more often with their wives whom they were gradually allowed to bring over from Russia.

After the initial savagery, the behaviour of the Russians became more disciplined. Those who entered Stanislavov first and found shops still well stocked, bought anything they could get, paying with roubles. They were particularly attracted to the ladies' long silk nightdresses, taking them for ball gowns. Now their wives, attired in these nightdresses, walked into the restaurants to the delight of the staff. The fact that they wore heavy boots made these flimsy clothes look even more bizzare. Sometimes, instead of boots they wore plimsoles and with them very pale pink, woollen understockings, which were still available. I should perhaps explain the role of understockings in pre-war Poland. Our winters are severe and, to protect our feet, we wore warm bootees which according to the foolish fashion of the day, reached only to the ankle. Something warm

33

was necessary to protect the rest of the leg. A Polish lady, with any pretence to elegance, would not be seen wearing sensible thick woollen stockings so, in order to solve the problem of both looking smart and keeping warm, thin woollen, flesh-coloured understockings were worn beneath the usual silk stockings. Worn on their own, the pale pink shade gave the legs a most unhealthy appearance. Dressed like that the Russian women seemed comical but, at the same time, they aroused sympathy. Some of them were very pretty and it was obvious that they wanted to look feminine and attractive, and were enjoying the first glimpse of luxury in their lives. As far as the Russian men were concerned, there was nothing more desirable than a wristwatch. Times have changed since then.

With the Russians in control, our situation was becoming worse every day. To the concern about food was now added a much more serious worry, as the wave of arrests expanded in ever-widening circles until there was hardly a family not affected by it. In addition, there was the problem of those Polish men who had succeeded in working their way through the enemy occupied territory, without falling into their hands. Hiding in woods and small villages, and moving under cover of darkness, they arrived in Stanislavov with the idea of getting into Romania. Some wanted only to save their lives, but the great majority wanted to fight the Germans if not on their own, then on foreign soil. These men needed shelter. Some who were still in uniform had to be given civilian clothes and then helped to escape. A few had families or friends in Stanislavov, but the majority relied on luck and the help of strangers. Usually they came at night as it was safer. Many women expected their missing male relatives to arrive at any moment.

We jumped out of bed on hearing any sound at the door, real or imaginary. We had to be extremely alert as there were informers among some ethnic minority groups ready to de-nounce a Polish officer or NCO to the Soviet authorities. The worst culprits were the small shopowners, particularly barbers or tailors, who tried to gain favour with their new

34

masters, probably in the hope of preserving their livelihoods. They were all the more dangerous because many spoke Russian or Ukrainian, which was also understood by the Russians.

I expected Nik to arrive hourly. I lost sleep listening for his steps at night, afraid that if I missed him when he was at the door, someone else in the building might see and betray him. I did not forget for a moment our agreement to meet in Stanislavov. Meanwhile there were some new arrivals to be taken care of – cadets from the Military Academy in Lvov who had been directed to us by a secret organisation SZP. (Service to the Polish Victory), requesting that they be given temporary shelter until their escape could be organised. They were in imminent danger of arrest. They were all very young mostly sixteen and seventeen years old. It was very worrying to see these boys, torn from their families, now facing an unknown future. In a way, however, it was easier to help them than the grown men because they could pass for pupils at the local school. One of our duties was to remove from their clothes anything that could betray their affiliation with the Army. We were supplied with false documents for them by the SZP in case they were stopped by the Russians and many of them were smuggled over the border before the Russians had established proper outposts and acquired a good knowledge of the terrain. Smuggling was very well organised and there was never any shortage of people willing to help, either for money or for the cause. Men who escaped endeavoured to let their families or friends know of their whereabouts through the Polish broadcasts of the BBC, so that there were always people listening in case there was good news for someone. Nooka and I were getting more disappointed as the days passed because there was no message for us. I was very anxious to know that Nik was by now out of Poland. I no longer wanted him to come to Stanislavov as it had become almost impossible to hide anybody from the spying eyes. I hoped that, having realised how dangerous the situation had become, he would cross the frontier to Romania. Although I had helped others and knew the right people to approach, I could not, even for a moment, think of our own escape until I knew that Nik was safely abroad. What would happen, for instance, if he came to Stanislavov and did not find us there? So I waited and hoped, as anxiety grew daily. Getting out of the country was becoming more and more difficult. Soviet patrols were well organised by now and their local knowledge was improving all the time. Even leaving the town itself was becoming harder because many people, especially men, were under observation and ordered to report for periodic checks. Arrests were increasing, the jails were overflowing with people of both sexes and there were hardly any men, young or old, to be seen. In front of the prison gates were long queues of women bringing warm clothes and food to their relatives inside. As long as parcels were accepted by the Russian guards, people had hope that the prisoners, whom they knew to be innocent of any crime, would be released one day. But when the refusal of a parcel was explained by a prisoner's transfer to an unknown destination – which really meant deportation to a forced labour camp in Siberia – then even that last ray of hope disappeared.

About that time Nella and I were greatly saddened by an incident which occurred soon after the last group of cadets had left us. Crossing the street I had to give way to some men being led under military escort. Such sights were not unusual, but I noticed that one of the prisoners was a seventeen-year-old cadet whose escape we had arranged. We had been sure that he was safely abroad by now and seeing him arrested shook me to the core. He had noticed me as well but without giving any sign of recognition, looked straight ahead and said, loudly enough for me to hear, 'I do not know anyone here'. I understood. Even in that terrible situation he wanted to let me know that he would not betray us. The Russian soldier nearest him, not understanding what he had said, looked round anxiously but noticing nothing unusual, walked on. Later we received a message through someone who had been arrested with the cadet, but later released, that he had brought his own misfortune upon himself. Cadets normally wore a badge on their cap in the form of the sun and, for sentimental reasons, he did not want to part with it and carried it in his pocket. It was found during a search on the train in which he was travelling. With such unmistakable proof of his identity, no false papers could help. We sent him food parcels for some time until we heard that he had been taken to another place. We never heard from him or saw him again.

I personally had yet another worry. The manager of the Savings Bank in Stanislavov and an old friend of ours, Jan Roszek, found himself in a very difficult situation and, knowing that I was fluent in Russian, came to me for help. Following the Russian invasion he was allowed to remain in his job and was treated fairly well though an NKVD man was appointed to supervise him. He had hoped he would be needed in his old capacity but soon discovered that the Russian banking system had nothing in common with ours. Having taken over all the bank assets, the only thing that the Russians wanted was confidential information about the bank's old clients, in other words collaboration. He was left in no doubt that if he did not comply, he would be arrested or worse. He decided to escape, together with his brother, Kazimierz, a vet, who had survived the German onslaught in the West, reached Stanislavov and was hiding from the Russians in Jan's flat. Jan's plan consisted of providing himself and his brother with a letter written in Russian on the bank paper, with official seals to which he had access, and the forged signature of the present NKVD boss, authorising them to inspect bank's propery near the Romanian border from where they hoped to escape. I was asked to write the letter and forge the signature, which I agreed to do. After their departure I went through the letter in my mind and realised that, in my haste, I had used an expression which would immediately reveal to any mildly intelligent person its pre-Soviet form. I was terribly worried now in case they were caught and, under very strong pressure, disclosed the name of the forger. In view of the fact that I had a child to support I wondered whether I should have endangered not only my future but Nooka's as well.

These two incidents, which could attract Soviet attention to us, made us stop our secret activities. In addition there was another reason for extreme caution. A room in Nella's flat had been requisitioned for a Russian officer. He was Alexei Kuratov, a cavalry man in his middle twenties, married with a year old son and came from the Don region. This we learned from him later as at first there was no verbal communication between us at all. He behaved very quietly, confining himself to the room allocated to him, walked as if on tip-toe, never slammed doors and did not bring any friends in – a fact we appreciated. In fact, we never heard him going out or coming in. He seemed a mysterious and menacing figure and his presence in the flat had an unsettling and depressing effect on us. Whenever he was in we talked in whispers, thinking that he might be able to understand Polish. I shivered at the thought of what would happen if Nik suddenly arrived. We suspected that Alexei was there to watch us, that he knew who we were and that it would not escape his notice if another person suddenly appeared. Even if he did not actually see that person, he would probably sense that something unusual was happening in the house and the unavoidable atmosphere of conspiracy would not have gone unnoticed by him. As future events were to prove, some of my suspicions were correct.

There were other problems as well. Apart from losing our home and all its contents, my luck failed in yet another way. At the news of the Russian approach, the wives of the military personnel were paid the equivalent of three months of their husband's salary so that they could buy food and other necessities still available in the shops. Unfortunately the person who had been left in charge of the funds out of which I was to be paid, sneaked abroad taking all the money with him. It probably did not do him any good, as the Polish *zloty*, at that time, did not have any value abroad, but it deprived me of the last opportunity to stock up on necessities, as well as of the chance to exchange the remaining Polish money for Russian roubles, while it was still possible. Thus having had little cash to start with I was now left with just enough to last me another day or two. As there were no cooking facilities in my room (and I could not possibly use Nella's small kitchen) we had to eat in restaurants, which was an expensive way to live. In any event I would not have been able to get ingredients for a meal as by now shops were empty either through confiscation by the Soviet authorities or because of the black marketeers who had been amassing food and selling it at vastly inflated prices. Peasants were still bringing their produce to the market but would only exchange it for clothing or various domestic appliances, so that particular source of supply was automatically ruled out for me. While I was racking my brains as to how to get money to pay for our food, an unexpected source of income opened up. There was a sudden demand among the professional men especially doctors and dentists, for people who could teach Russian. Knowing the language well, I soon had more pupils than I could cope with.

The Gamekeeper's Daughter

Late one evening someone rang the bell and I rushed to the door. A young, blond woman I had never seen before stood on the threshhold. I asked her what she wanted and she replied, 'I have come to see Mrs. Duszynski.'

'I am Mrs. Duszynski,' I said.

She lowered her voice to a whisper, 'I bring a message from your husband.'

On hearing this I almost collapsed. I had just enough wit to signal to her not to say anymore, took hold of her hand and led her into our room. I felt so weak that I thought my legs would give way, because I knew that Alexei Kuratov was at home. Joy and fear rushed through my head at the same time. I put my arms round the woman and hugged her to my heart. To me she was an angel; and I felt that I loved her already. I wanted to cry and laugh at the same time, to embrace her, even before I learned any details of what she had to say. My Nik was alive, and had sent me a message. There was hope I would see him again and we could be together once more. At last the tension and anxiety of the last few weeks found an outlet in tears. When I was finally able to control my emotions, we both sat down and she started to talk.

She told me her name, explaining that she was a gamekeeper's daughter from Czortkov, the town to which Nik went after leaving Stanislavov. During his work, her father came across a Polish officer who was very weak from loss of blood from a deep wound in his leg. He had probably been shot by a Russian guard while trying to cross the Romanian border and it was a miracle that he had not been captured. Her father tended the wound as best he could, brought him food and drink and, when night fell, he and his daughter took him to their cottage. When they learned who he was they tried to get in touch with me, but were unable to find me at the old address – hence the delay. She said that although Nik was still very weak, his wound was almost completely healed and he was making such a good recovery that soon it might be possible to smuggle him abroad. I listened with my heart so full that I could not utter a word and just kept pressing her hand in mine. I knew the dangers facing anyone sheltering a Polish officer: if discovered they would undoubtedly face arrest and deportation to Siberia or even death. The self-sacrifice of this family had been very great, and they still had the problem of getting him over the border. The longer he remained in the cottage, the more dangerous it became for them. The Russians were watchful and the chances of being detected grew stronger every day.

There was no question of sleep that night. Instead we spent it in whispered discussions about what should be done. The most urgent matter was to supply Nik with civilian clothes. There was no chance of buying any of these in Czortkov, as the shops were either closed or emptied. The gamekeeper's clothes would not fit because he was larger than Nik. Luckily, on leaving our requisitioned home I had taken a complete set of Nik's civilian clothes thinking he might need them. Now I thanked God for that fortunate decision. I collected everything into a huge parcel, although I knew it would be difficult to carry without attracting the attention of a street patrol. The young woman, however, did not seem to be unduly worried, and assured me she would be able to tell a plausible story if stopped. In any case, there was no other way and we had to take the risk. She had to leave early that morning before the rest of the household awoke so she would not be seen by anyone else. To avoid being seen together we decided that I

41

would try and travel to Czortkov alone, and hope my journey would not attract too much attention. There was a train from Stanislavov to Czortkov every afternoon and we agreed that her father would pick me up near the station in a horse and cart. She described her father to me and I told her what I would be wearing so we should not miss each other.

The next two days passed in an agony of suspense and anticipation. I was in such a state of excitement that I could neither eat nor sleep. Having discussed the situation with Nella who promised to take care of Nooka during my absence, on the appointed day I very discreetly left the house and was lucky to be able to buy a ticket and get on the train to Czortkov. At that time trains ran very erratically, but mine departed after only a slight delay – another bit of luck. I found the carriage filled with Russian soldiers who behaved far more freely and arrogantly than those in Stanislavov. Some of them tried to talk to me but I pretended that I did not understand them and, after making some unsavoury and vulgar remarks, they left me in peace. The journey took about two hours and by the time I arrived it was already dark. The station was littered with cigarette ends and other rubbish; it was obvious that no one had made any effort to clean it for quite some time. I waited until the soldiers and other passengers had alighted, then with a thumping heart, I went into the street. I looked round but could see no-one. No horse and cart were waiting for me. The town looked deserted and gloomy. Was there any sinister reason behind it or merely an ordinary obstacle such as an untimely visit of some friend which had delayed their departure? I tried not to panic, but decided to wait for a while. I went into the street again and again looking in all directions, but still no one came. It started to rain, and the station waiting-room was draughty and cold. I was wearing a warm suit and had a woollen cardigan in my overnight bag. Now I got it out and put it on, but it seemed very inadequate. It was unthinkable to spend the night at the station dressed like that: I would catch my death of cold. There was nobody in the station building apart from a man I took to be the stationmaster. He came out of a room at the back and looked around. He must have wondered what I was doing there at that time of the night when the last train had gone.

I approached him. 'Could you recommend me a hotel?'

'I wouldn't advise it. There aren't many here and those that are are very primitive. Apart from that, they are mostly used by Soviet soldiers and girls seeking an easy income. It would be dangerous for a woman like you even to cross the doorstep of such hotels.'

'What am I to do then? If I stay in this draught much longer I shall catch pneumonia.'

'I'll try to find a blanket and you can wrap yourself up. You can use my office. It's warmer and safer in there. We normally have the stove burning, but unfortunately we haven't got the necessary fuel at the moment.'

There was nothing more to do except to thank the man for his offer and accept it with gratitude. With a blanket and out of the cold and draughty room I would survive quite comfortably until morning.

Suddenly I heard the sound of horses' hooves in the street and a carriage stopped by the station. I looked hopefully at the entrance. But it was not the person I was expecting. Instead an elegantly dressed young woman walked in with light, brisk steps. She looked strained and was very pale. Ignoring me completely, she went straight into the back room, followed by the railwayman. Part of the wall between the office and waiting-room was of frosted glass and I could see them talking. She glanced in my direction several times during the conversation. When she came out of the room she hesitated for a moment before approaching me.

'Mr Y tells me that you are a stranger here and have nowhere to stay. I don't live far away and would be very happy to help you. You cannot spend the night here, so please come to my house. I am sure that tomorrow you will find things much easier.'

It looked if the good God Himself had sent this person to

43

my rescue. Her waiting carriage took us to her house. When I entered the hall I saw a Polish officer's cap on a shelf. So, like me, she was an officer's wife. The discovery made me feel much more at home. After a hot bath and dinner, my optimism returned. She was indeed the wife of a Polish officer but had heard nothing from him since the war started. Most nights she went to the station hoping to receive news of him through the stationmaster who was a go-between and in the past had delivered messages for other soldiers' families in Czortkov. Recently, however, all personal contacts had stopped, and she did not intend to continue her visits any longer since messages now only came via the BBC. In fact, she told me she had not wanted to go to the station that night, but some irresistible force had made her.

Saying this, she smiled sweetly and put her arm around me, as if to encourage me to tell her my problem. I was grateful, for, by now, I badly needed someone to share it with. She seemed surprised when I mentioned the name of the gamekeeper and his daughter. Her husband was an enthusiastic huntsman and, because of that, she knew most of the gamekeepers in the province, at least by name, if not personally but she had never heard of that name. When she saw how much the news had upset me, she tried to console me, saying the man might have been new to his job and that was why she did not know of him.

Having gone through the latest events in my mind, I now had some doubts about the veracity of the young woman's story. Krystyna (my benefactress) and I went over the woman's visit in detail and came to the conclusion that she must have come across my husband at some time or another, or how else would she have known, for instance, that he had been in Czortkov? She had known he smoked and had recognised his photograph on my desk. The more I thought about it the more desperate I became. I was determined to find the woman at any price. She must lead me to my husband. If he was wounded, I must be at his side – but what if he had died in the meantime and that was the reason she had not come to meet me? I was driven to distraction by so many conflicting thoughts. Krystyna remained with me most of the night, trying to boost my morale, but hers was not much higher. No wonder, as so many terrible things had happened to us in the last month and our worlds had been turned upside down.

There were moments during that terrible night in Czortkov when I felt particularly close to Nik. The town is situated on the River Dniester and two years previously we had made a trip down it by canoe from Stanislavov. I had the most wonderful memory of that journey and, forgetting about my present grief, I told Krystyna about it. Once again I relived those moments, without knowing they were part of an irretrievable past. It seemed to me that all the evil would go away, that my fears and suspicions were unjustified and that tomorrow I would see my dearly beloved husband. However, that self-deceit did not last long and soon we were again discussing the situation and trying to decide what to do next. We were firmly agreed upon one point: I must find the woman who was holding the thread leading either to my husband or at least to some information about him. Krystyna thought we could do no worse than contact the gun shop owner. Such a shop was required by law to keep a register of people buying arms and ammunition and the owner might have the gamekeeper's name on that list. Knowing him Krystyna felt sure he would not refuse to help us. My hopes rose again.

In the morning we went to find him, and luckily he was at home. Although the shop had been closed since the Occupation and all the ammunition requisitioned, he had managed to remove the books that contained the names of all his clients. He got out the books and turned page after page, carefully checking each name. My heart almost stopped beating each time he hesitated over one. Finally he closed the last book, put his hand on it and, raising his eyes to mine, shook his head. No, there was no gamekeeper of that name in or near Czortkov.

So the last ray of hope disappeared. There could be do doubt now that I had been shamelessly cheated. How was it possible that any woman could play so cruelly on another woman's feelings, just for the sake of swindling her out of warm clothes and shoes, no matter how valuable they might have been at the time? The loss of my clothes seemed of little importance now. I would have gladly given her the rest of what remained in exchange for information about my husband. The belief that she had such information filled me with the most terrible fear. If he was wounded and had fallen into the hands of such a cruel and greedy woman, what could he expect? She must have gained the information about him from somewhere – most probably from the documents and other clues found upon his person. Was he still alive, or did he die among or by the hands of strangers?

The peasant population of the region was composed mostly of Ukrainians. At that time, strong political ferment existed which had been started by members of the nationalistic Ukrainian movement and directed against Polish landowners. I was sure that in the atmosphere of hatred which now prevailed, those people would never try to save the life of a Polish officer. I recalled a small incident from our canoe trip. While passing one of the villages we saw a little girl of six or seven years old standing up to her knees in water. When we drew level, she recognised that we were Polish and started to swear and shake her fist at us. There was so much hatred in her expression and voice that, even now, I can still hear her terrible curses. That child's behaviour must have reflected the adults' attitudes. I knew also, that after the arrival of Soviet troops, at the incitement of the Ukrainian revolutionaries, even those peasants who until then appeared to be loyal and devoted to their Polish masters, attacked and murdered them and burnt their estates. So, could I have any hope at all?

Now that I knew for certain that there was no gamekeeper, I knew also that I could not leave Czortkov without finding out something about my husband. Someone here must know something. Suddenly I realised I knew the address of his quarters in Czortkov. He had given it to me when we parted in Stanislavov on the 15th September. Why hadn't I thought of it before?

46

With Krystyna's help I found the house and rang the bell. With every nerve in my body trembling from emotion and fatigue, I waited. Finally the door opened very slightly and a tall, grey-haired woman looked at us questioningly.

'I am the wife of Captain Duszynski,' I said. 'I understand that he was billeted with you. I am trying to find him.'

Her face lit up for a moment and then became thoughtful.

'Do come in. If you are looking for him it means he did not reach you in Stanislavov but I know he was going to join you there.'

My heart sank again. 'Please tell me everything you know.'

'Well, your husband stayed here twice. The first time was in August before joining his division and the second time in September on his return from the Polish Western front, after the collapse of the defence there. On the second occasion three other officers were stationed with him in this house. They were all awaiting orders from their Command when an alarming message arrived from the Supreme Command in Lvov cancelling all previous orders because of the advancement of the Soviet Army on the Eastern Polish frontier, which made further resistance against the Germans impossible. On the strength of that message the three men decided to cross the frontier to Romania. They had a car at their disposal and tried to persuade your husband to leave with them but he firmly refused saying that he had agreed to meet his wife and son in Stanislavov and could not leave without them ' And that was the end of the story.

All this had occurred some weeks previously and I was sure that he would not have changed his intention of going to Stanislavov. So something had happened to him on the way there. I knew there was no chance of solving the mystery here and that there was nothing left for me but to go home. All the threads that could lead me to Nik were broken. Krystyna and I parted in tears. These had been very worrying days for her as well.

Alexei – the Russian Lieutenant

The journey home was a real nightmare. I can't remember
how I got back. I felt completely broken. When I had left for
Czortkov I had been filled with worry and fear for Nik's fate,
but there had been hope in my heart that we should soon be
together again and I could do something to help him. In spite
of the constant anxiety that thought had sustained and filled
me with almost joyous anticipation. Now all that was gone
and my heart was heavy. I had no feelings, no thoughts, just a
strange tiredness and indifference to everything.

It was only when I found myself at our front door that
normality rushed back. What had happened to my son in my
absence? Was he terribly worried? Had there been any fresh
arrests and searches? Would I find my friend at home? Had
the Russian caused any trouble about my sudden disappearance?

I entered our room. Nooka was not there. I took off my
jacket and hat, put my suitcase on the floor and went to the
bathroom to have a quick wash. I could hear sounds of
animated conversation coming from the dining-room. Nella
came out, and looked at me searchingly. I shook my head.

'I did not find him, I have been cheated. Where is Henryk?'

'He is playing in the nursery with the children, they have
already eaten, and we are just in the middle of our dinner. Mr
and Mrs Hass are here.'

'Is everything all right?' I asked.

'So far not too bad,' she answered, 'but come and have something to eat with us, you must be starving.'

How true! Only now did I realise how weak and hungry I was and how cold. A hot meal was most welcome. I went to the nursery to kiss my son. I did not know if he had guessed where I had been, as Nooka always kept his thoughts to himself.

Apart from our old friends, Mr and Mrs Hass, Alexei Kuratov was seated in the dining-room. I must have looked very surprised because Nella gave me a meaningful look and smiled sweetly, indicating a place next to the Russian. I suppose she wanted to soften the impression this scene made on me by her smile. She was one of those people whose smile could transform a plain face into a pretty one, and a pretty one into a beautiful one. She belonged to the latter category. Unfortunately during those past weeks I had not seen her smile once and had almost forgotten about that miraculous transformation. Now I did as I was told, placing myself beside the Russian. I was the only person present who spoke Russian and, probably because of that, Alexei looked extremely pleased and helped me to my chair. I felt disinclined to talk. The only words I could speak were those of anger and despair, and that could do no one any good, so having replied to his 'good evening', I directed my whole attention to the bowl of hot soup.

Suddenly the Russian turned to me and asked quietly, 'Did you see your husband?'

I almost choked. Who on earth had betrayed me? Could it be Nella? Had she fraternised with him in my absence? Was that why he was now sitting at her table? These thoughts rushed through my head as I tried to recover my senses.

Finally, I asked, 'What makes you say such an extraordinary thing? I have not had any news of my husband since the war started. I neither know where he is nor what has happened to him.'

The Russian answered, 'Nowadays, if someone disappears from view as suddenly as you did, one can assume one of two

49

things; either that person was arrested or had to leave for a very important reason. Arrest is difficult to conceal, your friends would have known about it, but you suddenly disappeared and no one seemed to know where you had gone to or why. No one travels for pleasure these days, so I came to the conclusion that you must have received news of your husband and had gone to meet him.'

I listened to his words with mixed feelings. Feelings of alarm at the confirmation of my suspicions that we were being watched and of relief at knowing that, as my meeting with my husband had not materialised, I could not betray his whereabouts. The Russian was probably trying to trap me into making a confession by haphazard guessing.

Now it was my turn to ask, 'You have naturally informed the authorities about your conclusions?'

He replied, 'I am a cavalry officer, not a member of the NKVD. That kind of report is not included in my duties.'

There was rancour in his voice. I looked at him in surprise; his annoyance seemed genuine. After dinner, when everyone had left, I told Nella the story of my distressing journey in detail. Although sympathising with me, she did not seem surprised that the journey had been in vain, as, after my departure, she learned of similar cases of fraud. The methods were almost identical and the victims all Polish officers' wives. The perpetrator of those crimes was a Ukrainian servant girl who obtained all the necessary information from unsuspecting friends working in other households. She had obviously discovered it was easy to deceive people by playing on their emotions. I certainly had not doubted her sincerity and truthfulness for a moment, nor had any kind of suspicion crossed my mind. To have suspected deceit at such a moment was unthinkable, however naive it might have seemed afterwards. Nella's revelations about the woman made me feel ashamed of my gullibility. Nevertheless the knowledge that the trickster had never seen my husband and that the story about him having been wounded must have been pure invention, brought me immense relief. It was a great pity that, instead of choosing a more conventional method to carry out her thefts, she had chosen one which had caused so much suffering.

Since my returning from my distressing trip to Czortkov and the conversation at dinner with Alexei Kuratov, I began to trust him more, and finally told him about the visit of the 'gamekeeper's daughter'. He strongly advised reporting her to the militia in the hope that I might recover at least some of the stolen property, and also to prevent her from continuing her criminal activities. I followed his advice which not only produced no result, but could have ended tragically for me. The woman was found and spent a couple of days in jail, but by then she had already disposed of her loot and, in revenge, she told the authorities that during her visit she had seen a gun in my room. Obviously she knew that possession of arms was a very serious offence. I was put under arrest and my room searched but, as nothing was found, I was released the same day. I considered myself very lucky, because not long before I had got rid of two guns as well as the cadets' documents which, at their request, I had hidden in my room. On seeing one of them arrested, I had promptly burned the documents and buried the guns. Alexei seemed so upset that he had put me in such danger that it finally convinced Nella and me that he was well disposed towards us.

It was now two months since he had moved into the flat and we began to think ourselves fortunate in having him instead of anyone else forced upon us – more especially because we heard more and more about the troubles other people in the block had with their 'tenants'. He certainly had a way with the children and their friendship with him was progressing rapidly. The chocolate he was bringing and the tricks he showed them greatly contributed to it. Nooka told me that he could bend coins and other pieces of metal with his fingers without any difficulty. He could also lift two children at once high in the air on each of his hands and so on. We learned later that Alexei was an all-round athlete and winner of many awards in the Soviet Army. He obviously liked children and

51

perhaps playing with them relieved his longing for his small son. Such a friendship would not have been looked upon with indulgence had it not been for the fact that schools and nurseries, not functioning properly since the outbreak of war, had now closed completely. The children were bored and Nooka, with no proper home or school to go, roamed the streets with the other boys. Nella's children, who were at the nursery school age, were a real problem to her and she welcomed anyone who could help to amuse them. So, when Alexei asked if I would teach him Polish, I agreed. Our lessons consisted not so much of the language tuition as of talks in Russian about pre-war life in Poland. He assimilated my information with immense interest, showering me with more and more questions, although I could see that he accepted most of my answers with scepticism. It was all so contrary to what he had been told in Russia. Gradually, however his questioning became less and less aggressive and his interest switched from the political and sociological to more general subjects such as customs and family life. He also started to talk about himself.

His childhood was spent in Saratov, a town on the River Volga. He could not remember his father at all, although his mother had told him he was an officer in the Cossack regiment and had been declared missing during the Revolution. He really did not know his mother very well, either. Her job as a book-keeper in a factory, queuing for food and the compulsory attendance at political meetings, did not leave her much time to devote to him. He belonged to a group of hooligans who roamed the streets, robbing people of clothes and stealing food when hungry. Each member of the gang carried a knife and was always ready for a fight. In winter he usually stayed in the half room which was their home. Another family lived in the other half behind a partition made of blankets. In summer he mostly slept out of doors. His schooling was completely neglected and only later, when he joined the Communist Youth Organisation, *Komsomol*, and subsequently the army, did he receive some education. He excelled in sports, particularly riding and athletics. He moved noiselessly, like a cat, with light springy footsteps, as if wearing ballet shoes instead of his heavy military boots. He was slightly above average height, broad shouldered and slim waisted – a fact he liked to emphasise by pulling in his belt very tightly. He was not exactly handsome, but he had an interesting face, high cheek bones, a swarthy complexion and dark, lively eyes which never looked anyone straight in the eye but threw quick watchful glances all around. It puzzled me why he never kept his gun in a holster at his side, but hidden under his coat, on his chest. I noticed that often in the street on hearing footsteps behind him he would reach quickly for his gun and holding it in his hand, would turn abruptly to face the person. Once, when I asked him why he was so suspicious and jumpy, he said that it was most probably a habit left over from his turbulent and dangerous youth, but I wondered whether that was the real reason, or if it was because he did not feel very safe in his new surroundings.

Alexei's regimental duties only required his presence for a few hours each morning so, being free in the afternoons, he accompanied me on my tours of lessons and waited to escort me home. At first I did not mind that, as walking with him I felt better protected from the lascivious glances and occasional rude remarks of passing soldiers, who were not used to seeing Polish women walking alone after dark. Although Alexei had by now become almost a friend to us I soon realised that to those who saw me in the street, walking in the company of a Russian officer and speaking in Russian, the situation must have apeared quite differently. It would not take much to make a Russian spy and a collaborator out of me, and I had to stop it. During our next lesson I asked Alexei not to wait for me in the street any more, which he seemed to accept. After a few days' break, however, I found him waiting for me again.

In an effort to put him off I said acidly, 'I hope that at least you are adequately compensated for following me.'

As soon as I said it I realised my mistake. Alexei stepped back from me as if in horror. I thought for a moment that he was going to murder me but he said nothing, just turned round and walked away. It left me worried. The last thing I wanted was to antagonise him. I knew that Nella, who, on a previous occasion had expressed fear that Alexei's growing interest in me might bring complications, would be very cross if she knew what had happened. I had to do something quickly. As soon as I came home I wrote Alexei a note apologising for what I said, but I did not get a reply. As lessons had been suspended with the approach of Christmas I hardly left my room so our paths did not cross for a while.

Nella and I dreaded the thought of Christmas. We were determined to make it as traditional and pleasant as we possibly could for the children. We gave them a Christmas tree and quite nice presents, but they missed their fathers so much that all our efforts to make a cheerful holiday failed badly.

Having received no news of Nik since our parting in Stanislavov in the middle of September, I worried more and more about him as the days passed. Where was he now? Why hadn't he given a sign of life? With lessons temporarily stopped I had more time for thinking and often, to feel closer to Nik, recreated in my imagination scenes from our past life together.

These reminiscences, after giving momentary pleasure, made me feel the immensity of my loss and the tragedy of our present situation even more. The rule of the Soviets did not bring benefits to anybody. Although some of the poorer sections of the community and, possibly, some of the ethnic minorities had expectations of a better life under the Communist regime, their hopes were soon dashed and their expectations frustrated as their lot became much worse. After the invasion of Poland by the Russians there was a Ukrainian uprising against them in Zbaraz in February 1940 and the leader of the uprising was quoted as saying, 'Poles tried for twenty years to make us love them but did not succeed, but now, with the Soviet arrival we realise how pro-Polish we have become in just a few months.'

Nooka and I spent New Year's Eve of 1940 huddled, fully

dressed, under blankets on our beds, reading. The room was not heated and the temperature outside was −25°C. Finally Nooka got bored and went to play with Nella's children. I tried to continue reading, but my hands were getting stiff with cold, so I put the book aside and allowed myself to be overcome by old memories. A knock at the door and Nella's voice brought me back from my reveries. She had come to ask me to join them in the drawing room as Alexei was waiting with a cake and a bottle of champagne to wish everybody a Happy, New Year.

'A Happy New Year,' I said, 'with Russians and Germans on our soil?'

'We all know that, but do come; there is no point in offending Alexei.'

I had not seen Alexei since our encounter in the street and wondered how he would behave towards me. When he saw me entering the room, he jumped to his feet from the floor where he was playing with the children and greeted me with what I thought was an apologetic smile. I acknowledged his greeting. On the little table I saw a beautifully decorated cake with an inscription in Polish, 'Happy New Year'. At first I could not believe my eyes and thought it must be a dummy cake. But no, it was real. Alexei must have gone to a lot of trouble to get it, and it was a kind thought. While Nella cut the cake, Alexei opened the bottle, the cork flew high into the air and the wine cascaded into the promptly proferred glasses. We all wished each other a Happy New Year. Never before had such a wish seemed to me to be so filled with meaning. In my family the standard wish in the past, repeated every year by my husband, was 'May it not be worse'. Now, with all my heart, I prayed silently for a better year for all of us. May the war and occupation of our country end. May our families be reunited. May peace on earth return. Looking at this young Russian officer, I thought that his wishes must be very similar. He was only a little cog in a monstrous mechanism – an ordinary man, a husband and a father who must miss his family as much as we missed ours.

The children, having gorged themselves with cake, were sent to bed, but Alexei asked permission to remain with us a little longer. He suggested bringing his balalaika and singing Russian folk songs to us. We gladly agreed, as we liked Russian music and song, and also felt that because there was not much to talk about this would be an easier way to spend the rest of the evening. He soon returned carrying another bottle of champagne. As we did not want to drink any more, Alexei put the bottle on the floor and settled himself beside it. He started to sing in a soft, pleasing baritone. The songs were melodious and amusing. He explained that they were called *chastushki*, composed by peasants and, like the popular proverbs, contained a lot of unsophisticated wisdom and wit. When he tired of singing he asked us to tell him about our customs and amusements during the festive season. As Nella could not speak Russian, the task fell on me. He particularly wanted to hear about our *kuligs*. Being a cavalry officer, they probably interested him because of the part horses played in them. *Kulig* was the name for the sledging cavalcades which were very popular in Poland during the carnival. It usually started with one or two couples arriving in horse-drawn sledges 'unexpectedly' at a friend's house, where they had a few drinks and snacks and dragged their hosts on to another house, then yet another, with refreshment at each stop. When a long string of sledges had collected together, races would start. *Kulig* lasted well into the early hours and by the end everybody was happily tight on the traditional drink, *krupnik* (consisting of pure spirit, honey and spices) which had been served hot at each house they had visited.

Alexei listened to my stories with bated breath and appeared excited. He had almost emptied the champagne bottle and his eyes were sparkling. He began to sing again, but this time he was plucking the balalaika strings with such fire that I thought they might break, and his singing acquired a passion which we had never suspected in him. As we watched, he seemed to change from the correct, quietly spoken Russian officer into a swaggering, uncontrollable Don Cossack.

Suddenly, he interrupted his singing, jumped to his feet, lifted his glass and shouted, 'To hell with war! Long live lovely Polish ladies!', then he rushed out of the room and the flat. We thought he must have gone out of his mind. We looked at each other in horror: if he shouted like that in the street, he would be arrested immediately and that would bring problems for us – most probably a flat search and possibly prosecution. We waited in terror for the worst to happen.

After what seemed an eternity of unbearable tension we heard someone turning the key of the door, then light steps – unmistakably Alexei's. No soldiers' heavy boots, no menacing loud voices. He was alone.

He came in, and turning to me, said, 'Madam, the horses are waiting. It is a beautiful night and you must come for a ride with me.'

It was such an anti-climax, such transition from tragedy to comedy that I did not know whether to laugh or cry. But the transition was not as complete as I had imagined, for now, standing before me, gun in hand, was a drunken Russian officer.

'If you don't come, I'll shoot,' he said. The threat sounded real enough, particularly as Alexei could no longer think rationally after the amount of champagne he had drunk. I looked at Nella and Anna, who were equally terrified.

Trying to keep calm, I said, 'Please put that gun away. I'll come with you.' He did as I asked and I went to get my coat and a shawl for my head.

Waiting outside the house was a sledge drawn by two horses. Obviously Alexei had been influenced by my tales of the *kulig*, and either wanted to recreate an illusion of the past for me or to have a taste of the bourgeois pleasures himself. Despite the absurdity of the situation, I could not help noticing how truly beautiful the night was. The air was very still and the crisp snow sparkled in the moonlight. The sky was studded with stars and, under that heavenly illumination, the world looked pure and deceptively peaceful. I sank into the sledge, the coachman pulled at the reins and the horses moved to the delicate sound of bells. For a moment it seemed like any normal New Year, but the illusion did not last long. The dead appearance of the city, which normally at this time of the year would have been full of life and rejoicing, brought me back to reality. I looked at the windows of the houses; with few exceptions they were dark. Most people had sought refuge in sleep. Suddenly the words of a popular and sad Russian gypsy song came into my head:

'Coachman don't drive horses so hard, I have nowhere to hurry, I have no one to love.'

A feeling of great despair swept over me. Where is my beloved now? Why isn't he here instead of this crazy Russian? A lump came into my throat and, although I don't cry easily, I could not hold back my tears. I pulled the shawl more tightly around my head and buried my face in it to muffle my sobs. Alexei seemed alarmed and tried to remove the shawl from my face.

'What is the matter? Why are you crying?'

'I want to go home,' was all I could say through my tears.

He ordered the coachman to return and when we reached the house helped me from the sledge and up the stairs into the flat. He had sobered up and we parted in silence outside my room. 1939 had ended on a very strange note.

I dreaded the thought of meeting Alexei again as I restarted my rounds of lessons, but he did not show up. At home his behaviour had changed, he did not play with the children any more and avoided encounters with Nella and me by leaving very early in the morning and coming home late. Anna was the only person to see him and she said he was gloomy and unhappy and, judging by the number of empty bottles in his room, had been drinking heavily. Anna hinted that Alexei was lovesick and found it very amusing.

Just as I thought that Alexei had at last disappeared from my life he suddenly made a dramatic reappearance. Late one afternoon he knocked at my door and, without waiting for an answer, came in and walked straight to the desk where I was sitting. He was obviously drunk. His face was pale, and his jaws contracted.

He pulled out his gun, placed it in front of me, on the desk and said in a strangely quiet voice, 'Shoot me, go on shoot me!' Nooka was also in the room, and the thought of the effect the scene must be having on him made the whole thing even more distressing.

Searching desperately in my mind for something to say I managed to utter, 'Why? What has happened?'

He let go of the gun and repeated, 'Don't ask, shoot!'

Despite Alexei's unstable state I could think of nothing better than to repeat, 'Tell me what has happened.' As I spoke I cautiously turned the barrel away from us.

Then he said, 'I can't talk to you in front of your child. Come outside with me.'

While I was putting on my coat, Alexei replaced his gun on his chest, as was his custom. I gave my poor, terrified son as reassuring a smile as I could muster and left the room with Alexei. He summoned the first passing sledge and ordered the driver to go to the local park. We did not speak, and I wondered why he wanted to go to the park and what would happen when we arrived there. All kinds of wild thoughts ran through my mind, but how could anyone guess the motives of a madman.

We reached the park and I got out of the sledge and walked ahead of Alexei. It was getting dark, and there were few people about. Alexei, by my side now, suddenly pulled out his gun and started to shoot into the air. People fell to the ground or tried to hide behind the trees. I hoped that a militia patrol was close at hand, and would arrest the lunatic before he killed anybody. However having used up all his ammunition, Alexei returned the gun to its usual place. I breathed a sigh of relief, glad that this horrible adventure had ended without anybody getting hurt, but very uncertain and frightened of what was going to happen next. I wanted to get away as soon as possible, and home to reassure Nooka that all was well.

As I started walking towards the gate Alexei caught me by the arm.

'Wait. Listen to me. I was shooting to scare all the people away.'

'Why?'

59

'Because I wanted to talk to you alone.'

He grabbed me in his arms and, holding me very tight, his face very near mine, whispered passionately, 'I love you, I love you so much that I can't sleep, eat or work. I think of you day and night, and I can't go on like that.' He sank to his knees and put his arms round my legs. 'My love, my little dove (*golubka*) have pity on me, otherwise I shall go mad.'

By now I had recovered somewhat and tried to make light of it all.

'Get up, or you'll freeze to the ground.'

He tightened his grip, almost knocking me off my feet.

'No, I won't let you go until you promise that you will be mine.'

'All right, I promise.'

He sprang to his feet, and we walked out of the completely deserted park. There were no sledges to be seen anywhere and the pavements were very slippery. There had been a slight thaw during the day, and now the surface was covered with a thin layer of ice. Walking was difficult and as I slipped and almost fell once or twice, I did not object when Alexei linked his arm with mine and held me until we reached home.

'I shall wait for you tonight,' he whispered on parting.

I nodded. On the way home I had devised a plan of action. I had a very good and devoted friend Mila Soborska who owned a large house on the outskirts of Stanislavov. I decided to escape there that night. She knew about my previous problems with Alexei and had suggested before that Nooka and I should move there.

My son was very relieved to see me back home and we embraced warmly. He had obviously been very worried, but yet I had to find the courage to tell him that I was going to leave him again that night. I did not know how much he had guessed and understood, but when I said that I was going for the night to Mila's he took it in his stride and said that he would be all right left with Nella.

As I had hoped, Mila received me warmly, prepared a bed for me and asked no questions. I couldn't sleep all night for worrying what would happen when Alexei discovered that I had fooled him. But as usual there were surprises. I knew that Alexei left for his regiment about seven in the morning, so I had planned to return as soon as possible after that. It was a quarter past seven when I reached home and, to my dismay, I saw him in the street, outside the entrance to the house, waiting for me. I was paralysed with fear when he started to walk towards me, but I could not see anything menacing in his expression or behaviour. On the contrary, he looked humble and unsure of himself, and there was not a trace of the previous night's daring.

He simply said, 'I understand that you went to a friend's house. Why did you do it? Don't you know how dangerous it is for a woman to walk alone at night?'

I thought what a puzzling and unpredictable man he was.

'Am I a wild animal,' he continued, 'that you have to run from me like that?'

I was tempted to say that indeed he had behaved like a wild animal, but now I saw a mortified and dejected human being in front of me, and couldn't help feeling sorry for him. He was unshaven and looked as though he had not slept at all. But now whatever he said, I knew I could no longer trust him. He was totally unpredictable. Was he really in love with me or was it because he was separated from his family? Was it due to the confusion of finding himself in such different surroundings? Had his ideology changed and had there been a collapse in his loyalty towards his country and his superiors?

No one could know, perhaps least of all himself. Whatever the reason, I decided that it was high time we left Nella's flat – as much for her sake as for ours. So I gladly accepted Mila's offer of hospitality given so warmly and with the understanding so typical of her. We moved in the next day.

About a week later some of us were awakened by the sound of horse's hooves. I looked out and saw a man on a horse. He neared the entrance, then turned the horse around, jumped over the fence and disappeared into the night. As the house stood in a garden protected from the street by a high fence everyone, except Mila and me, thought that the noise must have come from the street.

The next morning we found a letter on the doorstep addressed to me. It simply said, 'Goodbye my love, forever.' It was a most welcome message. I never saw or heard of Alexei again, but the Russian officer who moved into his room in Nella's flat seemed to think that he had been sent to the Finnish front as, apart from his other skills as a sportsman, he was a good skier. Perhaps this was true but I thought, not without sadness, that an even worse fate might have befallen that knight-errant.

The Arrest

It was now 1940 but there was still no news of Nik and although an optimist by nature, I began to have the blackest thoughts. From the information gathered in Czortkov I knew that he left that town in September and now it was February. Could there be any hope of him being alive?

And then in the middle of February, I received a strange looking envelope addressed in Nik's hand. It was posted in the USSR and my heart sank. That was the last place I would have wished him to be. On the other hand I knew now that he was alive and that was the most wonderful news I could have had. He was writing from the Soviet POW camp in Kozelsk in the Smolensk province. Not a word of how and where he had been taken prisoner, but it was obvious to me that he was captured on his way from Czortkov to Stanislavov. No doubt it was our decision to meet in Stanislavov that contributed to that great misfortune. He couldn't and wouldn't break his promise and wouldn't for a moment contemplate leaving the country without his family.

Being the man he was he tried to comfort me by writing that the camp was in a healthy area surrounded by pine trees and was very good for his health. He knew that I would be worried by his susceptibility to bronchitis which dated from the time when, as a young soldier in the legions, he lived in trenches. He had also described conditions in the camp as quite good, with some kind of social life and occasional lectures and

63

concerts organised by fellow prisoners. Much later, in England, I learned from General J. Wolkowicki, who for a time was also imprisoned in the same camp, that conditions were appalling. Nik implored me to look after myself and Nooka until we could meet again and, releasing me from my promise to wait for him in Stanislavov, advised me to go to Wilno, where his family lived and to seek help there from the Red Cross, if necessary. Obviously he did not realise that it was impossible for us to move out of the province without permission from the Soviet authorities and that that was out of the question. Besides Wilno was also invaded by the Soviet Army and the activities of the Red Cross and other international organisations, were suspended. We were now totally isolated from the rest of the world. He was allowed to write and receive one letter a month, plus a very small sum of money which he quoted and begged me not to exceed. This made me wonder if such a transgression would have deprived him even of these paltry privileges. He asked me not to send him any warm clothes, saying that he took enough with him when he left, and that I should sell or exchange for food any clothes that were left. I cried when I read this. He was quite a heavy smoker, but neither cigarettes nor food parcels were allowed. My only comfrot was the belief that Nik would be protected under the international law relating to treatment of POWs and, that being quite young and strong, he should outlast the war.

I received two more letters from him, one in March and another at the beginning of April, 1940, and he now knew, from my letters, that we were living with the Soborski family.

About the same time most welcome news had reached me that Jan Roszek and his brother (now living in Canada) had successfully crossed the border.

Saborski's family owned a large nursery and flower shop in Stanislavov and, as a regular customer, I had become good friends first with the owner, Franciszek (whom I will call Frank) and later with his wife, Mila. Frank, a reserve captain, was one of the first men arrested by the NKVD, and was later deported to Russia and interned in Ostashkov, one of the three notorious Russian POW camps from which very few emerged alive.

When we moved to his house, only Mila, their two teenage daughters, Halina 16 and Janka 15, Frank's widowed mother and his sister Maryla with her eight-month-old son, Leszek were left. Frank was already in prison and Mila queued outside every day, along with many other women, with food parcels for their menfolk.

Maryla's husband, who, before the war, was the head of the section for Soviet affairs in the provincial administration offices, had had to seek refuge in Romania to escape the arrest and persecution which doubtless would have awaited him had he remained in Stanislavov after the Russian invasion. Frank's prompt arrest was probably due to his acceptance of the duties of the former Chief of Police who had left the country as soon as he heard of the approach of the Soviet Army. Frank hoped that he could maintain law and order in the town and save the inhabitants from anarchy until a replacement came. He was convinced that he was only doing his duty as a good citizen.

Although there were only women in the house itself, there were many men working in the garden. I was surprised to see so many of them previously unknown to me; there were more 'gardeners' employed now than before the war. I soon learnt that they were mostly military men in hiding. Passed off as labourers, they were biding their time, waiting for a signal from the ZWZ (Association of Professional Soldiers), the secret organisation working from Lvov, that the time and conditions were ripe for their escape. In addition to disregarding the risk involved in sheltering these men, the family also provided them with food from their rapidly dwindling reserves.

At first sight, Mila's plain exterior, short plump figure and round, kindly face did not reveal the intelligence, depth and subtlety, which were characteristic of her, as well as her generosity and all-round goodness. Although she was in charge of the business after her husband's arrest and 40 years old at the time, it was unquestionably her mother-in-law, the Old Lady, who ruled the household. Mila, with an endurance at which I marvelled, accepted it. The Old Lady must have been very beautiful in her youth. She was slim, tall and even now in her late sixties held herself erect. She had an oval face with regular, delicate features and a mass of grey hair which she wore in a chignon. I was told that when she was young her hair was jet black and reached to her knees. Now she had it cut quite short, as not only was it too heavy a load for her to carry on her head, but it also caused great problems when it came to washing or combing.

Her only daughter, Maryla, by contrast, was quiet, patient and submissive. I could never imagine her quarrelling with anyone. When she happened to disagree, she fixed her large, light-grey and very expressive eyes on the person concerned and slightly, very slightly, tightened her lips. Of couse, she never even thought of disagreeing with her autocratic mother, but her submissiveness did not seem to deprive her of dignity in the slightest degree. The impression she created was that she chose, rather than was forced into it. She was a perfect mother, showing infinite love and devotion to her little golden-haired son.

Frank and Mila's daughters were brought up with a strict discipline under the watchful eye of their grandmother, and I never heard them answer back or disobey her orders, although I could see that at times they resented them. Both girls were very good at school and most helpful in the house where no one was allowed to remain idle, even for one short moment.

Mila's hospitality came at a very difficult time in my life – not only because of Alexei's behaviour, but also because the number of my pupils had decreased, and paying for our meals in restaurants left me with no money for anything else. Sensing the situation with her usual subtlety and tact, Mila asked if I would replace her in the flower shop for part of the day in exchange for food for Nooka and me. I accepted with joy and gratitude. I love flowers and a part-time job suited me perfectly as I could combine it with giving lessons to my remaining pupils. I realised that it was a magnanimous gesture on Mila's part, as food was priceless in those days, but just how magnanimous I was soon to discover.

The shop had no chance of success – who would buy flowers in those times? In addition, plants brought from the hot-house died within a few hours in unheated premises. We offered them at greatly reduced prices to anyone who came into the shop but that did not cover even part of the running expenses, and just before closing time we gave away the remaining flowers to friends who happened to come in for a chat. I was sure that Mila knew she would have to close the shop very soon and her offer of a job was made with the thought of helping me without hurting my pride. When the shop finally closed, Nooka and I were already a firmly established part of the household, sitting down to meals with the rest of the family. Naturally I tried to help on the domestic side as much as I could and was allowed to do. Being independent by nature I was slightly apprehensive of the Old Lady and it might have been very difficult had it not been for Mila's firm but discreet support. I also contributed towards the cost of articles still obtainable for cash, such as bread, flour or sugar, which by then had been rationed.

Nooka and I occupied a room in the attic. It had no heating, and not much space in it either: two beds, a wardrobe and a dressing-table filled it, but that did not matter, as all our free time and evenings were spent downstairs with the family. I hoped in that way we would manage to get through the winter and perhaps even through the war, as we felt more and more at home among these warm-hearted, kind people. But whatever hopes I had were soon dashed.

Now I had a new escort waiting for me in the street, in the person of an NKVD man. Politely but firmly he would order me to follow him. My protests that my pupils were waiting for me made no impression on him. He walked quickly in front of me, pretending that we had nothing to do with each other. This walk usually ended up in some flat or a room each time in a different locality. Invariably there would be a table laid with all sorts of delicacies, fruit and a bottle of wine. Occasionally there was another man waiting in the room, but usually there were just the two of us, although I had the feeling that there might be others behind the door. I was asked to sit down and offered a glass of wine, which I always refused. The questions never varied. They concerned my origin and those of my ancestors. At one of the meetings it was said that they knew who my husband was and I must realise that, as the wife of a military judge, I was a highly suspected person and did not deserve any privileges.

'What privileges? You even prevent me from earning the little I can from teaching and, thanks to you, I shall lose all my pupils.'

'Privileges depend upon you. Why struggle by, giving badly paid lessons, which you can lose any day? We are offering you a chance. You could be very useful to us. All we want to know is what is happening among your circle of friends. You must admit we're not asking for much, but by doing what we ask of you, you would ensure a comfortable life for yourself and your child.'

I tried to explain that I did not possess any information which could be of interest to them. They replied that it was not up to me to judge what was or was not interesting to them, and that I would simply have to repeat my conversations with friends and acquaintances and to steer those conversations towards subjects which would be given to me.

Although these meetings were conducted in a courteous manner and without threats, I felt completely exhausted at the end of them. I kept wondering how long I would be able to withstand them. I tried to discourage my interrogators by saying that I was not skillful enough for the task, and that I had lost contact with all my previous friends. When this did not help, at one of the meetings I lost my temper, jumped out of the chair and rushed out of the room, slamming the door behind me. Now, when I know how cruel and ruthless the NKVD men could be, I am amazed at my 'arrogance' and their tolerance at that time. They must have been ordered to treat me patiently, hoping sooner or later to break my resistance.

After my outburst, the next session took a different shape. There were three men present and I noticed the absence of wine and tempting food. The session started as usual – I recited my name and those of my parents and grandparents. This was followed by gentle persuasion and flattery, such as, 'Why don't you take advantage of your knowledge of Russian, which would make it so easy for you to communicate with the authorities, your exceptional intelligence, and your extensive social contacts?' (which at that time were practically non-existent). The lack of response on my part visibly annoyed the Russians. There was a sudden change of tone, from friendly to sharp and official. Instead of addressing me by my name and patronymic (a friendly and respectful form of address in Russia), they started to use only my surname. I was told that they had received information that I was an active member of a secret organisation, had helped people to escape across the border and that my activities were directed against the interests of the Soviet state. This last accusation sounded ominous. One of the greatest crimes was to be called an enemy of the Soviet people and the state. When I showed great surprise, they gave me the name of a person who had, according to them, denounced me. He was a Pole, an acquaintance whom I had been seeing from time to time. At our last meeting he had tried to persuade me, not for the first time, to join the secret organisation and I had promised to think it over and give him my answer at our next meeting. How thankful I was that the present interrogation was taking place before I had been given any details about that organisation. However bad the threats, or even torture, might be, I could not betray any secrets. But I was thoroughly confused. Did my interrogators suspect my acquaintance and were they trying to get confirmation of his involvement from me? Or was he an *agent provocateur* instructed to set a trap for me? I rejected that latter thought outright because, if it were true, they doubtless would have waited until I had given him my answer. Having concluded that they could not have known anything, but were merely guessing, I very emphatically denied all knowledge of any secret organisation, insisting that our meetings had been purely social. At last they let me go.

So far I had never been summoned from the house, only stopped in the street. Suddenly, at the beginning of April 1940, just after dinner, when the whole family was gathered round a large table to spend the rest of the evening together, the bell rang sharply. A uniformed NKVD man stood at the door and ordered me to follow him immediately to the militia post. Until now only Mila knew of my 'visits' as I had tried to keep them secret in order not to alarm my son and the rest of the family. Now there was general consternation. Why and for what was I being summoned? I wondered whether this was the end of the 'velvet glove' treatment and what would happen to Nooka if I was arrested. I said a quick farewell to the family, trying not to appear worried, and left the house with my escort. There was one comforting thought: that in case a search was made, except for the two genuine ones, there were no 'gardeners' left. The others, we hoped, were safely abroad.

In the hall of the militia station were several local men obviously waiting to be called in and interrogated. When my turn came I felt very tired, as it was well past midnight and I had been standing in the draughty hall for several hours with no bench or chair to sit on. I entered a room in which there were two uniformed men who apparently knew all about me and my 'noble' ancestors because they did not go through the normal procedure. One of them, a captain, said straight away that they knew my husband was in a POW camp in Russia and, if I still refused to cooperate, life would be made very difficult for him. He wanted an immediate answer. I asked to be allowed a couple of days in which to think about it. He replied that I could equally well reflect in a prison cell and that I must not forget while in there that my husband's and child's fate depended entirely on me. After that, a second man summoned a soldier and told him to escort me to the local

70

prison. It was getting light by then but there was not a soul in the street and I thought I could vanish without trace, and no one would know what had happened to me.

My escort had a rifle and marched me to the prison gate like a criminal. When we arrived, no formalities were required and I was simply passed on to the prison guard and led through the semi-dark corridor towards a cell. The door was opened and I was pushed inside. I stumbled over someone's legs and provoked a shower of abuse. There was a fearful smell. I leaned against the wall, afraid to take even a single step. A very weak light filtered through a small window near the low ceiling, but it was not sufficient to see anything. Gradually as my eyes became accustomed to the darkness, I began to distinguish the various inmates. The sight was so nightmarish that I suspected it had been arranged especially in order to terrify me. The cell was filled with old, unkempt dishevelled harridans, packed like sardines. They created an impression as horrifying as the most frightening descriptions of the under-world from Dickens or Gorky. The appalling stench came from a bucket, placed at the far end of the cell, which was used as a latrine.

Now that I could see the cell occupants, they were also able to see me and, not recognising me as one of them, they joined in a chorus of the filthiest jokes and remarks. The sight of them going about their morning routine made me feel that at any moment I might be sick over them, and I hardly dared think what might happen to me then. The thought of remaining in the cell for any length of time threw me into panic. I had to get out of this hell by hook or crook. I started to bang on the door and screamed at the top of my voice that I must be let out.

I did not believe that this would produce immediate results, but surprisingly it did. The door was opened and I staggered out past the guard. I clutched at my throat to stop myself vomiting. After the cell, the air in the corridor seemed to me as pure as that at our country retreat and I took a deep breath. Again, not quite believing that my request would be granted,

I asked to be taken to the man in charge. I was led to a small room at the end of the corridor and told to wait. Shortly afterwards I was escorted to another room where I was received by the NKVD men, neither of whom appeared surprised to see me and who were not in the least interested in my particulars.

The senior one, said, 'You asked to see me?'

'Yes. Please let me out of here.'

I thought he looked at me mockingly. 'Why?'

'Please tell those who sent me here that I agree to do as they ask.'

He inhaled deeply from his cigarette, blew out the smoke slowly, got up from his chair and went out of the room. I waited anxiously for his return. The thought of returning to the same cell seemed worse than death to me. Actually, I was disappointed in myself and my lack of resistance. I tried to prepare myself for a negative reply and the return to that hell. Perhaps when I got over the shock and knew what to expect, I might react differently and recover my self-respect by finding the necessary moral courage to endure it. Nevertheless, when the man came back and said, 'You can go home. You will be informed when and where to report.' I must confess that I was very happy.

I scarcely remember how I got home, but I well remember the cries of welcome, the embraces and kisses that were showered upon me. The happiest of all were those from my son.

That night, after everyone was in bed, Mila and I held council. She alone knew that I had evolved a plan after the previous interrogation, when I felt that my days of freedom were numbered. From the moment I had heard that Nik was interned, there was nothing to keep me in Stanislavov. Nor did I think that my escape could affect his life in the POW camp and I was convinced that all the threats were merely an attempt to force me to collaborate. We both thought I was extremely lucky to have got out of prison and, at least temporarily, out of the clutches of the NKVD, as I badly needed time to put my plan into effect. When I was arrested I had been waiting for word that the preparations for Nooka's and my escape had been made and that the courier was available to take us over the border. It was to come from a priest, a very old friend of Soborski's family.

My first meeting with him took place in a church when I went to 'confession'. He gave me some instructions and warned that I might be expected to take an oath not to disclose the names of people who helped us, adding that I must think twice before deciding to take a child with me. After 'confession' I stayed in the church for a long time, praying fervently for God's help in making the right decision, for the success of the plan and for strength if it failed. Now Mila and I decided that I could wait no longer and she would go to see the priest the next morning and ask him to do everything possible to treat the case as extremely urgent and speed up the escape. She returned with the news that nothing very positive could be promised, and that, in the meantime, I had to play up to my tormentors. The priest still had grave doubts about the wisdom of taking Nooka with me. I was very down-hearted. Mila tried to comfort me by saying that if there was no other way and I had to go alone, I could be certain that Nooka would be looked after like their own son until we could meet again. We both cried unashamedly.

Journey into Exile

However, before anything more happened, events overtook us. During the night of 12/13 April 1940 we were awakened by furious hammering on the door which someone opened. Then came the sound of heavy boots on the stairs, and before I could throw on a dressing-gown, two armed soldiers burst into the room. One of them stood guard by the door, while the other, an officer, went straight to my bed and started to search nervously under my pillow. He was obviously looking for arms, but by that time I had none. I suddenly remembered Nik's sword which, before his arrest, Frank had buried in the garden and felt glad it was out of the heathens' reach. My poor little son sat on the bed, crying. The soldier searched the wardrobe, throwing everything out.

He found a folder with Nik's letters which were very precious to me. Whenever we had to part Nik wrote to me regularly once or twice a day. His letters mirrored our whole life together and I kept them because to me they were the most beautiful letters ever written. The officer handed the folder to the guard by the door. I begged him not to take them away but he replied that he was always very interested to know what a Polish officer wrote to his wife and was looking forward to having them translated. He saw Nik's photo on the dressing table and, with one swift movement, swept it away and put it in the folder. When I protested he said I would have no need for it because soon we would be together as they were taking

74

us to join him. At last I knew why they were here and the news made me feel happier. The officer told me that I had two hours at the most to finish packing and there was no time to lose. This was generous as most of our possessions were already in the wicker basket which I had taken with me when we were thrown out of our home, and in a small pigskin suitcase which I had bought in Vienna before the war. Now I added our eiderdowns, pillows, some warm clothes, helped Nooka to dress and lastly, still in the soldiers' presence, dressed myself. I had no idea what was happening to the others. Did they have to prepare for the journey as well, or was it only the two of us who were to go?

On coming downstairs I saw that they too were packing, which for them, was a far more complicated business. It was not easy to pack for six people in so short a time and to decide what to take from such a large house. They had been told that they were going to join Frank so Mila took his fur-lined overcoat and as many warm clothes as possible for him. The house was full of soldiers, which was hardly conducive to clear thinking. We rushed all over the house trying to collect what we thought would be useful in that new and unknown world. The Old Lady concentrated entirely on packing provisions. Her past experience of deprivations suffered in Poland during the First World War taught her that, whatever happens, people must eat. Luckily, the women in this household were used to making all kinds of preserves for the winter. There were still several jars of jam left, as well as large, hermetically sealed metal containers with clarified butter and lard. They were heavy but strong. These provisions saved us from starvation during the journey and sustained us later. Mila's last-minute inspiration to take her hand sewing machine proved an equal blessing. Our decisions about what to take with us were also limited by our physical strength. How many suitcases and other loads could be hauled about by two women, one old lady and three children? Maryla could not really be counted as she had to devote all her attention to her baby, who, shaken from sleep, clung to her and cried incessantly from fright at so many strange, unfriendly faces. The soldiers had evidently been ordered to accomplish their task as soon as possible, and continuously pressurised us to take our suitcases and bundles outside. Due to the fact that we had been given so little time, packing proceeded calmly and without tears, in spite of the shock caused by the night raid. We knew that this was no time to cry and that something very serious was happening to us.

We were ordered to load our baggage on to a large open lorry waiting outside the house. The night was chilly as spring was late that year and we shook from cold and shock.

Despite deporting nearly two million people during 1940–41 and the massive organisation this must have taken, none of us had any inkling of our fate that April night. The operation was carried out with complete secrecy and ruthless efficiency by the NKVD. In organisational terms it was a brilliant success.

Many more people were collected on the way until our lorry was full, mostly of women and children plus a few old men. Fear and despair were written on every face. En route we passed our old military headquarters now teeming with Russian soldiers. I could not look at them without a feeling of contempt and hatred. They were there because of a despicable, deceitful act, not as a result of victory on the battlefield. Our lorry went so fast that we were afraid someone would fall out or that a pedestrian might be killed. We saw other lorries like ours, also filled with women and children, travelling in the same direction. The convoy was driven out of town and stopped alongside the railway tracks. We were ordered to unload our baggage and threatened that if we did not do so quickly enough, we would lose it as the lorries had to return for more people. This caused indescribable chaos as people scrambled for their belongings, screaming and cursing. I still do not know how we managed to handle our cumbersome luggage without injuring our backs or spraining muscles. God must have watched over us.

There was an engine on the track with an incredibly long

76

trail of freight cars, all with open doors and sloping boards on which to climb inside. The distance from the ground to the car opening was about one and a half metres. We could not see the end of the train – none of us had ever seen anything like it in our lives and it required more than one engine to pull such a load. We were ordered to get in the car nearest us. The main concern of our little group was not to be separated and to get into the same car, which was not easy with so many people struggling to get in first. Finally, we managed it and all eight of us were there together with our belongings. Inside the car it was filthy, smelly and dark. It was normally used for transporting timber, hay or cattle and there were no fittings of any kind. To the left and right of the door were small openings in the walls for ventilation. Had it not been for these, we would have been in total darkness when the door was closed by the guards and barred from outside. We tried to see if there were any friends or acquaintances in the car, but they were all strangers and I felt lucky that Nooka and I were still with that wonderful family of whom we had grown so fond.

Before the door was shut, we were issued with one bucket of boiled water for the whole car. Our share came to about one pint of water and that was only because we had a jug with us, thanks to the foresight of the Old Lady. Those who had no large containers had to be content with a cupful. We were to appreciate the Old Lady's foresight even more when she produced some dry bread and distributed plum jam and lard. Oh, brown bread and lard – had anything ever tasted better than that? But, as the French say '*l'appetit vient en mangeant*' and we felt more hungry than before as, apart from Leszek who had been given a drink of milk, we had had nothing to eat since our meal the previous evening.

After a long wait, our train started to move slowly and I wondered how long we would travel in a closed car and what would happen if people had to relieve themselves. We soon discovered that provision had been made for such a situation. By the back wall of the car, opposite the door, a square hole had been cut into the floor. As it was completely exposed, the

77

person who wanted to use it had to go with an escort to shelter him or her from the rest by holding a blanket or piece of cloth in a 'matador' gesture. This arrangement intimidated many people and made them supress their needs causing problems later.

But there are some people who can turn any situation to their advantage. We soon noticed that one old man placed himself on the floor just opposite the hole and had been peeping under the 'matador' cloth. When discovered, he narrowly escaped being lynched and was chased into the furthest corner of our car. Gradually people became indifferent and more and more of them started to use the hole without escort or screen. *Privikniesh* was the most popular saying in Russian – meaning, 'You can get used to anything'.

After a day and a night of travelling the door was opened and we were told to get out and unload our things. We were glad to receive the order, thinking that this was the end of our journey. We were stiff and aching all over, having been unable to sit or lie down properly. However, our 'joy' was short-lived as we learned that this was only the beginning. The interruption was due to the fact that we had reached the Russian border and had to be transferred into different carriages because the Russian rails were a different gauge from the Polish ones. Again our hopes were raised. Maybe we would be transferred from cattle trucks into passenger trains. But this was not to be. Another freight train was waiting on the track, the only difference being that it was considerably shorter than the previous one. Again there was panic, made worse by the shouts and threats of the Soviet soldiers. The struggle to get our bundles had renewed our feelings of despair and helplessness and, worst of all, the fear we might get separated. Such a misfortune almost happened. At the moment when I was carrying the remainder of our things into the carriage where the rest of our party was, I was stopped by a soldier who ordered me into the next wagon. He would not listen to my explanations that my son and the rest of my family were there and brutally pushed me back. In sheer exasperation, not thinking of the consequences, I dived under his outstretched arms and ran. I thought I heard his footsteps behind me and expected to feel his rough grip on my shoulders at any moment. My legs almost gave way but somehow or other I managed to reach our car and several helping hands pulled me in. I only escaped because at the very moment of dodging the soldier someone shouted to distract him. That single moment could have weighed heavily against Nooka's and my future for, as we were to discover later on, different carriages in the train were going to different destinations. They were disconnected and shunted at various points along the route and I do not know how I would have been able to survive my exile separated from my son and friends.

Presently we attempted to settle down in our new mobile home. These cars had wooden bunks built on either end in two tiers. Each bunk could take eight people lying head to feet, packed like sardines in a tin. As there were just eight of us, we were able to secure one whole bunk for ourselves. On one side were Mila, Janka, Nooka and I, and on the other the Old Lady, Halina, Maryla and little Leszek. Not everyone was so lucky. There were more than fifty people in our carriage but the bunks could take only thirty-two for sleeping, so the rest had to sleep on the floor. Those nearest us used our baggage as beds and seats. It was not very comfortable but much better and warmer than sleeping on bare dirty boards. Some had no luggage at all: they were refugees from western Poland who, fleeing from the Germans, fell into Russian hands. What few possessions they had had, they had lost or traded for food on the way.

We had an assortment of people with us: Poles, Ukrainians, Jews and a very old, retired Armenian teacher being deported with his partially crippled daughter and sick wife. I wondered what harm these people could possibly have done to the Soviet invaders had they been allowed to remain in their homes. The Armenian was the only man in our carriage, the rest made up of women of all ages and children of both sexes. There seemed to be no rhyme or reason to the pattern of deportation. To some extent we could understand our 'punishment' because we were connected with the military, but most of the others were just families of small householders and shopkeepers. I think the idea was to replace the entire local population with Russian military and Party personnel and their families.

We started unpacking, looking for anything suitable for bedding, and I congratulated myself on taking our two eiderdowns. They were covered with pink satin and looked most out of place, but they were warm and large enough to cover all eight of us. As it was bitterly cold in the car, we never undressed but slept in our winter coats with scarves or other warm coverings on our heads. In spite of that, our heads froze as a chilly wind and snow blew through the cracks in the thin walls. As we moved into the north-east of Russia the temperature continued to drop. At the time of our deportation, the middle of April, spring was in the air and days were sunny and warm. Now we were entering a country covered by a thick layer of snow and the further north we moved, the further spring seemed to retreat. We did not have much chance to watch the scenery as there were always many volunteers to take a place by the small window on our bunk and have a glimpse outside. Priority was given to the children who were more easily bored than the adults, and even such meagre entertainment as watching the monotonous, flat scenery helped them forget their hunger. The thought of food never left us.

Every other day, the door opened with a crash and a soldier distributed a few loaves of heavy brown bread and a bucket or two of hot water. Thanks to the Old Lady, our party had reserves of food, but she kept them strictly under her control. Accustomed to a spartan way of living and being thrifty by nature, she now seemed to be a real miser. But she had reason to be careful. No one knew how long the journey would last and how much more misery we would have to endure in the future. Food could not last for very long. Most of all, she tried to keep her little grandson alive. In that intense cold, without sufficient food, he could not have survived. Occasionally we

80

stopped at stations to which peasants had brought some kind of rye leaven bread and boiled potatoes. Unfortunately they were not allowed to come near, even on those rare occasions when the door was opened for a little while. So even the lucky ones who had some roubles could devour these delicacies only with their eyes. I had no money and had almost forgotten how to use it, as I usually handed over my earnings as our contribution to the household expenses.

By now we had travelled for twelve days and were deep into Russia. Any idea of escape was now obviously out of the question. Previously, when our train stopped it was surrounded by soldiers and no one was allowed to get out, but now more and more often doors were left open, and we were able to stretch our legs and avoid using the hole in the car. The journey might have been easier, at any rate morally, if we knew at least some of the people in the car. As it was there was no point of contact, outside our close circle, and no mutual interests to stimulate the enforced companionship. There were two moments during the day when we all seemed to be united in spirit: waking in the morning and at night before settling down to sleep. At those times we all sang, terribly out of tune, traditional hymns which unfortunately, were often followed by plaintive and tear-jerking folk songs, in which some of the women passengers wallowed. We hated these outpourings.

Physical conditions grew worse all the time. We had spent more than two weeks without once taking off our clothes or washing. Despite freezing temperatures and severe draughts in the car, the stench of unwashed bodies and clothes, saturated with sweat, not to mention the smell of excrement, poisoned the air. Through the hole serving as a toilet strong gusts of wind blew constantly, and the danger of frostbite was added to the indignity of using it. As the area was never cleaned the frost at least performed a useful function.

In addition to all this, lice began to torment us, attacking our bodies and hair. People scratched continuously and searched their own and other people's hair and clothes. You could see that some were quite experienced in that art, especially those who were equipped with fine-toothed combs, which helped greatly in the hunt. This occupation became an obsession with many and helped to pass the time.

Hunger, boredom, and physical discomforts were our nagging enemies. It hurt me more than anything else to see my son going to sleep hungry, although he was better off than some other children in the car as the Old Lady gave him a morsel of something from time to time. We were stiff and sore from spending long hours in the same position on hard boards. We could not sit properly as our bunk was too near the ceiling and only very occasionally, when people on the lower bunk were asleep, could we let our legs down. At night if anyone turned over, we all had to do the same, as we were forced to fit together like a jigsaw puzzle. There was very little room on the floor so we tried to remain on our bunk most of the time in order not to disturb the others. We tried to invent all kinds of mental occupations to stave off our boredom, such as talking about books we had read, or remembering names of flowers or animals. Unfortunately we had no paper or pencils. Occupying the higher bunk enabled us to see the other people in the car, and watching them at least afforded some sort of distraction.

At last the scenery began to change. First there were foothills and then mountains on the horizon: the Urals! To us a reason for alarm. The Urals – the division between European Russia and the Asiatic. Were the Russians taking us along the route of previous generations of Polish martyrs to Siberia, the place chosen by them as *katorga* – penal colony for all the undesirable elements, political or criminal? To which category did we belong? Were they really taking us to unite us with our families?

From the moment I realised we had left behind the province of Smolensk, which contained Kozelsk, the POW camp where my husband was being detained, I suspected that we had been cheated. Now, on passing the Urals, I was certain. But why such subterfuge? Taken as we were in the middle of the night by the armed soldiers, our whole attention focussed on the crying children. How could we have considered any resistance? I felt another surge of bitterness and contempt towards our invaders. They had taken everything. Not just our country, but our homes and all our possessions. How convenient it was for them to move into a house or estate where everything was ready waiting for them. Everything – furniture, linen, saucepans, clothes, jewellery. I had saved some of my jewellery, but the Soborskis remembered that, in the hurry and confusion, they had left all theirs behind. We fantasised that some Bolshevik or other would go mad at the sight of all those gold watches, chains, rings and bracelets. Perhaps they would kill each other, fighting for them. Tormented by cold, hunger and the utter helplessness of our situation, I think we could be forgiven feeling that way. It seemed that God, whom they refused to acknowledge, was on their side, not ours.

In case anyone in the car had not yet fully realised the situation, the soldiers escorting our train took every opportunity to enlighten us, describing in a cruel and mocking way the places to which they were taking us and the kind of life that awaited us there.

In our little group I perhaps was the most adversely affected. Maryla knew that her husband was abroad, Mila had never had any information about her husband's whereabouts and did not expect to be reunited with him. But I did. For the second time in the last few months I was painfully deceived. That moral blow was much worse than any physical discomfort to which I was subjected in our journey. My greatest worry now was whether I should be able to renew my contact with Nik, and my heart bled at the thought of the effect the news of our deportation might have on him.

On the eighteenth day of our journey, 1st May 1940, the train halted and we heard a lot of noise outside. The car doors were opened one after the other and we were told that we had reached the end of our rail journey and that here we would be split up and taken by trucks to our various destinations.

By some miracle, no one in our car was seriously ill or had died during that terrible journey. We had had to call the

Russian woman doctor travelling with the train only once, when one of our women developed a very high temperature, but we heard later that there were several cases of sickness and one death – probably from pneumonia – in the other cars. There was also one birth and the Soviet Union acquired one more male citizen. The organisers of the trip could be proud that they had delivered the same quantity of goods as was initially dispatched.

People rushed to the doors to get their first look at the world in which they were supposed to live and, perhaps, die. It was a depressing sight. As far as the eye could see there was not one tree, not even a single bush. Just a hopeless, monotonous expanse of desert, but instead of sand and sun, there was dirty-looking snow just beginning to melt, and cloudy grey skies.

Apart from the Russian soldiers who had escorted us, we saw short bandy-legged men wearing fur hats with ear flaps and felt boots. They had Mongolian features and, with their long black moustaches, they looked fierce. They ran to and fro alongside the train shouting excitedly to each other in a language unknown to us. They were Kazakhs, inhabitants of the Kazakhstan Soviet Republic, to the extreme north of which we had been brought. The name of the railway station was Fedorovka, in the province – or *oblast* – of Kustanai.

Kazakhstan

At the time of our deportation, North Kazakhstan was an extremely primitive, poor country. Sparse settlements were isolated from each other and the rest of the world as there was no road transport and a very inadequate railway system. About one-third of the population was of Asiatic origin, the rest were Russians and Ukrainians, descendants of the richer peasants, deported in the decade following the Revolution as a work force for the newly created collective farms, called *kolhoz*.

At about the same time, the native population was forbidden by its Soviet masters to lead a nomadic life and was forced to settle into collective farms. North Kazakhstan was a flat expanse of steppe with a harsh climate of long, extremely cold winters, and short, hot and dusty summers.

On getting out of our car in Fedorovka I took a deep breath, and experienced a moment of euphoria probably similar to that felt by any prisoner suddenly finding himself freed. But on reflection I realised that all that happened was we were simply being transferred from a very confined prison to a larger one. With some roubles from Mila I went to look for someone selling food. I would have given anything just then to be able to bring back some milk or a loaf of dark, heavy peasant bread. Alas there was no one. Not far from the train I could see a few huts. Hoping I might get some food there I went towards them, glad that no one was taking any notice of me. I knocked at the door of the first hut, but there was no answer. I knocked again a little louder. The sound of a weak human voice reached me. I opened the door and found myself in the kitchen. On the edge of the back of the stove, where Russian peasant families usually slept, I saw a man shaking convulsively under a heap of clothes which were piled on top of him. I realised he was only half-conscious. The sight was so unexpected and upsetting that my first reaction was to retreat, but when I turned to go, I heard a muffled moan coming from the room behind the kitchen. Nervously I took a few steps forward and looked in. A woman was lying on a bed, obviously very ill with a high fever. By now I felt feverish myself. It must be typhus, I thought. I had heard there were frequent epidemics of it in Russia. I was quite familiar with that illness because I remembered my mother nursing patients in Petrovski Park during the typhus epidemic in the early twenties. I was not particularly frightened, as she had told me it could only be transferred through lice and in no other way. I looked closely at the woman but could not see any of the characteristic spots. I guessed rather, than heard her whisper 'Drink, drink'. I found a bucket of water, baled some out and brought it to her. She lifted herself with difficulty and, as she leaned on her elbow, moistened her lips with it. I forgot my hunger and the reason for my visit. I was deeply puzzled as to why those two people were left un-attended and what their illness could be. The woman must have read my mind for I heard her mutter, 'Malaria'. I had not suspected this, but understood why the hut looked clean and tidy. Had I arrived at a different time I would have probably found two people going about their duties, instead of that macabre scene. I had always been terrified of malaria because I believed it was a disease that, once caught, could never be cured; I preferred typhus.

After that I made no attempt to call at any other hut and returned from my expedition very subdued. I suspected that the Russians had brought us here so that the malarial mosquitoes could finish us off. My main concern was for the children. I did not want to say anything about my traumatic experience to my companions, but they knew me too well not to notice that I had had a shock, so it was better to tell them about it straight away instead of letting them guess and imagine far worse things. They tried to comfort me as best they could.

I saw the Russian woman doctor in one of the cars and stopped to ask her how widespread malaria was in these parts. Her answer did nothing to cheer me. I looked at the car in which she and some of the Russian soldiers had travelled to compare it with ours but there was not much difference between them. Theirs was also a freight car but with larger windows and an iron stove with several buckets of coal and, of course, they were able to get out whenever the train stopped. The doctor's bed was a narrow bench with a minimum of bedding and a small bundle instead of a pillow. There was nothing to show she had any other possessions with her. I expressed surprise, as, after all, she must have known the journey was to last about three weeks. She said she did not want to get used to 'luxuries' as one never knew what to expect in life and that one should take things as they came. I wondered whether such a way of thinking, instilled into a new Soviet generation out of necessity, was not that nation's greatest strength.

I heard the sound of engines and, turning, saw lorries coming towards us. Rushing back to our car I was just in time to hear orders to bring out our luggage. By now we were quite experienced in this and performed the task with the skill of professional porters. My wicker basket, however, nearly defeated us. It was large and its weight by far exceeded the strength of a few women and children exhausted by hunger and the long, tedious journey. Once more, however, somehow or other we managed it, and in spite of being dragged along the ground and pulled and pushed mercilessly, the basket was still in one piece. Its size and weight embarrased me at each transfer, and I wondered what I could have packed in it to make it so heavy. In the end, the good old basket proved its

87

weight in gold and during the journey it had served as a bed or seat to a great many people and so justified itself in their eyes as well.

The Soborski family's belongings were mostly packed in bags and easy to handle. Apart from the wicker basket and a small suitcase containing some of my jewellery, and papers, I had another piece of luggage: a hat box! Why I took it from our flat when I left so many necessities behind, I shall never know, except perhaps that I felt that hats were necessary for my morale. Now the lorry, filled to bursting with people and luggage, started to move away and, as it gained speed, we were horribly shaken as it jolted along the uneven road. We clung to each other in an effort not to fall about. Apart from our 'family', there were about twenty other people, which meant a tight squeeze. That hat box became a real nuisance and bounced around like a ball; I had to hold it by its leather strap. Suddenly, at the next jolt, the strap snapped and the box flew out of my hands, its contents scattering. Someone banged on the back of the driver's compartment and he, not knowing what was happening, braked violently. Sitting precariously on our bundles, we almost followed the box in its flight. Displayed on the snow were hats made of straw, lace and tulle, adorned with ribbons, bunches of artificial flowers and fruit, as well as several impressive pieces of paste jewellery. In our present circumstances the sight seemed so absurd that it provoked fits of ironic laughter. Our driver got out of his cabin, annoyed at the interruption, but forgot his anger and watched in stupefied silence as we hurriedly gathered together the strewn 'treasure'. He must have taken the sparkling glass for the real thing. Getting back into the truck we had our first taste of the hazards connected with vehicles driven by Russians. We did not know then that they never waited until all passengers were safely inside before moving. To our horror, the last person had to run and be hauled into the already moving truck.

After an hour or so of travelling we arrived in a small village which was to be our place of exile. It was called Novo-Troitsk and was only a short distance from the Siberian border. Administratively, the area belonged to the Kazakh Soviet Republic, but in all other respects it was a continuation of the desolate Siberian steppe. At the time of our arrival it consisted of fifty or sixty mud huts which seemed abandoned in the boundless, barren steppe. It must have looked a little less desolate a century before when the area fell finally under the Tsarist rule. The Russian administrators, who were sent to govern the conquered native population, and the traders and settlers who followed them, lived in quite large houses made from imported timber, and a few of these houses, although badly battered, were still there. They were now occupied by the top local people.

Originally the area had been populated by nomadic tribes of Turko-Mongolian origin which, with their sheep and horses wandered from place to place in pursuit of seasonal pasture. If they stopped for any length of time they erected dome-shaped felt-covered tents. In the decades following the Bolshevik revolution, their livestock was requisitioned and they were forced to settle in the collective farms. Many died of famine because they knew nothing about agriculture. To survive the winter in their tents, instead of moving to the warmer south, was unthinkable, so they had to learn to build huts from the mixture of mud, cow dung and grass, the only material available, as the import of timber had been stopped. Dried cow dung on its own or mixed with grass, served for cooking and heating. They hated their new way of life and the richest and most enterprising among them fled with their flocks across the border to China.

When we arrived in Novo-Troitsk, only a few Kazakh families lived there. The population was predominently Russian, almost all of them descendants of the *kulaks* (the prosperous peasants), deported from the Ukraine soon after the Revolution. There was not a trace left of the descendants of the Russians who had lived in Kazakhstan before the Revolution. They were dealt with, no doubt, in the usual way. Not that the later arrivals were treated much better. We noticed, for instance, that apart from the men employed by the local administration and the workshop, there were only women and children in the village; we learned that while most young men were away on military service, the older ones, probably considered to have been contaminated by the memories of old times, were arrested and removed to unknown destinations, almost certainly to the labour camps of the furthest north. Some of the more optimistic women still cherished the hope that one day they would return.

Being the 1st May, a national holiday, the inhabitants had gathered along the road to watch our arrival. As we learned later, they were bitterly disappointed, having expected to see a party of Polish generals resplendent in uniforms with medals and ribbons across their chests, and their wives attired in magnificent robes, sparkling with jewels and with long, ermine or sable capes covering them from head to foot. What an anti-climax it must have been to see worn out, tired and filthy-looking people emerging from weeks of travel without a wash! Nevertheless, there were still enough people willing to accommodate us and our little group accepted an offer from one of the women. She did not ask how many we were and it never occurred to me to enquire whether there would be enough room for us all. The temptation to settle down and rest was too great. I could see that she was slightly put out when she realised that there were eight of us, but it was too late then to change her mind and our belongings had already been taken off the lorry which, by now, had driven off.

We were dismayed to discover that the woman had five children at home. Her sixth child, a member of the *Komsomol*, was out, as he had a job in the *kolhoz* administration. As soon as we entered the hut the children started to leap about us and followed us into the 'living-room' which we were to occupy. Even without them, there was no room to move. Now, as we attempted to unpack, they were literally crawling on top of us, trying to touch everything and even rummaging through our luggage. Difficult as it was, things became even more unpleasant when the woman's son returned from work. He started to quarrel with his mother for taking in the 'bloody capitalists' and accused her of greed. I think he was right, as I heard him shouting that his job in *kolhoz* assured them of a sufficient food supply and other perks without taking in lodgers. There was another good reason for his anger; apart from the room we occupied, there was only one other room left for all of them, and that was the kitchen.

Looking round we wondered how and where we could sleep. There was one large bed with masses of pillows piled high, advertising the owner's prosperity, and we decided that the Old Lady, Maryla and her son should have it. The rest of us had no choice but to make use of the limited floor space. We asked our landlady for some boiling water and a loaf of bread. This, with some lard and jam, became our supper. Its enjoyment was somewhat marred by the jealous gaze of the landlady's children who had probably never seen jam in their lives.

Now all we could think of was sleep, no matter how or where; just to stretch, then close our eyes. Alas, it was not to be: the place was bug-infested. The parasites, appreciating their sudden change of diet, tried to make the most of their opportunity, so, despite our deadly fatigue, none of us was able to sleep a wink. It was clear that we would have to look for another place to live. This became even more urgent when, the next morning, our landlady declared that her son had warned her that if, on his return from work, he found we were still there, he would throw our things out into the snow. So we had to move out that same day.

By now my role as 'Minister of External Affairs' had been firmly established so the task of finding accommodation fell to me. Halina and I set off. Our efforts to find somewhere to live produced no result and this, as well as the general appearance of the settlement, greatly depressed us.

We explored the length and breadth of the village in our search for somewhere to live. The houses were so scattered that, wherever we looked, we could see far into the steppe where nothing relieved the desperate monotony of the land-

91

scape. We tried hard to persuade people to accommodate us, but no one was able to take in eight people because, like the owner of our present hut, they had only one room and a kitchen. We were determined not to separate.

In despair, we went to see the chairman of the *kolhoz*, but he almost threw us out of his office shouting, 'We are not responsible for you, we have not invited you here and do not intend to burden ourselves with the problems of the capitalist parasites. You have been persecuting the poor peasant people in your bourgeois Poland and now you are here to receive the punishment you more than deserve'. I was tempted to say that among the deportees were many of those 'poor peasants' and to ask whom they were supposed to have persecuted, but I was too shocked by his treatment of us to do that. We heard many such ridiculous accusations during our stay in Novo-Troitsk.

Under normal circumstances I did not lose heart easily, but being compelled to listen to insults and to go back empty-handed to people who were waiting anxiously in a very hostile house for my return, seemed more than I could bear. Had it not been for Halina whom I did not want to demoralise, I would have flopped down in the snow and sobbed my heart out until I had got rid of all the anger and frustration. But I had to take myself in hand and come to some decision. I knew that two of the families who had arrived with us had stopped in an empty, dilapidated timber house and it seemed now that the only possible solution was to join them there. We went to have a look at the house and to test the reaction of the people to our plan. Luckily they responded very warmly – the more the merrier!

The house was quite large, with three good-sized rooms and a kitchen, but it was in a very bad state. The glass was missing from most of the windows, the doors did not fit properly; wind blew in from all sides and it was bitterly cold. I was surprised that it had not been taken to pieces for the wood alone, as it would have provided the villagers with a lot of fuel, if not timber. Later I was told that the punishment for such an act was so severe that no one dared do it. The house had remained unoccupied because, generally, people preferred to live in small huts which were easier to keep warm. The other wooden houses went with the job to the top employees of the *kolhoz* and the militia who did not have to worry about such things.

The families we were going to join were those of a middle-aged widow of Ukrainian origin and the old Armenian teacher we had travelled with. The widow, Mrs Krilenko, had two daughters and a son with her. The Armenian had his wife and daughter. All seven of them gathered in one room, each family occupying one side and we decided to move into the adjoining room. Naturally there was no furniture, but the floor was made of wood which was far more pleasant to sleep on than mud. As the house was not far from our previous quarters, the Krilenko daughters helped us transfer our things quite quickly. We had some bread left from the previous day to appease our hunger, but we had nothing to quench our thirst except cold water, as there were no heating facilities of any kind. We had noticed that the bread was bitter and it was only because we were extremely hungry that not only were we able to eat, but also to enjoy it. We spread our bedding and any warm clothes we could unpack easily on the floor and, having washed our hands and faces in the snow, we were ready to go to sleep. Of course, we remained fully dressed, including our warm gloves and head coverings. Our companions, who had already spent a night in the house, assured us that there were no bugs and, hardened by now to the cold and other discomforts, we all slept soundly.

In these new circumstances, our shy, unassuming Maryla revealed talents which I had never suspected. She could improvise and do many odd jobs with very primitive tools – or no tools at all – which greatly impressed me, as I was useless at that kind of thing. From now on her role as 'Minister of the Interior', whether she wanted it or not, was recognised and exploited. Using wood from broken vodka crates which I got from a local shop together with some nails, she filled in the damaged windows of the two rooms and, having examined the distorted front door, fixed the hinge and patched it up. This cut down the draughts by half. In spite of these and other improvements, it did not take us many days to realise that there was no hope of making any sort of life in our present surroundings. We knew Leszek would not be able to withstand the cold much longer and there was no way of warming that outsize house. Once again we decided to look for a new home. Our dream was to find a little den with tiny windows and low ceilings half buried in the snow for protection from the gales and easy to heat – something entirely different from this house so proudly towering over the neighbourhood, although now it was a pitiful shell battered by gales.

As time passed, we began to despair of finding anywhere to live. Finally, when Maryla's baby son started to cough badly and developed a high temperature we felt that something must be done quickly.

I took my courage in both hands and went back to the village administration office determined to demand help in finding better accommodation. I was relieved to find that the chairman was not there, but the attitude of the others was not much better so I threatened that I would write to the provincial authorities who, I said, did not bring us here to die. (I was convinced that this was so.) This made some impression and, after a whispered conversation, they told me that there was a little uninhabited hut on the edge of the village and, if it was suitable, we could live there for a small rent. They explained its location and so, filled with hope, Mila and I went to view it. It was some distance from the rest of the settlement and looked very desolate. If we had wanted something small, we had found it. It was so small, in fact, that you had to come very close to it to see it as it merged into the steppe on the very edge of which it stood. We had to struggle before we could open the twisted, narrow door, which strongly resisted our efforts. It finally surrendered with a frightening noise. It led into a semi-dark space which apparently had been a kitchen as it had a small iron stove in the middle. There were two openings; one led into a barn which must have housed animals and which smelled terribly, and the other into a smallish room. The walls were made with turf instead of mud bricks and floors were of mud. Everything, including the absence of the large oven which was indispensable to the Russian and Ukrainian families, indicated that the hut had been built for the Kazakhs who had abandoned it before the winter came. Offering us this hovel was not the concession I thought I had won through my insistence, but an unexpected opportunity for the *kolhoz* to let it at a rent, however small.

But we were so anxious to settle down on our own and start some kind of a home that nothing could put us off. The hut was completely unsuitable, even by local standards, for winter occupation. However, we were now in the middle of May and it was evident that the snow and frost could not last much longer, and we both thought the isolated position of the hut would be an advantage in the summer, as it would give us more freedom of movement.

Having accepted the *kolhoz* offer, we started work on our future home. Early next morning we swept it, weatherproofed the windows and door as much as possible, polished the floors with a mixture of cow dung and water and cleared the barn to make room for our luggage. We hired a wheelbarrow and, by stages, transferred our belongings. This accomplished, I went to look for a bed for the Old Lady and succeeded in finding two iron ones, as well as straw to be used instead of mattresses. We bought as many vodka crates as we could, having previously discovered their usefulness, and now used the wood as the base for the mattresses so that the straw would not fall through the widely spaced bars of the bed onto the floor. We also spread some of the planks on the floor in the room where the rest of the Soborski family intended to sleep. This prevented earth from the floor getting into the bedding, and more importantly, served as insulation, because the floor was damp. We had to remove these planks every morning to make room, and replace them again at night. One of the beds was for the Old Lady, and the other, which fitted neatly into a

95

corner of the dark kitchen, was for me. Nooka's place at night was on top of our basket, which was placed against another wall of the kitchen. A few days later, looking through the things in my basket, which we now called Pandora's box, I found my favourite *kelim*, no doubt one of the things which added so much to its weight. I hugged it affectionately as if it were a long lost relative and, with typical wantonness, instead of saving it to exchange for kerosene or potatoes, I hung it on the wall over my bed to brighten the dark corner. Contrary to expectations, instead of cheering me, the sight of that lovely rug on the grey mud wall made me feel sorry for its degradation, and I buried my face in my pillow and wept secretly. This place was more dreary than any we had seen since we left the train, but nevertheless we all agreed that it was good to be on our own at last because now we could start to organise our life into some sort of routine which was absolutely necessary if we did not want to disintegrate.

Having settled the question of our accommodation more or less satisfactorily, I could now direct my efforts towards renewing contact with Nik. I learnt in the village post office that deportees had the right to send letters but no money or parcels. As establishing contact with Nik was the most important thing, I was reasonably satisfied with that information. Composing my first letter from our exile was far from easy as I tried to present our new place and conditions as cheerfully as I could, without making it sound improbable. His letters to me from Kozelsk served as a good example and now, having sent mine, I waited anxiously for his reply.

In the first fifteen days in Novo-Troitsk we had learned quite a lot. We had sold for roubles or traded for food some of our possessions and now had a supply of flour and potatoes. We knew who was willing to sell milk and even where to get the precious kerosene for the primus which the Old Lady had managed to bring, as well as for the lamp which a villager had sold us. Without a primus our lives would have been infinitely more difficult. It was a real blessing that the Old Lady had taken such an active part in the original packing and that, despite her advanced years, did not lose her head as many others would have done in such a situation.

In spite of all this the first two weeks in our new hut were particularly hard. The nearest water well was more than a quarter of a mile away and the road leading to it was slippery and muddy. Our iron stove would not work, either due to insufficient draught or to our total lack of experience with the local fuel. We had managed to obtain a small quantity with great difficulty and at a high cost as at that time of year everybody was running short. We gradually learnt how to get the stove going, but bricks of cow dung were not a satisfactory form of fuel, they did not produce enough warmth, smoked and smelled horrible. We prayed for the warm weather to come so that we could take the stove outside and do our cooking in the open.

In summer the fuel cost nothing as people used cow dung in its raw form, collecting it in the steppe in the places where cows grazed. Thus suitably enlightened, when the right time came, Halina, Janka, Nooka and I, equipped with sacks, went into the steppe in search of *kiziak*, the local name for cow dung. It took us some time before we found the first offering. We had to lift it with our bare hands, and the revulsion that I felt would be hard to describe. Even worse for me was the sight of our children carrying sacks with shit on their innocent backs. However, later on, we competed and boasted when anyone of us had beaten the other and brought home the largest number of 'pancakes'. I recall an earlier occasion when, coming home, I saw a magnificent *kiziak* lying on the road. Surprised no one had seen it, I quickly dug it out and proudly brought it home putting it in front of the burning stove. My pride soon turned to embarrassment when my *kiziak* started to melt away. It was very fresh and it was only because it was frozen on the surface that I could get it in one piece. I never made that mistake again. *Kiziak* had to be well dried and mature before it could be used as fuel and some knowledge was needed in selecting the right pieces in the steppe.

We had to admit that the saying frequently repeated by the natives in Novo-Troitski, '*Nichevo privikniesh*' (It is nothing, you will get used to it), had a lot of truth in it, especially when you had no other choice or solution. The other saying that reflected the philosophy of the Russian people, when life seemed unbearable was, 'You can't go into the grave alive'. Could there be a stronger way of expressing one's utter resignation?

By the end of May the snow had almost melted, making it much easier to walk and communicate with the villagers. Soon a flourishing trading business developed, and we were assured of a regular supply of milk, a very valuable supplement to our meagre diet, and occasionally we could buy butter and a few eggs when the hens started to lay. The milk was not sterilised and the cows not properly examined, but we no longer worried about such things.

In a short time after our move we managed to free ourselves completely of lice, which was an achievement, but I then had to face another enemy, fleas. For some reason the area round my bed was singled out as a breeding ground. It looked as if they were dormant during the winter, and, with the arrival of warmer days they came back to life with a vengeance. I became an obvious target, and dreaded the thought of bedtime, for as soon as I approached my bed, I was assailed by hundreds of them. I had to invent some method of defence. The best I could think of was to brush the fleas off with a very quick movement of both hands, and lift the leg promptly on to the bed, and repeat the same manoeuvre with the other leg. In that way I was able to rid myself of most of these parasites. Inexplicably they never jumped on to the bed. Maybe it was too high, or they avoided it because the once white sheets made them feel too conspicuous. It was also a mystery to all of us why they never went into the room where everybody else slept, but concentrated their attacks in one area and me. But woe betide anyone else who ventured into the forbidden territory! I wished I had stilts to transfer me over the danger zone to my bed or at least a tin of insecticide. But who had ever heard of such a thing in Kazakhstan? As if this was not enough, very soon the mosquitoes and other flying insects made their appearance. Somehow, nothing in this country seemed to have any sense of moderation, and now they came in millions and tormented us day and night, not only stinging but getting into eyes and ears as well. They eased off only for a couple of hours at dawn and this was the only time I could get some rest. Once, after several sleepless nights, my body burning from their bites, I jumped out of bed, ignoring the fleas, to see how the others were faring. I was amazed to find they were all alseep with mosquitoes sitting on their faces and any other exposed parts of their bodies. I had always been a very light sleeper and now, ashamed of my over-sensitivity, sheepishly returned to my bed. During that period more often than not, I preferred to fight the mosquitoes outside the hut and go back to my bed at daybreak after their activities ceased.

During the day everybody suffered equally from mosquitoes and midges which made going to the well particularly unpleasant. To make the trip worthwhile the normal procedure was for two people to take three buckets, one on either side and one in the middle carried between them. An escort of two additional people was necessary to defend the water-carriers, whose hands were occupied, by waving pieces of cloth, bunches of wormwood or other grass as available. Both the water carriers and escort came back utterly exhausted from this mission and with half the water spilled. Similar protection had to be given to anyone doing the cooking on our small stove in the open. Even smoke did not deter the pests. Kazakhstan was a cruel and uncharitable country.

The Surgeon and the Vet

The time we spent in our little hut was not without incidents. It was very cold both in and out of doors. A thin layer of snow still covered the steppe and the distance from the village did nothing to make life easier. We existed on a mixture of heavy, dark flour and half-frozen potatoes cooked together in a mash which filled and warmed us up but never satisfied our hunger for very long, particularly as we were trying to eat in moderation in order to stretch our supplies because of food shortages in the village. No wonder that our favourite topic of conversation was food – especially meat. We dreamed of it and talked about it incessantly.

One afternoon we heard an unusual noise and commotion outside the hut and, rushing to the door flung it open to see what was happening. Three or four dogs sprang back with loud yelps as the door hit them and, there at our feet, was a fully grown hare which they had just killed. Before the dogs could recover from their pain and fright, someone grabbed the hare and slammed the door shut. Finding a hare lying on your doorstep at such a time seemed nothing short of a miracle and we firmly believed it must have been sent from heaven.

One night we were awakened by loud moans and cries for help from Mila who was writhing in pain. Apparently she had suffered from gallstones for some years and now she was having a really bad attack. The situation was desperate as there was no doctor or even a qualified nurse in the village.

Soon after daybreak I ran to the village to enquire whether a lorry might be going to Troitsk, a small, neighbouring town about thirty kilometres away, where the nearest hospital was situated. By an amazing stroke of luck one was being sent there from the local tractor repair depot and, because of the exceptional circumstances, I got permission for Mila and me to travel in it. It was a risk to take a gravely ill person by truck on such a rough journey, and I prayed that Mila would reach the hospital alive. My prayers must have been heard as, in spite of severe shaking and bumps on the road, her pain eased off and she stopped crying. I held her hand in mine for comfort, and, from time to time, she opened her eyes and gave the semblance of a smile, which to me was very reassuring.

When we reached Troitsk I had to use a great deal of persuasion to get the driver to take us to the hospital which was out of his way. Having overcome this obstacle I was now terribly worried in case the hospital refused to take Mila in on the grounds that not only did we not belong to the town, but we came from a different Soviet Republic. Troitsk, like the rest of Siberia, was part of the Russian Soviet Federated Socialist Republic while Novo-Troitsk belonged to the Kazakh Soviet Socialist Republic. But here again luck was on our side, and we owed it to the head of the hospital who was also its principal surgeon. Judging by his appearance, accent and manners he did not belong to this miserable town and like us must have been deported, only in his case by his own people. I was sure that had we been able to confide in each other we would have had a lot to talk about. He examined Mila and said that an operation was necessary and that he would perform it himself. This was a great relief as he inspired confidence in both of us. I returned home in the same truck, exhausted but reassured that Mila was in very good hands and that I would be able to comfort the rest of the family, especially her two daughters who had been deeply shaken. Poor Mila had to be left in hospital for at least three weeks. Postal deliveries had not been working properly so there was little hope that she would receive a letter from us. There was not much chance, either, of visiting her, as trucks rarely travelled, and it was not easy to find out when they did and even harder to get a lift. But the unexpected happened.

Early one morning a cart, pulled by two oxen, drew up in front of our plot and a young man greeted us in Polish. We were overjoyed to meet a compatriot, and welcomed him, glad to be able to offer our modest hospitality. His name was Piotr Jasinski and he came from a neighbouring village to which he had been deported, along with his mother and sisters. He was that rarity, a young man among women and children and his family were very fortunate to have him with them. On hearing that he was going to Troitsk, sent by the *kolhoz* on some errand, I realised this was my chance to visit Mila, and asked him if he would take me with him. He readily agreed, but warned that the journey by oxen would take many hours and would be extremely tiring and dull. But nothing could put me off. By now it was full summer and, as the day promised to be very hot, I decided to wear a very light summer dress and a large hat, from the famous hat box, to protect myself from the scorching sun.

Our journey to Troitsk lasted several hours and it was well past midday before we reached the hospital. We fixed a time and place to meet for our return and as I had an hour to kill before visiting time, I decided to have a look at Troitsk. With its dusty roads and one-storey wooden houses, mostly with a small porch at the entrance, it looked like a town from the American West. The people in the street were almost exclusively Russian. I asked the way to the market place, hoping to buy some food, but when I got there it was closed. I tried the shop but, except for vodka, it was empty. I saw a man selling ice cream from a hand-cart and joined the queue. The ice cream was very watery and sickly sweet, but it refreshed me. I got back to the hospital just as the doors opened for visitors. Mila had not expected me and was overjoyed. I thought she looked quite well, although much thinner. The operation had been one hundred per cent successful and she was feeling fine. Our friendly surgeon could not have done

102

more for her and she felt she owed a lot to his care. The news that all was well at home was a great tonic for her and I was very happy that I had decided to come. Before leaving I gave her some money in case she needed anything. We shed a few tears on parting and I promised to find out when she would be discharged. I tried to contact the surgeon but was told he was not available. In the office they instructed me to fetch her in ten days' time and I went back to the ward to let her know.

On leaving the hospital, I was alarmed to see how much the weather had changed. The sun was pale behind a curtain of yellow dust and mist. The temperature had dropped several degrees and the wind was blowing. As soon as I put my head out of the door my hat was whipped off and I had to race to get it back. When I reached our agreed meeting place Piotr was already waiting. He looked worried and shook his head in disapproval at my flimsy attire. But even he had to admit that this change in the weather was unexpected. We climbed into the cart quickly and Piotr prodded the oxen, which could move only at their normal, lazy pace. It was getting colder by the minute and the gale force wind blew clouds of dust. Then it began to rain. Piotr got a sack from the cart to cover my shoulders, but soon it was wet through and I started to shake like a jelly. He offered me his thick jacket. I refused. He insisted, saying that, instead of staying on the cart, he would walk and that would keep him warm. Finally, he took off the jacket, put it on me, covered himself with another sack and got off the cart. I was very touched by his kindness but angry at my thoughtlessness in starting such a long journey so inade- quately equipped. Who would have known that the weather would change so suddenly? We had not lived in this country long enough to understand its whims. There was no hope of finding shelter – wherever we looked there was no trace of habitation, and it would probably take most of the night before the oxen could reach Novo-Troitsk. Normally the nights in Kazakhstan, at this time of the year, were warm but this night, cooled by the sandstorm, was different. It con- tinued to rain, the cart creaked and the oxen shuffled along apathetically. Piotr constantly prodded them to no avail, and I sat on the cart, curled up with my knees under my chin, trying to keep as warm as possible. Again and again I thought of Piotr's sacrifice and remembered a French saying: '*Une bonne action ne va jamais sans punition*'. I had experienced the truth of that saying myself more than once. Despite the cold and uncomfortable position, my eyelids felt heavy and I was ready to fall asleep when we heard the distant sound of an engine. A moment later we saw headlights behind us. We hoped it would be someone from our village. Piotr stopped the oxen and signalled the vehicle to stop. I jumped down and saw two men in the driver's cabin. Piotr asked them if they were going to Novo-Troitsk. One of them put his head out of the window and said, 'Why do you ask?'

'Because we're going there, but there is still a long way to go and this woman is very cold. Perhaps you could give her a lift?'

'All right, she can get in. There's an old *babushka* sitting under the canvas, they will be warmer and cosier together,' they added laughing.

There was no need to repeat the invitation. I was so glad that I could return the jacket to Piotr and in no time I was in the open truck next to *babushka*. Without the jacket I was cold and shivering again. Crouching on the floor next to the *babushka*, we pulled the stiff canvas sheet over us to keep off the rain. I envied her her padded jacket and hugged as close to her as I could. After we had travelled about half an hour the truck suddenly stopped. One of the men asked if I was cold. I said I was all right and anyway, we could not be far from home now. He insisted that I join them in their cabin because it was warmer and more comfortable. I suggested they put the *babushka* in front, hoping I could then wrap myself entirely in the canvas.

'She'll be all right; she's dressed warmly, not like you. Don't argue. Just change places whilst you have a chance.'

It was far more comfortable in the cabin with the warmth of the engine and the men's bodies on either side of me, but it was stuffy and smelly. I could see the road now and recognised the crossing in front of us. To my amazement, instead of turning left, they went to the right.

'You've taken the wrong road,' I said, 'the road to Novo-Troitsk is to the left.'

'But we aren't going to Novo-Troitsk.'

'Then why did you say you were?'

'We didn't. Your chap asked us to give you a lift and that's what we're doing. You don't think we'd go to Novo-Troitsk especially for you?'

'Stop the truck. I want to get out. I can walk home. I know the road from here.'

This was true. It led to a small railway station where I sometimes went to get candles, soap or kerosene. Now that the wind and rain had stopped and daylight was coming, I could run all the way home and not be cold. The two monsters ignored me and continued on their way. By now we were a long way from the crossing and I was in despair. Suddenly the truck stopped with a jolt and I almost hit my head on the windscreen.

'We're stuck in the mud,' said the driver. 'We must find something to put under the wheels. Perhaps there will be some straw in there.' He pointed to a half dilapidated hut. 'Come and help us.'

I wanted to stay with the *babushka* to find out where we were were going, but they would not let me. One of them grabbed my hand and pulled me out of the cabin. The other pushed me from behind.

The moment we entered the ruined hut the man behind caught me by the shoulders and brutally twisted me round. He pushed me to the ground and fell on me with all his weight. I began to fight, kicking and shoving him away with all my might and strength. The other man got hold of my arms, spreading them so that I could not move. I realised there was no chance to defend myself physically and had to think fast to save myself. I stopped fighting and, with the man's face directly over mine, I looked him straight in the eye and said, 'Do you want to go to the labour camp?'

This acted like a bucket of cold water upon him. He froze and I knew there was not a moment to lose.

'The man who was with me noted your lorry's number and if he doesn't find me when he gets back to the village, he will report my disappearance immediately to the NKVD and you must know what the punishment is in the Soviet Union for rape.' I did not know myself if there was indeed any punishment, but the mention of the NKVD (which brought terror to everyone's heart)· worked like magic. Both men lost their appetite for playing games. Looking at each other in bewilderment, they released me.

One of them said, 'Let this Polish bitch go. She can rot in the steppe.'

Certain that I was in command of the situation, I said, 'If I perish, you won't get away with it. The NKVD is responsible for each one of us and they will find the culprits, if only to defend themselves. In any case, the *babushka* would have to give evidence and would say I was in the truck with you. But if you take me back to my village, I won't tell anyone what happened.'

Although they swore horribly, they knew I had won. I was certain the tale about being stuck in the mud was a lie, but fate can play tricks, and when we got back to the lorry, it was stuck fast. The men had to get spades to dig it out and it was almost an hour before we could move again, during which time I had been sitting in the drivers' cabin. As soon as they could move the lorry, they ordered me into the back. The *babushka* showed no sign of surprise or emotion when I rejoined her. Now I was really worried. Would they turn back and take me home or had they decided to continue on their way, leaving me in the steppe? I clasped my fingers in agony praying silently for deliverance from my plight. Seldom have I experienced such a feeling of relief as when I saw the driver turn the truck round. I did get some malicious satisfaction at the thought of him having to explain the reason for his delay and excessive use of petrol, which was considered a serious offence. When I finally got home, everyone was asleep.

106

Several hours later Piotr appeared and, to my great relief, he was just very tired, not ill, and able to joke at our adventure.

I told no one of my ordeal. Mila was my only confidante and, of course, she was not there. I was immensely pleased that I could reassure the family about her condition, the success of her operation and the prospect of her returning home soon. But the next day we had a dreadful shock. A message came from the hosptial to tell us that Mila had been discharged and must be collected forthwith. We were horrified. I could not understand what had happened since yesterday, when everything appeared normal. If her condition had deteriorated since then, surely the surgeon would not have sent her away, I was certain of that. Had she died? I rushed to the *kolhoz* office, but no one would talk to me. Possibly they knew nothing either. With a heavy heart and suspecting the worst, I asked if a truck was going to Troitsk. 'Even if it was, it doesn't mean that it would pick up a Polak woman. We have enough of our people who want to travel,' came the reply. I could not expect to be lucky more than once. The only hope left was to turn to one of the Kazakhs and beg him to come to Troitsk with his horse and cart. Having tried every family in the village I finally succeeded in persuading an old Kazakh from whom we bought eggs. I promised to pay him with a nice piece of Persian lamb from my fur coat out of which he could make a hat with earflaps. I did not relish the prospect of that journey again so soon, especially since I had no idea of what awaited me. However, I did trust my old Kazakh and travelling by horse was faster than by oxen.

We started very early next morning and this time I took enough clothes to cover any eventuality. At my request, the Kazakh upholstered the cart with padded kaftans and straw to protect Mila from bumps. The kaftans were probably full of lice and smelled of rancid fat, but that was of small importance just then. The most important thing was to bring Mila back alive.

I found Mila in great distress and she burst into tears when she saw me. When she had calmed down a little she told me

107

that after my visit the NKVD had taken the surgeon away, no one knew where or why. There were rumours that his arrest had been caused by the exceptional care he had taken of Mila, which had had an immediate effect on the hospital personnel's attitude towards her. She was shunned by everyone and told she must leave. But who would take her, how and when nobody said. My unexpected arrival was a great relief to her and the thought of going home, even in her state of health, seemed a deliverance. The arrest of such an able and kind doctor was an irretrievable loss, both to the hospital and to the patients, who adored him. Mila told me the surgeon had never treated her differently from any other patient, that he had always shown the same consideration to every one of them and had worked day and night, never sparing himself. He must have been the victim of denunciation and the thought that, however unwittingly, she had contributed to his downfall really upset her. I tried to comfort and reassure her while she dressed. If someone had decided to destroy him, either wanting his position or for some other reason, they would have done so anyhow, and she should not feel guilty. In Stalin's Russia people disappeared for no reason and, more often than not, it happened to those who, ethically and morally, stood head and shoulders above the rest.

The journey back seemed to last even longer. All the time I was frightened that the jolts might harm Mila and open her wound. I also wondered what would happen when the time came for the stitches to be removed, and who would dress her wound in the meantime. The only 'nurse' we had worked as a postwoman and I doubted her ability even in the unlikely event of her kit containing the necessary equipment. It was wiser not to think about it just then. We arrived safely with an exhausted but happy Mila. A more miserable 'home' would be hard to imagine, but she was back among a loving and loved family and what could be better than that to speed her recovery? We had to be optimistic and optimism served us well. As to removing the stitches, as so often happened in our present life, help came unexpectedly and in a rather amusing form.

Soon after Mila's return, news reached us about the

impending visit of a veterinary surgeon. He was coming from Kustanai, the capital of our *oblast* to do a survey of cattle in the region. Kustanai was about 120 kilometres from us. The vet's job was to inspect the local cattle and issue a report regarding their health and sanitary conditions. The fate of the chairman of the local *kolhoz* and other dignitaries depended upon this report, as, if unfavourable, they could pay for it with their jobs or even with their freedom.

The whole settlement was in a state of excitement as it began to prepare for the vet's visit. Strangely enough, the first and most important task was not getting the cattle and barns into good shape, but accumulating a large supply of vodka. This was not too difficult as vodka was delivered regularly to the local shop, was cheap and not rationed, so anyone who could afford it bought plenty. But if the idea was to win over the vet by plying him with vodka, it proved a total failure, as he happened to be a good Moslem and therefore teetotal. It was not wasted on the locals. Parties, the excuse for which was the vet's visit, lasted well into the night and the accordion and the drunken voices of the revellers were heard throughout the village.

I met the vet on my way to the village. He was quite young, perhaps about thirty, short and incredibly thin. His skin colour and slanting eyes were typical of the Mongolian race, but unlike other Kazakhs, he was clean shaven, which made him look much more civilised, and when he smiled he showed strong, white teeth, a rarity among the Russian population who ruined their front teeth by shelling sunflower seeds – a pastime in which they achieved an amazing degree of speed and skill. The vet stopped and greeted me in Russian, which he seemed able to speak well. He must have known of the presence of Polish deportees in the area because he showed no surprise at seeing me but asked if there was anything he could do to help us. I explained that we did not own any animals and asked whether he had examined Natasha's cow. We bought our milk from her and drank it without boiling it first in order to preserve the vitamins and save fuel. This was unwise as we had been told that the local cows could be infected with tuberculosis and brucelosis. Natasha had three children, who, although we suspected were ill-fed, had no coughs and looked healthy and must have drunk the same milk, so we reckoned it was safe to buy from her and no one else. He had not reached her household as yet but promised he would let us know. He did not ask where we lived, but in that little place he had no difficulty in finding us the very same evening. Apparently the cow, although very thin, was perfectly healthy and, as we liked Natasha very much, the news pleased us greatly for her sake and ours as well.

While he was drinking a mug of Kazakh tea (made from a compressed tea block) he saw Mila in bed and asked about her illness. We told him the whole story, except for the doctor's arrest, and expressed our concern about the removal of her stitches which we thought should be done very soon. He thought for a moment and then suggested that he could do it.

'There is no special art in it,' he said.

His instruments would be adequate to carry out such a small operation. We were a little taken aback and looked at Mila. She had a gift of making everything appear simple and her decision was quick and firm. In our present situation the solution was as good, or better, than anything else and we must trust this cow doctor. He gave the impression of being quite intelligent and must have had some studies and an understanding of hygiene. Mila was a fatalist and thought that if she was destined to live, then nothing could harm her. In due course the vet returned with his instrument bag. Unlike the rest of us, Mila was quite calm. As her scar had healed beautifully and there was no sign of any infection, we made the necessary preparations. An indispensable vodka crate, covered by a freshly washed linen towel, served as a table for the instruments and vodka was used as a disinfectant. Forceps and other necessary instruments were boiled in a well scrubbed saucepan and we managed to provide enough soap for the doctor to wash his hands. As we had no running water, we poured it over his hands from a jar, and a toothbrush replaced the non-existent nail brush. 'The operation' went off smoothly to everybody's delight, and afterwards Mila was as fit as a fiddle.

The vet obviously became attached to us, because he came to see us every day during his short visit. We owe one of our most pleasant memories, or rather, our only pleasant day in Kazakhstan, to him. During one of his calls, we complained about the dreariness of the surrounding scenery and he asked whether we would like to spend a day by the river where there were trees and birds. We thought he was joking, but when he assured us that he was serious, we got terribly excited about the idea and the children started to jump for joy. Then, suddenly, it occurred to us that he might have to pay for his kindness later on, and told him about the surgeon in Troitsk, warning him about possible repercussions. He just laughed and said no one in the village would denounce him as they depended too much upon his report. In any event, the surgeon's case was quite different because he was a son of a different social order and had been sent away to be re-educated and learn to be a loyal citizen of the new regime. The vet thought that the surgeon must have been under suspicion and constant surveillance of the political police, but that he, Ali, was above suspicion, having been educated entirely in communist institutions. Also, the fact that he lived in his own Republic working for his own people made him more independent from the central authorities and gave him comparative freedom.

It was planned that I should go on the excursion with Halına, Janka and Nooka. Naturally Mila could not go so soon after her operation, the Old Lady did not contemplate going at all, and Maryla did not want to go without Leszek for whom the journey would have been too tiring. They did their best to provide us with food and water for the day. Ali and the local Kazakh picked us up with a horse and cart.

We travelled for many hours through the steppe with no protection from the sun and, tightly packed, we were far from comfortable. When we finally reached our 'oasis', the sight of the winding river with its clear water, weeping willows and

111

the twittering of birds made us forget the discomforts of the journey. I held my breath, enchanted by the view, but the children wasted no time before they were splashing in the river. Ali and the driver went to have a swim and I joined the children for a paddle and cooled my face and hands in the water. Afterwards we all enjoyed a picnic of bread, cottage cheese and eggs, although the water in the bottle was warm, as we had already discovered en route. We spent only about three hours in that lovely place, as the journey there and back had taken up most of the day, but it left a strong impression on us all.

Ali's visit to the village reminds me of another incident which could have ended badly for me. It began with that trip. While I sat under the tree by the river, Ali noticed a lump, the size of a small pea, halfway up my shin. He asked me if it hurt and I said no. However, he explained that it might enlarge in time and, if it pressed on a nerve, it could cause pain. Obviously encouraged by his success with Mila he felt he could now treat humans as well as animals and asked if I woud like him to remove the lump while he was still in the village. Thinking what could happen if, indeed, the lump did grow to the size of a plum (as he said it might), I agreed. As he was leaving in two days' time 'the operation' had to be performed the next day.

We went through all the preparations as before and I placed myself on the basket with my leg stretched out. Brave as always, Halina agreed to assist and her duty was to hold my leg tight because the operation had to be performed without an anaesthetic since there was none available. First the scalpel was used to cut the skin covering the lump. I hissed slightly as he made a vertical incision which caused fairly heavy bleeding. Halina began to feel faint and, fearing that she might be sick, Ali released her from duty. At this point it became obvious that Ali was extremely short sighted, and with glasses on the tip of his nose, he fumbled in the wound, which was bleeding profusely trying to pull out the little cyst which refused to budge.

112

He decided that a horizontal cut was necessary and that he needed much better light than we had in our gloomy hut. He bandaged my bleeding leg and, as there was no transport, I had to hobble to the other end of the village where he had a room in one of the old wooden houses which he used as a temporary dispensary. Halina, who in the meantime had somewhat recovered, and Ali supported me on either side.

The room, empty except for the little medicine cabinet on the wall, looked very clean, the wooden floor was well scrubbed and there were two large windows letting in plenty of light. The complete lack of furniture startled me. I wondered if I would have to stand throughout the whole operation. Hobbling on one leg through the village had exhausted me and I was beginning to feel faint and afraid that I would be overcome by nausea from exhaustion and pain. It definitely looked as if I would have to stand and the only place where I could place my leg would be along the window ledge. Supported by Halina on one side and leaning against the wall on the other, I prayed that all would soon end well. I tried to put on a brave front in order not to scare Halina whose physical and moral help I needed badly.

The vet bandaged my leg tightly below and above the wound to stop the bleeding, rubbed the scalpel with alcohol and, with his nose almost touching the wound, skilfully made the second incision and, with the pincers, pulled out the cyst which he triumphantly showed us. He made no attempt to stitch the skin but just folded it back into place and rebandaged my leg. I do not understand why I did not faint as, while he was bandaging my leg, I trembled in every limb and poor Halina had to use all her strength to hold me upright. Now at last I could sit on the window ledge, which was not before time as my legs were giving way. Although I was in pain, the knowledge that the operation was over gave me strength and I limped home with Halina's help. Soon we were telling everyone this crazy story and trying to make light of the whole affair.

The shock caused by the sudden change in our circumstances must have deprived us, at least temporarily, of the faculty to think clearly, as not one of us had realised the foolishness of

113

allowing a vet to perform such an unnecessary operation in our dreadful conditions. There was always the danger of gangrene or other complications setting in. Against all odds, my leg healed very well and soon I was able to remove the bandage at least at night. I kept it on during the day to protect the scab which I hoped would soon fall off. Mila regained her health completely and the knowledge that there was no fear of another attack of gallstones, cheered her very much.

July arrived, and with it the sweltering heat from which there was no escape. The steppe which only a short time ago had been green, now turned into a desert under the scorching sun. Tormented by heat and horse flies, the cows, with tails erect, stampeded home, raising clouds of dust as they abandoned the pastures at midday. Sudden and very hot gusts of wind blew dust and made breathing very difficult. At night we were drenched in perspiration, and often now I was joined outside the hut by other members of the family who, like me, were not able to sleep. We could not sit for a moment because of the mosquitoes, but as nights were as light as days, we wandered along the edge of the steppe until, completely worn out, we returned to our beds of torture hoping to snatch a few hours of badly needed sleep.

Finally, one evening, to our immense relief, the rain came and lasted throughout the night, cooling the roof and walls of the hut which had been like an oven. For the first time for many weeks we all slept soundly, but in the morning a painful discovery awaited us. Someone had cut a large hole in the wall of the barn and pulled out a bag containing two men's coats and other articles of men's clothing which belonged to Mila's husband. As the hut was made of turf it was not difficult to cut a hole, and the sound of the rain on the roof must have muffled any noise the thieves made.

The loss was irretrievable as we could have got several bags of flour and other foods normally unobtainable for roubles, in exchange for the clothing. Apart from the loss, it was a terrible shock because we knew that, with equal ease, the thieves could have got through the hole and murdered us all. Being so far from the village no one would have heard our cries for help. We dared not stay another night and decided to move into the village. The independence and isolation, so highly valued by us, had its disadvantages. While we racked our brains as to where to go next, Natasha, from whom we bought our milk, heard of our misfortune and offered us accommodation in her home. Glad and very grateful, we accepted. We reported the theft to the militia post and the man who came to examine the hole expressed admiration for the skill with which it had been made and said it had been done by professionals who would have known how and where to dispose of the stuff quickly, and that tracing them would be quite impossible.

With a hired hand-cart we gradually transferred our possessions to Natasha's hut. In spite of the recent rain, the ground was dry again and I well remember the dust raised as I pushed the cart. I have a special reason to remember, but at the time I paid no attention to it. In the upset and confusion of that terrible day I forgot to bandage my leg and the dust penetrated the wound, with the inevitable resulting infection. As there was no one sufficiently competent in the village to help, I had to put my faith in Providence and my strong constitution. Unfortunately it was soon clear that the infection would not disappear by itself and I would require medical attention after all. After the incident with the surgeon in Troitsk I did not want to go there and the only alternative was a clinic in Kustanai. I had to get permission from the NKVD man to buy a railway ticket and, thanks to the postwoman nurse, who certified that I was in need of medical attention, permission was granted. To show our gratitude, Maryla, who was an expert at handicrafts, promised to embroider a *kosinka*, a kind of headscarf for the nurse.

Travelling in the Soviet Union was not only discouraged but often forbidden except when on duty, or for health reasons or official holidays. Trains ran irregularly and infrequently and, not surprisingly, the long distance trains did not stop at places like Yemankino, our nearest station. A person like me, even with the necessary permission to travel, depended greatly upon the whim of the station master who could refuse to sell a ticket on any pretext. We knew him from our visits for kerosene which sometimes, and in great secrecy, he let us buy. He seemed an exceptionally nice and sympathetic person and I hoped he would be willing to help. I took my little suitcase with a change of clothes and some food and set off on my way through the steppe to Yemankino, wondering what would await me there. Luckily, both the station master and his wife seemed glad to see me and soon I was sitting at their table, treated to pies filled with cottage cheese, served with sour cream and yoghourt with potatoes and we chatted like old friends.

These two were different from most of the Russians we met who held official positions. They seemed free from the fear of mixing with strangers and altogether reasonably contented. Maybe their comparative prosperity and independence made them so. They grew their own vegetables, had a cow, hens and geese. In addition, some of their supplies of food must have come from people who depended on the station master for their tickets, and in exchange for kerosene which was as much (if not more) valued as vodka. Most of all I enjoyed their bread which was white and not bitter like ours. I had to stay with these friendly people for a couple of days while I waited for the train, and they allowed me to have a bed in their room.

It looked as though the station master was not sure until the very last moment whether or not the train would stop at his station. Every time it was signalled I was ready to board and became more and more frustrated especially as my leg was beginning to hurt. At last the long awaited moment arrived and, equipped with reservation slip entitling me to a berth, I got in.

Long-distance Russian trains now seemed comfortable to me. Berths were arranged in three layers one above the other in a sort of open compartment for six people each, on both sides of the car. In the middle was free passage-way. I got the berth in the centre and it was just long and wide enough for me to stretch. Bare boards were uncomfortable for sleeping,

*Eugenia's mother and
father (Vilna, 1910)*

*Eugenia, aged 6
(Moscow 1916)*

Eugenia, aged 28 (1938)

Polish military inspection (Rowne, 1929). Nik is fourth from the right

Nik (Passport photograph, 1928)

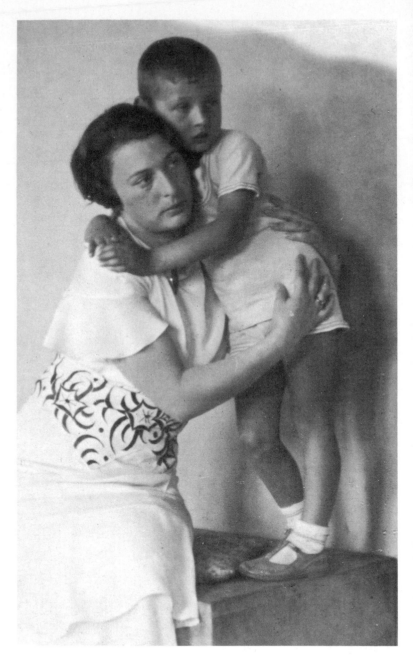

Eugenia with Nooka (1934)

Eugenia, Nooka, and Max the dog near Jaremche Waterfall (1936)

The house at Jaremche Waterfall (Summer 1939)

The village, Kazakhstan (Summer 1940).
Drawing by Janka

Inside Natasha's house (1940).
Drawing by Janka

Natasha's house (Summer 1941).
From left to right: Halina, Mila, Nooka, Maryla with Leszek, and Janka

The village in winter.
Drawing by Janka

Eugenia (Tehran 1944)

but luckily they were not infested with vermin, which, I was told, was often the case. There was neither a restaurant car nor restaurants at the stations, but sometimes one could buy food from peasants at the frequent stopping-places. Passengers usually took food supplies for the whole journey and that became their main luggage. At each station there was a large container with a tap, for *kipiatok* (boiling water) for making tea. Each car was designed for about forty people, but sometimes more travelled in it. At night we were issued with a candle and, as the windows did not open, the car became very stuffy and the candle hardly contributed to its lighting.

I dozed through most of the very slow journey, the scenery being so dull, just steppe burned by the sun. When not eating, my fellow passengers mostly slept. Occasionally they tried to start a conversation with me but, afraid of possible provocation, I answered in monosyllables and was finally left alone. The passengers were predominantly Kazakh peasants, but there were also some men in uniform and at some stops I saw uniformed railway officials getting into 'soft cars', which of course were not for people like me to travel in.

Kustanai was not impressive. It had the same dust roads as in Troitsk, on which cows, goats and hens wandered. The dust was indescribable. The houses were built mostly of wood, and quite old and neglected, but they were palaces by comparison with our huts. The vet had given us his address, although none of us had ever contemplated going to Kustanai, but here I was, walking along the dusty road, holding my little suitcase, followed by a crowd of ill-kempt, half-naked Kazakh children attracted by the unusual sight of a strange white woman. I suspected that, like monkeys, they imitated my movements because whenever I turned round, they suddenly stopped and burst into fits of laughter. Nevertheless, one of them, a little older than the rest, showed me to the vet's house.

Ali lived in a house with elaborate carved eaves which one entered through a covered porch with benches on either side. He lived with his mother who received me in a very friendly way. Ali was out and although I could not understand a word she said, she obviously knew who I was. She brought water for me to wash, gave me some pancake bread and *kumiss* (fermented mare's milk) to drink and, gesturing, persuaded me to lie down on the bed and covered me with a shawl. I had hardly slept during the journey as the bench was hard and my bones ached, and the station master had warned me against sleeping because of the numerous thieves on trains. So now, feeling safe in this hospitable house, I fell asleep. When I woke I saw Ali sitting on a chair. He seemed pleased to see me, thinking perhaps that he was the reason for my visit, but when I told him about the infection he was very upset. I tried to reassure him by saying that the operation had been a complete success and it was only due to my negligence that the leg was in such a bad state. He looked even more upset when he examined it and said he would take me to hospital straight away. I asked him to book a room in a hotel, but he was adamant, saying that his mother would be offended if I rejected their hospitality and that the hotels in Kustanai were terrible, filthy and bug-ridden. His argument was very convincing, especially as his house was very clean, which was a pleasant surprise, for I knew only the Kazakhs' houses in Novo-Troitsk and they were primitive and dirty. Added to which, Ali's house was partly furnished in European style which made me think that he must have lived at some time or other in European Russia, most probably when he was at university.

The head of the hosptial in Kustanai was a Russian and reminded me of the doctor in Troitsk – a sad association. When he saw my leg and heard the story, he was most indignant.

'Who was the idiot who attempted such an operation? That cut so near the bone might have caused very grave complications.'

I was ashamed to admit that it had been done with my consent by a vet and, not wanting to cause trouble for Ali for overstepping his professional boundaries, I kept quiet. The doctor's words alarmed me, because the danger of whatever complications he had in mind was still there and Kazakhstan was no place in which to be ill. Having cleaned and dressed my wound, the doctor gave me a lotion which he called the 'Physiological solution' and told me to return the next day. Ali's mother had supper waiting for us, consisting of delicious lamb kebabs, rice and freshly made pancake bread, followed by Kazakh tea with fat swimming in it served in little bowls. Not wishing to offend the old woman, I forced myself to drink that revolting tea. I would have enjoyed *kumiss* much more, but doubtless she had tried to do what was best in her opinion and, apart from the tea, the supper was a real treat for me. Lamb was unpopular in Poland and now I could see how much I had missed.

Ali's mother appeared to be quite intelligent, judging by the questions with which she plied me through her son acting as interpreter. She wanted to know about our life in Novo-Troitsk but most of all about our previous life in the distant 'Lehistan' (Poland). I tried to answer with caution as I was sure she would not be able to refrain from repeating it all to the avid listeners who would, most certainly, congregate on their porch. I was in no doubt that, as anywhere else in the Soviet Union, the NKVD informers were alert and I did not want to run the risk of being accused of spreading harmful propaganda and thus endanger Ali and his mother. I was sure there was a limit to that freedom of which he spoke so confidently when he invited us to the 'oasis'.

I spent a comfortable night as my leg no longer throbbed and when I went to the hospital the doctor seemed pleased. I was very surprised to see how much better it looked. The improvement was so rapid that after a few days only a red scar remained and I was allowed to return home. It must indeed have been a magical solution to have worked such wonders, and the hand of Providence must have been in it.

On the eve of my departure a reception was held with Ali's neighbours and relatives, with plenty of good food and not so good tea, and the following morning Ali's mother presented me with a badly tanned red fox pelt which, years later in

Europe, was eaten by moths. She also gave me a piece of roast lamb and some pancake bread which saved me from going hungry on the return journey as this time there were no peasants selling food at the stations.

We reached Yemankino late at night and I got off, still with my suitcase intact, and was met by my friend, the station master. They put me up for the night and next morning, very eager to see my son and adopted family, I walked home. On arrival I was happy to find everything in order and everybody in good health and in better spirits than when I left them and I was able to boast about the successful outcome of my journey. And so, our life in Natasha's house began auspiciously.

At Natasha's

The most important institutions in Novo-Troitsk which gave
employment to a number of local people were a tractor repair
depot, the *Kolhoz* administration office and granaries, the post
office and the shop. In the centre of the village was a small
pond filled with salty water, which was all that remained of an
earlier inland sea, which meant there was only one fresh-water
well serving the whole village. There were a few such ponds in
the neighbourhood and, during the short summer periods,
while there was still some water left, the children splashed
about, not minding that horses were being washed there at the
same time. But the water evaporated very quickly and the dry
pond with its flat banks and lack of vegetation, looked very
sad.

Natasha's hut, consisting of barn, kitchen and living-room,
stood on a piece of barren land with one side facing the street
and the other the steppe. It had the great advantage of being
near the shop and post office and only a few minutes' walk
from the road leading to the station and Troitsk. The entrance
led straight into the barn, where a cow was kept. To the right
of the barn was the door to the kitchen and from there an
opening led into the main room, which we were to occupy.
There were three small windows altogether, one in the kitchen
facing the street and two in the living-room from which we
could see the ruin of an abandoned hut.

The main part of the kitchen was occupied by a large oven,

121

at the back of which was a recess where Natasha's family slept. This oven was used primarily for cooking and baking bread and was similar to an old-fashioned baker's oven, but we were very glad to see that there was also a small kitchen range, with the chimney breast backing into 'our room'. We hoped to be able to do some cooking on it without having to use too much *kiziak* and at the same time to warm our room. Apart from a small narrow table and a stool, there was no other furniture in the kitchen. On the wall there was a 'hand washer', consisting of a small metal tank with a tap at the bottom. When the tap was pushed upwards, the tank released water which was all we had for washing ourselves.

The main room had quite reasonable furniture, probably originating from pre-revolutionary times, as there was no local timber and in the past twenty years no one except *kulaks* (wealthy peasants) and their families had been imported from other parts of Russia. In the centre of the room was a large wooden table with a long bench behind it. Quite a nice looking wooden bed stood against the wall on the left and two chairs completed the furniture. There was an icon with some faded paper flowers and ribbons on both sides and a mirror on the wall between the two windows. The mirror was not much use as it had lost most of the silvering and was covered in spots.

Natasha's hut, like most in the village, was built of bricks made of a mixture of cow dung, mud and dry grass. The bricks were dried in the sun. 'Cementing' was done by using the same indispensable *kiziak* mixed with water. Grass grew on the earth roof of the hut in early summer, delighting the goats who treated it as pasture, climbing on to it easily from the side which sloped almost to the ground level.

Natasha badly needed an additional income. Her husband was away on military service and, as a private receiving extremely poor pay, he could not help her and their three small children financially. She worked for the *Kolhoz*, as did all the other villagers not employed in one or another local institution. For this work she received a share in the produce harvested by the *Kolhoz*, plus a small wage and an entitlement to buy rationed food and articles such as soap, kerosene and, occasionally, even plimsolls or a piece of material at low government prices. Her wage in roubles was insufficient to pay for rations for the four of them and, as we discovered later, time was also required to purchase these articles as they were always in short supply and queues were long. Poor Natasha very often missed her chance, as only on rare occasions was she allowed to leave work to take her place in the queue. As she was the only adult member of the family, and as no one outside the family was allowed to collect the rations for her, she nearly always had to pay much higher prices for her supplies.

Our arrival did not inconvenience her very much as she and her children never used the main room. She was hardly ever at home, and with us there she could at least be sure that no harm would come to the children left alone all day. In winter the children, especially the two older ones, spent most of the day in the recess at the back of the kitchen stove. There was another reason why sharing her hut suited both Natasha and ourselves. In summer she was left with a small surplus of milk and eggs. She made the milk into butter which, together with the eggs, she normally sold in Troitsk market, where prices were higher. In us she had willing buyers on the spot, she never charged us the full black-market prices and we never tried to pay her less than she asked. We were also very fair at fixing prices for the articles she sometimes wanted from us instead of roubles. She was a sweet person, small in stature, but agile and graceful in her movements. She had had a very hard life but never complained nor grumbled, although at times she lost patience with her children, but in most situations she showed a calm dignity which inspired respect. To us she was a friend whom we all came to love and during our entire stay with her there was never any unpleasantness.

Our room was roughly four metres square. We solved the accommodation problem in the following way: the wooden bed was for the Old Lady to sleep in and rest on during the day; across the foot of it was my basket which served as Janka's bed. To the right of the entrance, between the protruding breast of the kitchen range and the wall, was a recess into which had been built a brick base for sleeping, and we decided that this would be the warmest and most suitable place for Leszek to play in the daytime and also room enough for Maryla to sleep on at night. An adult could only sit on it as the ceiling was low, but a small child could move freely. The 'bed' was about a metre and a half from the ground and, to get there, Maryla had to use the Soborski's basket which was placed against it. That basket was Nooka's bed. Between it and the opposite wall there was just enough room for my iron bed, above which I hung my colourful *kelim*. Mila and Halina slept on the floor in the middle of the room. At night, in order to create more space, we moved the table close to the wall. even so, mother and daughter had to sleep half underneath it, which was not only uncomfortable but even dangerous, if they woke up suddenly and hit their head. Sleeping on the floor was possible because Natasha's hut had the great luxury of a wooden floor. There was a trap door in the centre of the room which led into an earthen cellar where we could keep potatoes and, during hot weather, perishable food.

Since our arrival in Novo-Troitsk we had gone through various very trying experiences. Life at Natasha's was an improvement. There were no fleas excepting those that thrived in the fur of the huge old tom cat, Vaska. Mosquitoes did not worry us either as, to get to our room, they had to make a roundabout journey through the barn and the kitchen and were lost on the way, or put off our scent by the variety of smells exuding from the barn. In the previous hut they came through cracks in the windows and the door, but here the windows were tight and permanently fixed for the winter with a second set of frame glass and we were asked not to open them. This did not worry us as the doors of the kitchen and the barn were left open most of the time but even an unventilated room, the air mixed with strong animal odours, was infinitely preferable to the mosquitoes.

Natasha's easy disposition and her obvious pleasure at having us with her gave us a feeling of comparative security of our tenancy and made us start planning for the winter which, we were told, could begin as early as September.

First there was the question of supplies of flour, potatoes, lard or clarified butter, candles, kerosene for the lamp and primus and cow dung for cooking and heating. All this needed money and up until now we had not been earning any, but had lived on the sale or exchange of our possessions which, at the present rate, could not last much longer. We held a family council and decided that Maryla and I must try to get jobs. Mila was still too weak after her operation, but could look after Leszek, and the Old Lady, helped by our children who would gather *kiziak* in the steppe and bring water, should have no difficulty in running the household.

We soon learned that the man in charge of the local petrol pump needed an assistant. Maryla applied and was immediately accepted. The pay was ridiculously low; for a month's salary all she could buy was a quarter of a kilo of butter on the free market, but the advantage of the job lay elsewhere. It entitled her to 400 grammes of bread daily which was not to be scorned. It soon transpired that there was another, even greater advantage in holding that job. The *Kazakh*, Maryla's boss, gave her, from time to time, a bottle of kerosene. This was almost certainly a bribe, as he could not conceal from her that he had been helping himself to that precious liquid. These helpings of kerosene meant a lot to us. At this time of year the days were very long and, as we did all the cooking on *kiziak*, we did not need kerosene for the lamp or primus, but we knew that it would be a very different story later in the year.

Encouraged by Maryla's success I decided to try for an office job in the tractor repair depot. I could read, write and count in Russian so, in applying, I referred to the Constitution, according to which everyone in the Soviet Union had to be employed in a job which was in keeping with their education. Knowing that they were very sensitive on this point, I quoted the Constitution at every opportunity, as they so constantly and hypocritically did. Time passed and as I had not received a reply to my application, I decided to go to the depot myself.

My appearance there caused obvious dismay. I explained the reason for my visit and was told to wait on the bench in the hall, while the management of the depot called a meeting. I learned much later from one of the participants that there were two opposing views among the employers. Some insisted that if they refused to take me on they could be accused of breaking the Constitution, which would be considered un-patriotic behaviour, as bad as sabotage, particularly if, by any chance, I had been sent by the NKVD in order to test them. Others thought that they should not allow a deportee, and possibly a spy, to penetrate their ranks. As I spoke Russian like a native of that country, they decided that I must be a daughter of a Russian White Guard officer (how true), who had fought against the Red Army during the revolution and that that argument should be enough, if one was necessary, to persuade even the NKVD authorities that their refusal was justified.

Obviously no conclusion had been reached but, to my immense joy, I was told to report for work the following morning. I flew home on borrowed wings, intoxicated with my triumph, imagining the privileges that the job would bring.

I reported fifteen minutes early next morning and, to my surprise, found all the other employees already there. Apparently there was a serious punishment for being even one minute late. I was allocated a small dark corner with a rickety table and an equally deficient chair, and assigned to work on accounts. My boss was a young, puffy-faced Russian with small, spiteful eyes. I knew he was the son of the *Kolhoz* chairman and thus a very important person in the village. It was an unpleasant discovery as I had noticed on previous encounters that he was extremely arrogant and full of hatred towards Polish people. But there was nothing I could do, and he was the person I had to ask for instructions. I waited for

126

some time but finally had to interrupt the work in which he appeared to be so engrossed.

He looked at me askance. 'What do you want?'

'I came to work. I am supposed to work as a book keeper.'

He pretended to know nothing about it. 'At the moment there is no work to do, the books have been checked and closed.'

He returned his attention to his work and I, feeling frustrated and angry, went back to my table. I looked around hoping to see at least one friendly face, but everyone seemed to be deep in their work, heads down over their papers and it was obvious that they had been instructed to have nothing to do with me. I could not understand such an attitude. Why take me on if there was no work for me to do? The day seemed to drag terribly. I had brought a piece of bread for my lunch and I ate it, washing it down with *kipiatok* – boiling water. I noticed that the others made a kind of instant tea by putting crumbled pieces of pressed tea into it. The Kazakhs drank it with the addition of some fat. They were employed only in menial jobs or sometimes as lorry drivers. All office workers and mechanics were Russian and what struck me particularly was that, although the white-collar workers pretended to be swamped with work, never talked to each other and hardly ever left their desks, they in fact spent hours over the same sheet of paper. I was very happy when the whistle announced the end of the working day, as it had been the most boring day of my life.

The whole routine was repeated the following day, except that I found some account books on my table but no one wanted to tell me what to do. In vain I turned to the boss and other employees for enlightenment. They told me they were far too busy to teach me. At last, the boss called me to his desk and forbade me to talk to the others, whom, he alleged, I was hindering in their work, and added, with a sarcastic smile, that if I were as educated as I claimed to be, I should not need anyone's help. By now I was so disillusioned that I wanted to tell him to get stuffed and to go home but I remembered in time that such an action would be considered sabotage with all its foreseeable consequences. I continued to sit at my table trying to decipher the books which made no sense to me and pretended to work like all the others. Again the whistle meant salvation. I collected my books and went to the boss to ask where I was supposed to leave them. He asked what work I had done during the day and I said I had tried to understand what I was meant to do but, without explanation, found it impossible. In reply the youth gave me such a look of contemptuous irony and venomous triumph that for a moment it was all I could do not to slap his face. Luckily I managed to control myself.

He said, 'You can see for yourself that this work is much too difficult for you. We gave you a job in accordance with our Constitution which gives everyone a chance to work, but we cannot tolerate spongers and dunces in our factory, so do not come here any more.'

I had to admit that firing me was a relief and the best possible solution for me. I understood also how skilfully they had solved the problem I had created by my application. With similar perfidious reasoning, Soviet diplomats had been winning essential issues for years in the international forum.

Back at home I met with sympathy and understanding which revived my spirit.

Maryla's work at the pump did not last long either. Someone must have suspected the boss of giving her kerosene and now he had to stop. With that perk gone and with Maryla often being woken in the middle of the night to go and fill a lorry's tank and listen to the drivers' uncouth jokes, she was pleased to give the job up when the replacement arrived.

As our hopes of employment faded, we had to think of some other way of earning a living and here Mila's sewing machine proved our salvation. What a brainwave on Mila's part to have brought it with her! It weighed a lot and made the Soborski's basket almost as heavy as mine, causing grumbles during the journey, but in our present circumstances it proved to be worth more than all the gold left in the bedroom drawers of their home, as it became a stable source of income.

128

It was Natasha who started it all. As soon as she saw the sewing machine, she asked Mila to make her a dress out of some cotton cloth, in exchange for butter or milk. Mila was delighted to say the least. There was no dressmaker in the village and Russian women could only do the most primitive sewing because of the shortage of materials. In summer they all wore long skirts with shapeless, collarless loose blouses and in winter black, padded jackets, bought ready-made, with the same skirts. Natasha caused a sensation in her new dress and orders began to flood in. Mila, who was used to making her children's clothes and had, during our stay in their house in Stanislavov, even made a winter coat for Nooka, now worked from dawn till dusk trying to take advantage of the long days and the demand, while it lasted. Maryla, I and occasionally the girls, tried to help as much as we could. Even in such a dismal place as Novo-Troitsk and despite the very difficult life, women had not lost their desire to look attractive.

Mila's best clientèle was, naturally, the 'aristocracy' of the village, of whom the first and foremost was Masha, daughter of the *Kolhoz* chairman and sister of my ex-boss in the tractor depot. She was a comely young woman, tall and well built. She held her head high on her full strong neck, had a typically round Slavonic face with a snub nose and ruddy complexion, but when dealing with us, her good looks were marred by an expression of disdain and hostility. She behaved as if she were doing us a favour, and in a way, she was, since it was a favour to be paid by her for Mila's work, especially in food. As a close relative of two powerful men she could have had dresses for nothing had she wanted, and we often wondered what prevented her from doing so. Certainly not kindness or a sense of propriety. She usually fixed the amount herself, and it did not matter to us how much we received, but that we were paid at all. We were always very careful not to offend her. Her father, an old and stalwart member of the Party, was an extremely influential person in the village and held in his hands all the fruits of the villagers' labour. It was he who allocated the harvest and, as these rations were the basis of the villagers' existence, he was virtually the master of their life and death. He had always shown hostility in his dealings with us, which doubtless influenced the attitude of his children.

The other important person in the village was a militia man whose duties included overseeing both us and the villagers. He did not get on well with the Chairman which probably helped keep the Chairman in check. He never attempted to convert us to communism or point out our 'crimes' like most other officials. Once, his tongue loosened by too much vodka, he said that if we had committed a crime against the Soviet Union, we had already been sufficiently punished for it. From this we concluded that he did not overestimate the benefits derived by us from being transferred from the capitalist hell to the Soviet paradise. His wife was also one of Mila's customers. She was a shy, unassuming woman who appeared to understand our plight and in time we came to like her, although, because of her husband's job, she had to be careful not to be accused of fraternisation.

Our financial situation improved when we started to get orders for head scarves called *kosynka*. It was a matter of pride for every Russian woman in the village to have an embroidered head scarf. In the past, Russian women, especially the wealthier ones, wore a very ornate head-dress called *kokoshnik* which was an indispensable part of the national costume. It was usually made of velvet on a stiffened base to keep the shape, and was adorned with precious or semi-precious stones and sometimes trimmed with expensive fur. The less ornate *kosynka* was a relic of that tradition.

There was no longer any velvet so it had to be made out of what was available, in this case, thick white linen decorated with embroidery instead of precious stones. We were surprised to learn that the women in the village could not embroider, so they wanted to take advantage of our skills. At first the sole designer and embroiderer was Maryla, but, as the demand grew and she could no longer cope with the orders, I started to help. The embroidery was the Richelieu type with which I was familiar and, with Maryla's guidance, it was not difficult for me to pick it up. As there was no silk thread we used ordinary white sewing cotton. We disliked it but the village women were delighted with the results and soon in addition to *kosynkas*, we had orders for embroidered petticoats.

Here Maryla had a chance to display her talents. She drew designs from her head straight on to the material. Petticoats had to be embroidered around the top and bottom edge and each woman wanted an individual design. We were told that petticoats would be stored in a chest and used for special occasions or saved as dowry for daughters. We were paid for our work with butter, eggs, cottage cheese and, occasionally, if a pig had been slaughtered, a piece of meat or pig's fat. We became so well provided with food that not only did we have enough to eat for the first time since our arrival, but we could help our less fortunate or less enterprising compatriots in the village.

Among the Polish deportees was a pleasant woman, Mrs Kozlowska, the wife of the previous Chief of Police in Stanislavov who had succeeded in escaping to Romania just after the entry of the Soviet troops into Poland. He was the man whom Mila's husband had temporarily replaced, for which act he had been arrested and deported. Mrs Kozlowska had two children, a girl of eight and a boy of nine. They had travelled in the same train as us but in a different car and had arrived in Novo-Troitsk in a different truck. She was one of those lucky people who had hit the jackpot, owing her fortune to a special pack of cards marked with the signs of the zodiac which she had brought with her. One day soon after our arrival in the village, in order to amuse herself, she had spread out the cards and when her landlady saw the mysterious signs and pictures she assumed that she was a professional fortune-teller and begged her to read the fortunes of her husband and son who had been arrested some time ago, and from whom she had received no news. Mrs Kozlowska could not possibly refuse and, to comfort the woman, told her that she would very soon hear from one of them. The prophecy

131

came true and Mrs Kozlowska's reputation as a clairvoyant was established. From then on she had a steady flow of visitors who brought her all sorts of food, and her ability to read people's fortunes from cards created such an aura of magic that even the naughty Masha went out of her way to please her. The villagers believed that she could cast a spell on them and that their fates depended on her readings.

Nooka and Mrs Kozlowska's son became good friends and in summer saw each other quite often, but, although we liked Mrs Kozlowska very much, our busy life did not leave much room for social contacts, and I went to see her only once. We had met in Stanislavov when I visited her in connection with some charity work and I remembered her beautiful home. Seeing this family now in a miserable mud hut shocked me deeply. I returned home very sad, filled with pity for them, but when I began to share my thoughts with the others, I did not meet with much understanding. 'Do you think that our hut is any better?' I looked around and started to giggle. If anything we were rather worse off, but was there not proof here that one could lose sight of one's own misery after a time, and wasn't it a blessing? For me, our hut had almost become a cosy home.

Our 'prosperous' life with its sufficiency of food was too good to last. One day Maryla and I, together with some other women of similar age, were summoned to a meeting and informed that in the Soviet Union 'those who did not work did not eat' and that the time had come for us to prove, by our work for the State, that we had earned the privilege to live in one of its Republics. From the next morning, therefore, we should start working in the cornfields. We had no idea what and where our work was going to be, especially since we had not seen any fields near us.

Early the following morning a Kazakh duly arrived with a horse and old creaking cart shouting, 'Wenches come out to work', which, we learned, was a normal form of address. Some of the women were already in the cart, which also carried a barrel of water. The Kazakh explained, in broken Russian, that the corn in these parts was overgrown with weeds and that our job would be to pull them out. We had to travel for at least an hour to reach the cornfields, an awesome thought as the sun was already scorchingly hot. When we finally arrived, the sight of acres of golden fields made my heart beat faster, and everyone else looked bewitched as this was the first time that the scenery of Kazakhstan had reminded us of the Polish countryside. But there the similarity ended. It was an enormous area and bringing just a few women to weed it was a preposterous idea.

The field was divided into strips by pathways to allow access for weeding and harvesting. We were instructed to walk along the pathway weeding the strip on one side and then turn back to do the same on the other side. The weed, which we had to pull out by hand, was wormwood and extremely bitter. The bitterness permeated our skin very quickly. When I tried to wipe the sweat off my face, and in doing so touched my lips, they burned terribly and this, plus the heat, gave me such a thirst that I could think of nothing but the barrel of water which I had seen on the cart. Although I had only covered a very small area, I felt I had to go back and have a drink no matter what happened. Most of my working companions, previously hidden from sight by the rows of corn, were already there. They all complained of bitterness, thirst and mosquitoes. Unhappily, the bitterness did not deter the mosquitoes. A tin mug was attached by a chain to the barrel but it was too hot to touch, as were the metal hoops on the barrel, which gave us a foretaste of what the water would be like. Indeed the only good thing that could be said was that it was wet and the first sip gave an illusion of relief, but as soon as the mug left the lips, the thirst returned with redoubled force and it was impossible to quench. We understood why the bread baked from the local flour was so bitter. We tried to rest a little by the cart, but the Kazakh urged us to return to work, probably more from a sense of duty than from fear that anyone could check the results of our labours in such an immense area. In any case, sitting by the cart was no better than working; the mosquitoes were stinging just the same, the shade created by the cart earlier on had vanished with the sun high in the sky and time dragged more slowly.

Exasperated and in a mood of utter resignation befitting slaves, we returned to crawl along the rows of corn, pulling the hated woodworm, realising the futility of our labour, but trying somehow or other to kill time until our return home. Oblivious of the mosquitoes and heat, the Kazakh was asleep and snoring under the cart, dressed in his padded jacket. Perhaps he knew better and this was the best defence against mosquitoes and sun. In the meantime his little horse nibbled the grass. The weeding job lasted a few weeks and during that time we had to be up at sunrise which, plus the exhausting journey there and back, made us feel weaker and weaker. Finally, when someone fainted, it was decided that we were useless at that kind of work and we were sent to hoe a potato field.

The work in the potato field was much better in every respect. It was nearer the village, which meant we did not have to get up so terribly early and there seemed to be some purpose in what we were doing which made for a degree of 'job' satisfaction. There was also a much appreciated perk in the form of a few potatoes which we were allowed to bake on the camp fire at noon and sometimes we managed to smuggle a few back home with us. And we were free of the bitter taste of wormwood and the perpetual thirst.

Working near each other we sang Polish songs, made jokes about our employers and sometimes almost forgot our misery. However, we knew that this work had to end soon and wondered what our next assignment would be. The answer came soon enough, when we were sent to a meadow to cut and harvest the hay. This work was much better organised. People worked in groups called brigades into which we were incorporated. Our boss, Ahmed, was the only good looking Kazakh in the village, and, judging by his above average height and much lighter coloured skin, probably had some European blood. Although young, he was head of the brigade and the

Kazakh community. Our work was to scythe or cut grass with a sickle, bundle it and finally load it on to lorries. Only Mrs Krilenko and her two daughters knew how to do the work, having done it previously on their smallholding and Maryla, handy as usual, somehow managed the sickle. I betrayed a complete lack of ability in that direction, and, seeing my futile efforts, Ahmed said that I must work as a cook. My duty would be to prepare a mid-day meal for about twenty people in his brigade. The idea did not appeal to me for two reasons. Having enjoyed working with a group in the potato field I did not want to be isolated from the others and I also doubted whether I would be any better in my new capacity than I had been in the field. I tried to get out of it, but Ahmed was adamant and refused to change his mind. He said he was sure I would manage as the meal was very simple and never changed. It consisted of a kind of macaroni made from flour and water, then rolled and cut into small strips, called *lapsha*. This was boiled in salted water and then dished up with some of the water in which it had been cooked. Without meat or vegetables it was very insipid but, to a certain degree, satisfied hunger and thirst. The water for the *lapsha* was boiled in a huge cauldron over the camp fire and, as usual, the fuel was *kiziak* and some dry grass stalks. Lighting and looking after the fire was the duty of an old Kazakh who cursed incessantly as it smoked and frequently went out, and bringing the water to the boil was not an easy task.

After my first day's work I knew my misgivings were justified. Working the flour and water into a dough for twenty people was no joke, but it was nothing compared with the strength and skill required for rolling it out into very thin layers and cutting them into strips. As there was no table I had to do this kneeling down, using a smooth board on the ground. After a very short time my arms, knees and back, unused to such a position, hurt so much that every few minutes I had to stop working to let the pain subside. I tried hard to roll the dough as thinly as I could, nevertheless when Ahmed returned from inspecting the work in the field (which he did on horseback), he did not look at all happy. The real crunch came when the workers arrived for their mid-day meal. After tasting the *lapsha* they got very angry and swore at me in Russian, which leaves nothing to the imagination!

There was one rule that had to be strictly observed in making *lapsha* – it had to be as thin as paper. This was understandable as it was impossible to cook thick *lapsha* on a *kiziak* fire satisfactorily. I had to admit that my *lapsha*, swimming in what looked like clouded dishwater was difficult to swallow as it was very thick and not cooked through. Revolt was in the air and I was more than willing to resign immediately, but Ahmed refused to release me. I got home with red and swollen palms and a few blisters. Maryla came back very tired, her arms and back aching, but otherwise unharmed. At home Mila painted my blisters with iodine left by the vet, and this really helped.

Before leaving for work the following morning Mila dressed my hand with strips of linen. I was terrified at the thought of the ordeal awaiting me. It was not so much the work itself that frightened me, but the reaction of my 'customers'. I needed a few days more practice before I could master the art of cooking *lapsha*, but could not expect people to be patient and forbearing in the meantime. For some of them this mid-day meal was the only hot one of the day, and even for this several kopecks were to be deducted from the share of the harvest they were supposed to receive from the *Kolhoz* administration at the end of the season. We had also been promised that we would be paid in the same way.

With help from Ahmed, who stayed behind to roll the dough for me, I gradually learned to produce a good *lapsha* which satisfied everybody, but his extraordinary behaviour gave rise to jokes and jeers among the members of his brigade. This did not seem to worry him in the least, and although I no longer needed his help, he continued to spend more time near the cauldron than supervising the workers in the field.

One day he stopped by our hut to talk to Nooka, asking him if he would like to come to the field with us and help the old man with the fire, in return for which he would be allowed to ride a horse. Nooka, who had enough of petticoat rule at home, reacted enthusiastically and from the next morning started to accompany us. He did not do much for the fire, but became an expert bareback rider. At that time we were suffering from a prolonged drought. Outside and inside, the huts were covered with a thick layer of dust raised by the strong winds blowing from the steppe, and our eyes and throats were permanently irritated. For Nooka, getting away from the village was a heaven-sent opportunity. I, too, was glad that he could have some fun in our otherwise joyless life and spend a few hours in healthier surroundings.

With the ending of summer the work in the fields was over and Maryla and I returned to our previous occupation as embroiderers, hoping our private income would be supplemented by the reward for our work for the *Kolhoz*. But before this could happen we badly needed roubles and food and so, once again, I had to dig into my 'Pandora's box' to see what I could sell or exchange. Opening my basket was an interesting experience. Everything in it brought memories and associations, I could never make a choice quickly. I used to turn and hold every item in my hands, reminiscing before putting it aside, and often rummaged about in it for hours. Most of the remaining contents were personal clothing, bed and table linen and a few pairs of shoes, but I also found Nooka's and my skating boots with skates attached. Obviously I had thought we could continue that sport in any circumstances. There was my fabulous black evening dress which I had worn just over a year ago at the regimental ball. What use was it now?

Suddenly Mila said, 'You know, it would make a beautiful *sarafan* for Masha.'

Sarafan was Russian for a sort of pinafore dress worn with a blouse. At first I thought she was joking. Who would wear such a thing in the village, and what village girl, used to bright colours, would want to wear black? Still, there was no harm in trying and, as Masha was coming that afternoon for a fitting, I

137

spread out the dress on the Old Lady's bed and we prepared ourselves to watch for Masha's reaction. She came in pompous and cool as usual, but as soon as she saw the dress her eyes and mouth opened wide. Lifting the shimmering material she let it flow through her fingers with an expression of rapture and disbelief. We had no doubts about the success of our plan, but pretended not to notice her excitement and concentrated on our work. I am sure that each of us was trying mentally to translate the value of her rapture into sacks of flour and cereals. This time she did not dictate the price to us, but willingly accepted our terms, and departed with the dress pressed gently to her bosom. The following Sunday we saw Masha promenading down the dusty roads of Novo-Troitsk attired in her new pinafore dress and white organdie blouse with puffed sleeves which she had bought from me previously. She was surrounded by a crowd of admiring youths with balalaikas and accordions, and young women who must have felt very envious.

Even though we had finished hay making, Ahmed still visited us daily, staying for hours without speaking, merely following me with his eyes. This irritated me and caused the youngsters to make ironical remarks. In our crowded conditions, and with people popping in and out, his presence was most inconvenient. Not wanting to offend him, we tried to be patient, hoping he would soon tire of us.

But suddenly, one day he spoke in pidgin Russian, saying, 'My wife told me to bring you and your boy into our home. You will not have to do any work or worry about bread for your son. You will be our princess and we your faithful slaves.'

It seemed like some proposal of marriage, with his wife's approval. I did not know yet whether Kazakhs were allowed more than one wife, but I did not feel like joining his harem. Very cautiously I started to explain that I was older than he (I was then twenty-nine) and that soon my face would be covered with wrinkles and my hair would go grey. But he seemed unconvinced and visibly impatient. He grabbed me and began to pull me out of the room. I managed to get Mila's

138

ruler and hit him across the back. I felt him stiffen, more from the insult than the pain, and for a moment we were all terrified, thinking he might hit me back. However, he simply let go and rushed from the hut. I stayed indoors for the next few days, afraid to meet him. Soon afterwards the snow fell and life in the village came almost to a standstill. As Ahmed lived at the opposite end of the village, the chances of meeting before next summer were small, and by then new and unexpected developments beyond our control had changed our lives.

By now our little group had automatically formed a perfect commune where functions were divided fairly and sensibly. We were very fortunate because our temperaments and abilities ideally complemented each other. We greatly valued and needed each other's help and affection, and time and time again I thanked Merciful God that, in our misfortune, He had allowed Henryk and me to be with this lovely family.

As far as I knew, things did not always run so smoothly in the families of other deportees. Since our arrival in Novo-Troitsk we had been left to our own devices. Everyone had to struggle for their own survival, which did not promote good will. The daily worry and misery, the uncertainty of our situation, the mental strain and physical discomfort, the persistent hunger, the extremes of temperature, made people irritable and sometimes hostile to each other. Although we were all in the same boat, our reactions, and abilities to face hardship varied greatly, creating distinct differences between people which gave rise to jealousy and spite.

As our settlement was spread over a wide area and as it was no pleasure to wander along dusty roads in summer unless absolutely necessary, and almost impossible to do so in winter, we saw and knew only those people with whom we were brought into contact either through work or who, for some reason or other, sought our company.

The exiles we saw most often were the Armenians and the Ukranian widow, Mrs Krilenko, because their house was close to our hut, and probably also because we had previously

139

shared it with them. We felt great sympathy and pity for the Armenian family. The husband and wife were very old and their thirty-five-year-old daughter was an invalid, so they were all unfit for work. They must have lost their heads when the armed Russian soldiers burst into their home in Stanislavov and been unable to decide what would be most useful to pack; they were barely strong enough to carry what little they had. They still had some roubles, but we wondered what would happen when those were gone. Being unable to work for the *Kolhoz*, they could not expect to receive any food from it and would probably have to rely upon charity from those more fortunate than themselves. Mrs Krilenko and her two hefty daughters had worked hard and productively in the fields and now felt secure in the hope of adequate reward from the *Klohoz*.

Mrs Kozlowska, the fortune teller, came to see us once or twice when she visited the shop. She had been doing very well with her fortune telling and there was no reason to think that things would change for the worse for her and her two lovely children. With Mila's dressmaking and our *kosynakas* and petticoat embroideries, as well as the promised share from the harvest for our work for the *Kolhoz*, we were among the prosperous.

There was another person whom we knew only fleetingly and whose fate was a warning to us. She was a pretty young woman deported with her small son. She had a terrible temper and soon after our arrival, had quarelled with almost everyone, fellow exiles as well as natives. She was filled with hatred for the whole world, particularly Russians, and shouted abuse of Stalin and the communist régime at every opportunity. She doubtless thought that, having been deported to the threshold of Siberia, she had nothing more to fear and could express her views freely. Although we were convinced that many of the local people, and certainly all of us, heartily agreed with her, we feared that such behaviour in public would end badly and tried to warn her of the danger. We did not realise then just how real that danger was. She reacted angrily and would not listen. She did not stay long in the village. Two uniformed men came one night and arrested her, taking the child with them.

Every day we expected to be called to receive our share of the harvest from the *Kolhoz*, but when nothing happened we formed a small delegation and went to see the Chairman. At first he refused to see us which made us think things were not going to be as we had hoped. When we would not leave, he emerged, looking very indignant. 'Were we so stupid as not to know that harvest this year was very poor and that almost everything had to go to the government and that even their own people would be getting very little?'

When we protested, saying that we would die of starvation in winter, he shrugged his shoulders and went away. This was a terrible blow, and the knowledge that we had been cheated and ruthlessly exploited made it even worse.

Not long after, I was dealt a much harder personal blow, when my second letter to Nik, written in June, came back marked 'Gone away'. This was shattering news. Why had he left and where had he gone? How and when would I be able to find his new address and write to him again? However infrequent and restricted by censorship our letters had been, they meant everything to me, as no doubt, they did to him. His two letters from Kozelsk camp, which I had received in Stanislavov I knew by heart, and they were a constant source of comfort and hope to me. Naïvely I believed Nik's rosy description of the camp and trusted that he would survive imprisonment. In spite of this new blow I had to find the moral and physical strength to keep faith and surmount all the difficulties. Most of all I had to keep Nooka in as good health as possible, until all three of us were together again. I was determined never, never to let doubt about our reunion creep into my heart.

A few nights later I had a dream. I was in an empty church, kneeling at the foot of the steps leading to the altar. At the top of the steps I saw a statuesque figure which I recognised as my mother, although in reality she was not very tall, and her

141

normally light complexion was now dark like that of the Black Madonna of Czestochowa. Her eyes were abnormally large and glowing. She had in fact died four years previously, and it seemed to me in my dream that she had come as a messenger from another world. With her outstretched hand she pointed to something in the distance. I turned my head in that direction and saw the wall of the church part to reveal a cemetery with row upon row of graves. By one of them I saw a woman in deep mourning and, looking closer, recognized in her my mother-in-law. Stricken by a terrible thought, I looked at my mother in horror and she, bowing her head low, said, 'Yes, my daughter, your husband is dead.'

To everyone's alarm, I woke up sobbing. They gathered round my bed trying to discover what was wrong but I could say nothing except, 'My husband is dead, my husband is dead'. When I finally recovered sufficiently to describe my dream, they tried to reassure me saying that it was due to the ear infection I had at the time. I desperately wanted to believe them, and on reflection the dream did not seem to make sense. Why would there be all these rows of graves instead of just one?

Winter

Winter in North Kazakhstan came early in 1940. Snow fell at the end of September and the ground became ice-bound. It was hard to imagine how we could survive in our hut with limited reserves of fuel, *kiziak*, and food sufficient for two months at the most. We knew that winter in these parts was not only very long and severe, the temperature falling to minus 50°C, but in addition that very strong winds and snow storms were a regular occurrence. These snow storms, called *bourans*, paralysed daily life, and if we had to go out of the hut during one, the whole world disappeared from view, and we found it advisable to tie a rope to ourselves, like dogs on chains, to find our way back to the hut. It was only too easy to become disorientated and wander into the steppe, which could be fatal. As storms came without warning, trips to Troitsk and other places were cut to an absolute minimum. In summer, people moved along beaten tracks but in winter these disappeared under the snow. Gradually the snow on the tracks would compact and the only means of recognising the way was by feeling the hard path under one's feet. Winds that blew dust in summer now carried snow from the endless steppe and often buried the entire village.

Natasha's hut was more exposed to wind than many of the others, and every morning we had to clear snow from our little windows and the path to the door. Sometimes we awoke in complete darkness, despite the late hour, and had to rely on someone's help to dig us out, as the door had been blocked from the outside and no efforts of ours to push it would produce any result. Happily, there was always someone to come to our rescue so we were never buried for very long.

A great disappointment was the breakdown of the kitchen range on which had rested our hopes of heating the room. At first it had worked reasonably well but, with the advent of strong frost, the freezing wind that blew through the chimney in the night cancelled out the benefits derived from using it during the day. We decided to block the chimney on the roof with an old sack which we kept in place with stones. Normally it was Nooka's job to block it at night as he managed better than anyone else to do this tricky job on the slippery roof.

One night someone awoke with a bad headache and we felt it must have been due to the poisonous fumes from the blocked chimney. With Nooka fast asleep, Janka was sent to remove the sacking and, being very sleepy and angry at having to go on the roof, she pulled the sack so hard that the stones fell inside the chimney, blocking it completely. From then on, the range could not be used and the primus became our only means of cooking. The big oven, which required an enormous quantity of *kiziak*, was lit once a week for baking bread. In the meantime, our hut was without heating and was unbelievably cold. The inside walls were permanently covered with hoar-frost and, except for our felt boots, we all slept fully dressed.

Poor Natasha had had no time to prepare *kiziak* bricks and was left with no fuel at all. To earn a share of flour and potatoes from the *Kolhoz* sufficient for herself and her three children she had had to work from morning till night in the fields during the summer and in the granaries in winter. The *Kolhoz* did not provide people with fuel: everyone had to prepare their own, and the families with older children, or those lucky women who had their husbands with them, were able to cope, but Natasha, being the only bread winner, was in a hopeless situation. She complained to us that this autumn her share of flour and potatoes was very poor as most of the

144

harvest had been taken by the government. We often wondered how she and her children would have survived the winter had we not been there, as she could not have gone to work and left them alone all day.

On the days when bread was baked, our hut was warmer, at least for a little while. Nevertheless I disliked those days. For some reason, known only to herself, the Old Lady insisted on making bread in the evening, getting up in the middle of the night to work the dough and finally, at six in the morning, lighting the oven. On such nights there was an understandable commotion so no one had enough sleep and next day we were all tired and irritable. Since in our present circumstances sleep was a great blessing, I asked her to abandon this strange routine. It took quite a time before she finally yielded. The argument that succeeded in breaking her resistance was the unnecessary use of kerosene for the lamp because reserves were dwindling rapidly. It transpired that the reason for her behaviour was that in Stanislavov bread was always baked early in the morning to be served fresh at breakfast and she found it difficult to break with that tradition. In the end she admitted that it did not make much difference when we ate the bitter bread which felt like a stone in our stomachs, and that it was probably more healthy to have it ready in the evening and eat it the following morning. I suspected that behind that resistance there was something more than just the force of habit. Bread-baking was the only activity, in our present life, where the Old Lady was in full charge, and she naturally resented any interference. It must have been difficult for that autocratic woman, used to ruling her household, to submit to anyone else's will.

The days on which the oven was lit were real holidays for Natasha and her children. Apart from the warmth, Natasha sometimes managed to get time off work and cook not only bread, but cereals and potatoes which lasted her family for the entire week. If not, we did it for her. We never saw them eating hot food on any other day.

The other creature that enjoyed baking days was Vaska, the

145

cat. As soon as the bread was out of the oven he went inside it, only to leap out again in a panic, his fur singed from still glowing embers. It did not prevent him from doing exactly the same thing the next time as the temptation was too great for him. This regular scorching could be considered a sign of Vaska's stupidity, but he proved his extraordinary intelligence on many other occasions. Vaska was a very good mouser and his favourite hunting ground was under my bed, where he was least disturbed. One day, when he was lying in wait and we were sitting round the table occupied on our particular tasks, we saw him rush from under the bed and jump on top of it. Standing on his hind legs, he started to move along the bed, beating the *kelim* on the wall with his front paws. We watched bewitched, thinking that poor Vaska must have gone mad, but when he reached the end of the *kelim* a mouse appeared from behind and in a split second Vaska had it in his mouth.

Vaska was extremely patient and forebearing with Natasha's children. We often saw them pulling his tail, dragging him on the floor and generally teasing him, but when he had had enough he hissed once or twice and usually that was enough for them to leave him alone. Sometimes her son, Kolka, did not take the warning seriously and then he would receive such a powerful blow that blood would stream down his face and we would hear his yells for hours. Vaska was a very powerfully built cat and had huge paws and claws. His scratches went deep and he often ripped Kolka's nose or cheek, only by a miracle missing his eyes. We also took for a miracle the fact that his wounds healed so quickly although we, with our very primitive means of disinfection, were the only ones to attend to them.

Vaska was the scourge of all the neighbourhood dogs and if any of them happened to come near our hut he immediately went for them. His tactics were to jump on top of the dog and, with his claws well implanted in its flesh to keep himself steady, he rode on its back, while it howled with pain and fright, until it was driven away. Needless to say any dog who

146

suffered such treatment never reappeared. As most of the village dogs were ownerless, no one ever showed any resentment about Vaska but women had other reasons for complaint.

Some of the hens laid their eggs in odd places and Vaska kept watch over them. As soon as a hen started to cackle announcing her achievement to the world, Vaska was there before the breathless owner, whose embittered and unprintable invectives were heard for a long time afterwards. But by then there was no trace of either egg or Vaska. These exploits were only possible in summer; during the winter Vaska had to rely entirely on mice. During the cold weather I often wrapped my feet at night with Ali's mother's fox pelt, but when this was not enough, I allowed Vaska to get on my bed near my feet to warm them and, very occasionally, I even let him get under my blankets although he was often covered in soot. During the Siberian winter I preferred the dirt to the cold. Vaska never jumped on the bed without first asking permission. Sitting on the floor and looking at me imploringly he would produce a melodious soft 'miaow', very surprising for such a large cat, which I took to mean, 'May I?' We often wondered how it was that such a rustic cat could have such good manners.

During the winter months we seldom saw the sun and the days on which it did appear, as well as the intervals between blizzards, were used for stocking up with what food we could get and topping up our water supplies. Bringing water from the well was one of Nooka's duties. At first the girls tried to do it, but the task proved beyond their endurance. Janka, the least resilient and perhaps the least willing of the lot, came back in tears, numb from frost. As for Halina, she simply declared that to do that job you had to be a boxer or an acrobat and, as she was neither, the job was not for her. Why a boxer? Because during the short period of bearable weather, villagers rushed to the well and there was much pulling and jostling; and an acrobat because the approach to the well was a mountain of ice up which you had to climb before reaching

147

the winding roller with the hook on which to hang the bucket. Even if you succeeded in doing all that and pulling the water out of the well, three-quarters of it were lost in going, or rather, sliding down, and often the entire contents of the bucket were lost when a person slipped or tumbled, thereby adding another layer of ice to the mountain. Needless to say, some of the water went on our hands which froze instantly and very painfully. Back at the hut we melted snow for washing our faces.

Those who had the stamina and courage to undress completely in the icy kitchen rubbed their bodies with snow watched by Natasha's puzzled children. I used that method and found that our hut seemed warmer afterwards. For understandable reasons, visits to the well were very rare in winter. For cooking we used snow which we melted on the primus, but even the water brought from the well often had to be treated in the same way as it froze very quickly in the hut where the temperature was far below freezing point.

The food situation was gradually becoming more and more difficult and again we had to rely on our concoction of flour and potatoes. Our sources of income had dried up as no one was now interested in a new dress or an embroidered petticoat, and hardly anyone was willing to part with precious food in exchange for luxuries. But others were even worse off. The Armenian teacher became a daily visitor. He usually came during our meal time in the hopes of a bowl of something hot and we tried not to disappoint him. He always brought an empty bag into which we discreetly put a piece of bread or a few potatoes, but in spite of that, on his way out through the kitchen, he snatched whatever food there was and, as long as we could afford it, we put some extras there. We had been told that all three were begging for food in the village. The family was now so thin, and pale that it seemed there was not a drop of blood left in their bodies. Their clothes were painfully inadequate for the freezing Siberian weather so they wore blankets as well.

When Mrs Krilenko visited us she usually complained

about her daughters who, she said, were resourceless, lazy and relied on her totally to provide food for the whole family. The only work they knew was on the land; they did their best during the summer season, but now, bitter from being cheated out of their due, they had sunk into complete inertia. The family owed a lot to Mrs Krilenko's friendship with the Kazakhs. There were two young Kazakhs who had eyes on her fair daughters and were more than willing to take them in marriage, bringing them gifts of eggs, pancake bread and so on. The older Kazakhs liked Mrs Krilenko for her own sake, helped her in different ways and were pleased when she accepted their invitation to share a meal with them. You had to have a strong stomach to do that, but she was tough; besides, if you are hungry, any food served in any way is a treat. We all agreed that on the whole the Kazakhs were kinder and better disposed towards us than the average Russian: perhaps they were less frustrated. Though deprived of the right to lead a nomadic life, they were still in familiar surroundings, while the Russians must have greatly missed their motherland, the countryside with lakes, woods and hills and could never be happy in the monotonous steppes of Kazakhstan.

One day Mrs Krilenko came not simply for a chat and hospitality but with a problem. Apparently, in addition to the two young Kazakhs, an older man had started to come almost daily. He would not speak or bring anything, but just remained by the door for hours. Although he was quite old and had a wife, she suspected he intended asking for the hand of one of her daughters, as it was not unknown for a married Kazakh to take a second wife. We asked if she knew which of her daughters was the object of his desire, but she had no idea as the Kazakh looked at neither of them in particular but concentrated his gaze on her, which she imagined might be because the decision depended upon her. As it was hard to believe that with such strong competition from her daughters the Kazakh was infatuated with Mrs Krilenko herself, we accepted her explanation as perfectly normal.

It so happened that this Kazakh was our nearest neighbour who came to sell us eggs or cheese or sometimes just to pay a social call, so Mrs Krilenko asked us to try and find out what he really wanted as his continuous presence was becoming unbearable. We fully sympathised with her, because as well as the inconvenience of having an unwanted guest, we knew he had a horrid habit of scratching his head for lice which he caught between his nails and then squashed with gusto with his teeth. Most of the Kazakhs dealt with the parasite this way and they had no inhibitions about doing so in public. We suffered agony because of it as, while we could avert our eyes, it was impossible not to hear the crunching sound. We promised to investigate, and the result was quite unexpected. Mrs Krilenko had a massive gold front tooth which the Kazakh wanted. In exchange he offered her a bag of flour. We were most embarrassed when we passed the message on to her but, if anything, she was relieved. In the circumstances, a bag of flour was worth far more to her than her tooth. The sequel of the story was sad, however. When, after a long struggle, Mrs Krilenko managed to pull the gold jacket from the tooth, the Kazakh, seeing that it was only a thin shell instead of a solid piece of gold, withdrew his offer.

Excursions for food and fuel during these long wintry months were invariably carried out by me, and I was sometimes accompanied by Nooka. I particularly remember one occasion when Nooka and I were returning from Yemankino proudly carrying a tin of kerosene which our friendly station master had let us have at a low government price, when a blizzard overtook us. In an instant snow gummed our eyelids making us blind and the wind almost threw us off our feet. The gripping cold and lashing snow made breathing difficult. Nooka and I linked arms so we would not lose each other and tried hard to keep to the beaten track, which we could still feel under our feet. We were forced to double up, as the only way to move forwards was to push our heads against a very strong adverse wind. In no time the soft flakes turned into needle-sharp ice spicules which hurt our faces, clustered on our bent heads and fell into the gap between head and collar. I was wondering whether by now we were suffering from frostbite, but there was no time to stop and examine and rub the endangered parts. Shaking the snow from our heads was the most we could do. I tried desperately to work out how far we had to go to the village; according to my calculation, based on the length of time since we left Yemankino, we should have been very near. I could not even share this cheering conviction with Nooka as we could not hear each other above the noise of the wind.

Suddenly, I heard wolves howling. Nooka must have heard them as well as I could feel his arm stiffen. This was almost too much to bear, but it forced us to double our efforts, almost beyond endurance, and to press ahead. We both knew that wolves and exhaustion were two of the greatest dangers in the steppe in winter. If a person felt tired and sat down he never rose again, and we had heard many tragic stories about wolves attacking poeple and horses in the wilderness. So we gathered all our remaining strength and will power to suppress our exhaustion and fear. Then, as sudden as the howling of the wolves now came the fierce and hysterical barking of a dog. To us, at that moment, it was the most delightful sound in the world. From his barking we even recognised which dog it was and, lifting our heads, we saw the contours of a hut, whose woman owner we knew well. The relief was so great that at once we both felt completely drained of energy and were incapable of making another effort to reach our hut which, we knew, was very near. We knocked at the door and were let in. We flopped down, unable to utter a word, but the woman did not need an explanation. After a momentary rest we were able to leave. The blizzard was not as bad as some, so we could find our own hut without too much difficulty, and a few minutes later we were safely home.

From time to time we had to go to market in Troitsk to exchange some of our belongings, for food or roubles. The usual route was to walk to Yemankino and from there travel by train to Troitsk. With our 'connections', getting a railway ticket was not a great problem, but sometimes we had to wait a long time for the train.

In the market, as at the auction, a lot depended on luck; if many people were willing to buy, the prices rose. Sometimes, however, the trip was a failure and we returned home with heavy hearts and a full bundle of unsold things, which seemed to weigh far more than on the outward journey.

There was one trip to Troitsk which was more memorable than all the others. We awoke to an exceptionally cold day (−45°C or so), but the sky was blue, there was no wind whatsoever and the sun was shining. Apart from the strong frost, it was the day we had been waiting for, so Halina and I picked up our bundles, which had been packed beforehand for just such an occasion and departed for Yemankino. It was essential that we make that trip, as our food reserves were almost exhausted, and no one in the village wanted to sell their food. On reaching Yemankino, we were numb with cold and got a shock when the usually so friendly station master's wife, instead of greeting us, took one look at us and pushed us violently out of her hut. Only when she began to rub Halina's face with snow, telling me to do the same, did we understand – our noses and cheeks were snow white from frostbite. We had not suspected this relying on the calm and sunny weather. As we hoped to get away from Siberia one day, we were indeed grateful to her for enabling us to return with our noses in place. From then on we were continually alert to the danger and constantly rubbed our faces with snow. Treated to hot cups of tea and nice bread, we regained the necessary strength to continue the trip.

This time we did not have a long wait for the train and by midday we were on the wooden market platform. Usually there was very little chance of getting there. During our previous trips the local people, who arrived earlier, had always set up their wares there. The platform was the best place in the market, and as it was raised above the rest the stallholders were visible from all sides. Its wooden floor was cleaner, drier and warmer than the earthen base which, depending on the

152

season, was dusty, muddy or covered with solid or melting snow or slush. On that particular day the ground was frost bound, hard, dry and clean, but the market looked different as it was empty. The terrible frost had frightened off even the seasoned Siberians. Occasionally one or two frozen passers-by looked in and quickly withdrew. The temperature fell below −50°C. We could not possibly give in and go home with nothing so, against all odds, we spread our treasure on the floor and, in order not to freeze to the platform, started to run backwards and forwards like two monkeys in a cage, rubbing our hands and faces and stamping our feet. Once or twice someone stopped to watch this spectacle, but no one showed the slightest interest in our merchandise and, having lost hope of finding buyers, downhearted, we started to collect up our things. Just then an elderly Russian woman, wrapped up to her ears against the biting cold, came up to us.

'My heart bleeds just looking at you. What made you come on such a day? Don't you know that Grandfather Frost does not know mercy. A little longer and he would have frozen you to death? If you wish you can come to my place to warm up. I live not far from here.'

This was another miracle. As fast as our frozen hands allowed we tied our things into a bundle again and without stopping, we followed the woman. She lived close by in one of the more presentable old houses which was clean, warm and cosy inside. We took off our outer clothing in the little hall and went into the living-room where a bubbling, samovar made a most welcome noise.

A moment later we were sipping tea and gorging ourselves on white, fluffy bread spread with clarified butter. We almost forgot about our unsold things, the minus fifty degrees temperature and the return journey still awaiting us. On arrival in Troitsk that morning, we had taken a good look at the station waiting-room, knowing that before returning we would have to spend some time there, and we had noticed that there was a large iron stove giving out a lot of heat. This knowledge was a great comfort to us. What was more, we knew that in

Yemankino we had a warm shelter with the station master and a night's lodging if necessary, so that we would not have to walk through the steppe at night if the train was late. The kindness of people like our hostess and the station master in a country where life was a never-ending struggle for survival had a special significance as it strengthened our faith in the existence of a higher Being. On that faith depended our survival in that inhuman land as well as the retention of our mental and moral strength.

Our hostess was extremely interested in our experiences and we recounted the whole story from our deportation to the moment of our meeting in the market. She, in turn, opened her heart to us. With tears in her eyes she told us about her husband's arrest by the Cheka soon after the Revolution and his disappearance from this world. Now her happiness and pride lay in her only son, who had finished his medical training with distinction and was a chief surgeon at a hospital in one of the main cities in Russia. She deplored the fact that she was not allowed to live near him, the explanation given to her by the authorities was that there was no suitable accommodation. He had permission to visit her in Troitsk every few years and to send her money and food parcels. Thanks to him we were now eating butter with our bread and sometimes she even received honey and jam. Her son had recently informed her of his intention to get married, his future wife being also a doctor working in the same hospital. Although she was happy for her son, she was slightly worried in case her future daughter-in-law did not approve of her husband's visits to his mother. We tried to comfort her, saying that a good son, as he had proved to be, cannot change towards his mother after marriage.

We felt she was happy to be able to talk about her life and worries to us, and these mutual confidences, during which we laughed and cried in turn, brought us so close together that we found it difficult to believe that we had met only a couple of hours previously. When the time came to leave, she insisted that we stay for the night. She thought that by morning the frost might have eased considerably, as often happened here, and we would be able to sell our goods to people who would crowd into the market having been kept at home for many days by the cold. The invitation was very tempting. We had nothing to lose and maybe much to gain, so we accepted gratefully on condition she selected something for herself from our goods. Finally, after many protests, she chose a little scarf.

Having no spare beds, she made us as comfortable as possible on the living-room floor. Halina slept well but my sides ached from the hard floorboards and I was glad when morning came. We had a marvellous breakfast of buckwheat and crackling and, filled with energy, having kissed our wonderful hostess many times, we left. On parting she made us promise that on our next visit we would stay with her, and what could have been nicer than that?

Although it was early morning, it was much warmer than the previous day with the temperature back to $-30°$ and no wind and some sunshine; it did not seem at all bad. We were lucky to find a spot at the corner of the platform despite protests from those already there. The buckwheat filling our stomachs must have played a part in building up our self-assurance. As our new-found friend had hoped, the market soon filled with people. We had to keep a careful watch that nothing was stolen as thieves were everywhere. People crushed the displayed articles, held them against the light, smelt them and almost put them into their mouths to taste. These were desirable objects but very expensive, so a decision was not easily made. For example, I asked two hundred roubles for a silk petticoat which was the equivalent of the price of a kilo of butter on the free market and also one month's salary.

While Halina and I cast anxious glances to left and right trying not to lose anyone from sight, a young, pretty woman wrapped in expensive fur, pushed her way through the crowd. Without further ado she wrenched the articles which she obviously fancied from the hands of the people surrounding us, saying, 'I will buy all this. Tell me how much it costs.' The impression that her words created would be hard to describe.

155

Some took it for a joke and laughed loudly, but the majority, including us, were simply stunned, not knowing what to think. How was it possible that anyone would agree to buy things at any price, straight away, without first bargaining? It did seem strange. Besides, who would carry a sum of money necessary to pay for all that? As if answering our thoughts the young woman nonchalantly handed the articles to Halina, saying, 'I have not got enough money on me, so would you come home with me and I will pay you there.'

On the way she told us that her husband was the head of the local hospital and that they had only very recently arrived in Troitsk. From her dress and manner she definitely did not belong to this place and I wondered what had brought them here. Could it have been demotion rather than promotion? Obviously she liked pretty things and could not miss an occasion like today. They lived on the first floor of a modern building which had the luxury of a bathroom, but the finish was shoddy and the paint was peeling in many places. The old houses built of wood were so much nicer. This one looked like some sort of a brick building with a cement rendering on the outside.

She introduced herself as Nina Pavlovne Semionova, settled her bill and asked us to call on her when next we came to Troitsk market. Who would have thought that this trip which had started so badly, would end so pleasantly and profitably? We hurried to the market to buy food to take back with us. First of all such essentials as flour and buckwheat, but also some luxuries like clarified butter, cheese and pork fat. Prices were ridiculously high, but with our newly acquired wealth we could afford them.

On the way home, intoxicated with success, we gave no thought to the miles of steppe which we had to cross before reaching our village. We decided not to stop at the station master's but to go straight home where by now everybody would be worried by our long absence. We were also anxious to tell our story. How we had found a wonderful friend in Troitsk and a 'millionairess' who had paid high prices for our goods and was willing to buy more. The other important consideration was the weather. At the moment it held good, and there was no sign of a blizzard, but who could know what tomorrow would bring. But when we were still only half-way between Yemankino and home, we became tired and weary, weighed down with heavy bags, and dragged our feet along with difficulty. We could think of nothing but sitting down and resting which, we knew, we must not do under any circumstances.

As had so often happened before, rescue came unexpectedly. One of the friendly Kazakhs, returning home with his horse and sledge, caught up with us. He allowed us to put our bags on the sledge which was an immense relief, as was the fact that we were no longer alone. Even if the blizzard did overtake us, we now could hold on to the sledge, and the horse, which never lost its way, would take us safely home. This trip to Troitsk was the last one that winter as we realised the great dangers of venturing out at that time of the year on such a long and uncertain journey. We had been lucky that time, but it could have ended very differently.

We now had a reasonable supply of the food necessary to last us for some time. Bags of flour and cereals were stored under the beds and the cellar was filled with potatoes. We had brought some roubles from Troitsk with which to pay our rent and buy food from those villagers needing money and willing to sell. I took every opportunity to get any food that was obtainable in the village for roubles or by barter, and in this the Old Lady's and my opinions differed, as she thought that we could quite happily survive the winter on the mixture of flour and potatoes, saving our roubles and the rest of our possessions for later on. This caused a slight tension between us, but after a little while we resolved it amicably by respecting each other's wishes. As a result, on rare occasions, Nooka and I ate different food from the rest; this was very embarrassing for me, but the best solution as we both felt quite strongly about it. Luckily it made no difference to my relationship with the rest of the family.

157

There was great joy and excitement at the arrival of first a letter and then a parcel from Mila's sister in Poland. As they were a large and loving family, parcels began to arrive every few weeks. The thrill of receiving such treasures as bacon, salted pork fat, real tea, sugar and biscuits and, later on at our special request candles, soap, pencils, ordinary needles and ones for the sewing machine, exercise and text books, would be impossible to describe. Parcels invariably brought tears of emotion and gratitude as we realised that the situation in Poland could not have improved since we left and that people were making great sacrifices to send them. We could not learn much from the letters about what was happening, in Poland and the rest of the world. Eventually, both sides managed to incorporate a few disguised hints, but we had to be careful as it was obvious that all letters were censored.

I was very surprised when my first parcel arrived as it was sent by a Dr Jupiter, one of my former pupils. He was Jewish, and after the war, I learned with great sorrow that he had been murdered by the Germans after their entry into Stanislavov on the way to Russia in 1941.

As Christmas approached, parcels brought presents of warm gloves, socks and underwear as well as food. Despite great shortages of food and clothes in Stalin's Russia, nothing was ever stolen from these parcels, so strict was the discipline and so strong the fear of punishment. To remind people who their lord and master was, Stalin's portrait was hung in all public places, even in a village as small as Novo-Troitsk. It was well known in Russia that, given the opportunity, people stole left, right and centre, but for some reason, probably prestige, parcels from the 'newly occupied territories' were taboo.

Through the centuries, Christmas in Poland was celebrated in a great style. The most solemn moment being when the family gathered round the dinner table on Christmas Eve. Four weeks prior to this we refrained from eating meat on Wednesdays and Fridays and on the 24th of December we ate nothing at all until the actual dinner, which could start only after the appearance of the first star. Hungry and excited children would watch the sky anxious not to delay their meal by even one minute. According to custom, only an even number of people should sit at the table, or someone present might die within the year. If for some reason, the number was uneven, a stranger, be it even a beggar, would be asked to join. Ideally, dinner would consist of at least twelve meatless courses among which borscht with tiny pies filled with mushrooms and *kutia* (a dish of cereals and honey) were a must. Before sitting down, a wafer blessed by the Church was shared by all and at the same time Christmas greetings were exchanged. A thin layer of hay was placed under the tablecloth to remind us of the circumstances of Christ's birth, and under the napkins were presents (small and sometimes very valuable for the adults.) The children's presents together with all those too large to go under the napkins, were arranged under the tree to be distributed after dinner. Young children did not see the tree until it was lit, as it was brought in and decorated by the grown ups and kept in a locked room in great secrecy, so that the moment of opening the door had a special magic.

In 1940 our Christmas in exile had to be different, but we were determined to celebrate it as best we could. Clever Maryla made a tree out of the cardboard boxes in which the parcels arrived, and the children coloured it with the pencils sent from Poland. Together with Nooka's and Halina's help, Janka, who obviously inherited her aunt's artistic talents, made a Father Christmas, angels and stars using pieces of cardboard and any odd bits of materials left over from Mila's dressmaking. Empty egg shells, which we had been collecting for a long time, provided a wealth of ideas for decorations.

The Old Lady made quite a tasty borscht from the half-frozen beetroots for which we searched all over the village. The flour from Troitsk, because it was not bitter, was used for the pies, and the dried mushrooms for them arrived from Poland. Everybody who sent us a parcel remembered to include in it a blessed wafer. We shared it with lumps in our

159

throats and tears in our eyes, repeating the same wish, 'To be in Poland by next Christmas. For women to be reunited with their husbands and children with their fathers.'

On Christmas Day we did not feel like getting up early. The room was dark and cold and, by staying in bed longer, we hoped to save on kerosene and food. Natasha's family had given no sign of life either, but we heard strange noises coming from outside. Halina went to investigate and tried to open the outside door, but it would not budge. She could hear muffled sounds of human voices and it became obvious that we were buried under a snow drift following the blizzard which had raged all night. We were lucky that people had come to check. They told us afterwards that had it not been for a chimney which was still visible above the snow it would have been almost impossible to find the position of our hut. We had been buried before, but never so completely. The road and our hut were now obliterated by the snow and looked like a continuation of the steppe. It took many people to free us from our prison, and we wondered what would have happened had help not arrived.

In spite of the appalling lack of hygiene, a cold and humid hut and poor food, not one of us had so far been seriously ill. We attributed this to frost killing the bacteria, which would explain why Natasha's children never coughed or had high temperatures during the whole time we stayed with them. They were never free from catarrh or running noses and, not having seen a handkerchief in their lives, licked the mucus and swallowed it which, far from harming them, seemed to build an immunity to more serious illnesses. Summer and winter they went about practically naked, their only garment being a very short shirt hardly reaching their bottoms. Ninka, a girl about one year old, who could not walk, spent most of the day at the back of the oven, but sometimes when she got very bored, we put her on the kitchen bench where she could watch everybody. As she was not potty trained, she relieved herself wherever she happened to be. Taking pity on her, and being unable to stand the stench and the repulsive sight, we cleaned her and the mess which was not easy in our difficult conditions. Sometimes, having done this several times a day, we would feel that we had had enough and would then go to our room leaving the rest to poor Natasha.

In winter, the two older children had a pair of *valenki* (felt boots) to share between them. Seven-year-old Valka, being the older and the stronger of the two, treated them as her property and that right somehow got established in her mother's mind. Five-year-old Kolka, however, thought that there were situations when he had an indisputable right to them and one such was when he had to succumb to an urgent natural need. This could only be done outside the hut in the open and even Valka had to admit that while it was all right to go out into the minus forty degree temperature in just a short shirt, his feet had to be better protected, and lent him the boots. This invariably led to terrible rows and I remember witnessing one in particular.

Kolka, blue in the face and body and shivering all over, came back from an enforced outing and, having enjoyed the delightful sensation of warmth from the boots, flatly refused to give them back to Valka. A furious battle ensued and Kolka, kicking and beating his sister off, finally won, so Valka, who had to give in for the moment, decided to wait until her mother's return. As soon as Natasha crossed the doorstep, worn out by the day's work, Valka announced, 'Mum, Ninka shit herself.' That was a good strategic move as nothing could arouse Natasha's fury as surely as the prospect of having to clear up Ninka's mess. Not wasting a moment, Valka added tearfully, 'Kolka took my boots and won't give them back to me.' Natasha, glad to have a scapegoat on which to vent her rage, turned on Kolka and, grabbing him by his feet, began to shake him out of the boots, but being short and very tired, she could not lift him high enough so that his head banged repeatedly on the hard mud floor. Kolka screamed at the top of his voice. Seeing this terrible spectacle and seriously worried about Kolak's skull, I was ready to intervene, but it was all over in a flash with Kolka on the floor still screaming but with no visible signs of injury to his head and Valka smiling triumphantly, hugging the boots which her enraged mother threw at her. Such scenes occurred frequently and Kolka's head must have been made of iron. Indeed, we felt all four of them had iron constitutions: an incident which happened in the summer serves as further proof.

We had just returned from weeding, dead tired, when we heard Kolka's desperate cries and rushed out of the hut to see what had happened. The sight was frightening. The lower part of his face was covered in blood which ran profusely from his nose. After washing his face, we saw that a piece of flesh had been torn from his nose and was held only by a strip of skin. There was no doubt that hospital help and stitches would be required if his nose was to be saved. With great difficulty, we got out of Kolka that he had been bitten by a dog. Natasha was not at home so one of us went to fetch her from the local *Kolhoz* dairy, where she was working. We expected hysterics or at least tears, but there was nothing of the kind. She examined Kolka's face which, I must admit, looked much better after we had removed the blood, and declared, 'That's nothing. It will heal before his wedding' – a standard saying in Russia whenever a child was hurt. When we suggested she took him to hospital she said, 'I have no horse or ox to take him there and neither *Kolhoz* or the factory would give their transport'. With that she returned to work leaving us to worry. What if the dog was rabid? Or if an infection developed? As carefully as possible we joined the torn piece to the rest of the nose and put a dressing on top, trying to frighten Kolka by telling him that if he removed it his nose would fall off. For quite a long time after that a huge scab remained on his nose, but when it finally fell off there was a perfectly healed nose, although slightly more bulbous than before, with a brightly coloured scar which we thought would probably remain well past his wedding.

The question of our children's education naturally worried us. There was a primary school in the village, but the girls were too old to go there and only Nooka enrolled, but after

162

attending for a short time, had given up. It was clear that there was nothing he could learn there, as even his knowledge of Russian, compulsory in Polish schools during the occupation, was far superior to that of the local children. In addition, the school was unheated and during very cold weather it was closed. So, with the experience of home tuition received in Moscow and plenty of time on my hands, I decided to teach our children and other exiled children who wished to join, which proved very popular. At first I was worried when the older pupils sought my help in solving arithmetical problems such as, 'Train A left a station at such and such a time going at such and such a speed and train B . . .' I had never been able to deal with these puzzles successfully, but suddenly I found no difficulty in explaining and solving them as if some cells in my brain had opened up to release knowledge stored in my subconscious mind. It seemed as if I had acquired some strange powers in our wretched conditions.

We were allowed to receive from Poland text books on all subjects except Polish language, history and religion. We overcame these difficulties by holding discussions, each pupil contributing either by talking about books they had previously read, reciting poetry, or relating some historical or biblical event. At times, a discussion about a certain character or an incident in a book would lead to heated arguments which I found very satisfactory as it was proof of the children's involvement. Although he was the youngest in the group of ten-years-old Nooka was able to take part in the discussions, and I was surprised to learn how many books he had read before our deportation. Naturally, I was very proud of him. He and the two girls spent hours discussing in great detail the trilogy of our famous Nobel Prize winning author, Henryk Sienkiewicz, and this provided entertainment for all of us, especially when no other activities inside the hut were possible. Nooka got on well with the girls. There was a considerable age difference which probably helped. They differed greatly by nature: Halina, who had been a very active and useful member of Girl Guides, was cheerful, energetic, always willing and ready to help others, independent and averse to any show of sentimentality; on the other hand Janka seemed to be really happy only when near her mother. Clinging to her at every opportunity, she reminded me of a young monkey attached to her parent's body. She seldom smiled and seemed to be slightly cross with the whole world, although I had never known her to be really angry, even when she had to perform tasks imposed upon her by her indomitable grandmother, who was inclined to interrupt the activities in which she was engrossed. While Halina enjoyed robust health, Janka was less strong physically and, after spending a winter on the Siberian border, was beginning to show signs of illnesses from which she was to suffer greatly in later life.

In winter it was difficult to decide whether it was better to stay inside the damp, cold but sheltered hut, or to go out in search of fresh air and fight the biting wind and terrible frost. I have always been a fresh air fiend so I was pleased in a way that, being in charge of food supplies, I was forced to go out occasionally. Halina often volunteered to go with me, and I welcomed this as I always enjoyed her company. Nooka, following the example of the village boys, constructed some 'skis' out of the wood from vodka crates, which he tied with pieces of string to his felt boots, and braved the weather whenever possible. Although he had skates and proper skating boots, there was nowhere to practise as the lake was indistinguishable under the layers of snow. Maryla, Mila and Janka hardly ever went further than behind our hut.

On awakening each morning, we used to tell each other our dreams. One of the most repetitive themes was food. Permanently undernourished, we cooked and consumed the most delicious food in our sleep and anyone listening to our conversation might have thought that the main reason why we wanted to return to our country was for the food. I could not contribute much to these fantasies as either I did not dream at all or forgot about them as soon as I woke. Then, suddenly, one short and uninteresting dream repeated itself and became

164

imprinted in my memory. In it I saw a bomb falling; it did not take us long to associate it with the arrival of a parcel for me. The first 'bomb' fell just before the arrival of Dr Jupiter's parcel, but at the time I did not understand its meaning. When a parcel arrived in Novo-Troitsk, the normal procedure was to receive notification from the post office and then go personally to collect it. For me, this procedure became unnecessary as I would awaken with the words, 'There is a parcel for me,' and rush to collect it. I never made a mistake and my inexplicable foreknowledge was a source of constant wonderment to the post office manager, who could not understand who had let me into the secret. I should mention that there was no pattern in the way parcels arrived for me; sometimes I had nothing for months and sometimes two parcels arrived together.

By now everyone at home firmly believed in my sixth sense so when I had another puzzling dream, we tried to interpret it. It was very short – just three words written on a page of the Bible: 'Kazakhstan – India – England.'

It took us some time before we decided that it must mean we would go to India from Kazakhstan, although we could not imagine how or why. We had always assumed that when at last freedom came we would go straight back to Poland the same way as we had come. But the idea of going to a hot and sunny country from these frozen steppes seemed most attractive. England, which in our minds was a country permanently enveloped in mist and fog, did not appeal to us at all, so we simply ignored that part of the dream. Not having much to write about, Mila described my dream in her letters to her sisters in Poland who found the idea very amusing and wrote back asking us to bring an elephant or rubies and emeralds from maharajas' palaces in India. We exchanged many letters and jokes on this subject, treating it as complete nonsense.

Soon after the New Year the Old Lady fell seriously ill. She coughed a lot and had a high temperature. There was nothing we could do to help her and, watching her suffer was heart-breaking, particularly because she was as brave and uncomplaining in her illness as she had been throughout our exile. We suspected pneumonia, but there was no doctor to diagnose the illness, and our local nurse-postwoman was useless. There was no question of taking the patient to hospital in Troitsk as she was unlikely to survive such a long journey in that terrible frost. What she needed was good food and warmth, neither of which was available. Maryla's sad eyes now acquired a tragic expression as she watched her mother's health deteriorating. There was an additional ordeal for that very religious woman; the knowledge that should her mother die she would not receive the last rites, and would be buried in that dismal remote village without church service or a priest.

The Old Lady died in her sleep three weeks later. Maryla made a cross and a coffin out of the only material available – vodka crates – and lined it lovingly with the softest and warmest clothes she could find. Mila and Janka moved to the Old Lady's bed and thus room was made on the floor for the coffin, with Halina now occupying Janka's basket. The coffin was placed alongside my bed, so near to it that if I stretched my arm slightly, I could touch it. There was no church and no proper cemetery in the village, just a plot of ground where the dead were buried. Although the plot was not far from Natasha's hut, we nevertheless needed a horse and a sledge to take the coffin there. We approached the *Kolhoz* office for help, convinced that burying the dead would be one of their duties, but all we got were jeers. The only other people in the village who had horses were Kazakhs but we were far from sure that they would help us. We thought that being Moslems they would be reluctant to take part in a burial of a Christian woman.

However, before we could find out a series of strong blizzards occurred, and it was impossible to go into the steppe. The days passed and the situation became desperate as the body began to decompose and could no longer be left in the hut. We had reached a state of panic, not knowing what to do next when, one afternoon, the blizzard suddenly stopped.

The air was calm and the sky clear and although it was inadvisable to be in the steppe so late in the day, this was an opportunity not to be missed. We were immensely relieved when our friendly Kazakh, moved by our plight, agreed to come with his horse and sledge. We placed the coffin on the sledge and, the horse followed by a small group of our compatriots, moved off. All was well while we stayed on the road with its hard-packed snow, but the cemetery lay to the side of it and the surrounding snow was soft. As soon as the horse stepped on it, it sank to its belly which happened at every step. Very soon it became exhausted and refused to move. There was nothing we could do but unharness it and try to pull the sledge ourselves. This was not much better as now we in turn sank into the snow and, however hard we tried, we could not advance at all. The Kazakh, seeing the futility of our efforts declared that he had to return home with the sledge as it no longer served any purpose anyhow. At the same time the other mourners left and only the family remained with the coffin.

Frozen through and completely exhausted we rested our heads on the coffin and cried. The last straw came when we heard the howling of wolves and saw their eyes glowing in the dark. The only thing left to us was to leave the coffin where it was and return home. Mila, Maryla and I could not sleep at all thinking of the coffin left at the mercy of the wolves. The vision of them chewing through the thin wood and devouring the body tormented us all night. As soon as day broke, filled with terrible apprehension, we went to the cemetery. But the coffin was intact and there was no evidence of the wolves trying to get at the body, which to us felt like a miracle. A little later our good Kazakh came with his son and, together we succeeded in pushing the coffin on the snow towards the edge of the cemetery. The two Kazakhs dug a hole and the saddest funeral ceremony one could imagine was thus performed

Nooka told us his part of the story. He had been separated from us after we had unharnessed the sledge, as he was instructed to take the horse to the Kazakh's home. On the way the horse appeared to be very nervous, possibly aware of the wolves before we heard them, and when Nooka tried to remove its wooden yoke, so that he could ride it, it panicked, ran off the beaten track and got stuck in deep snow, and so was Nooka when he tried to catch it. All his efforts to get the horse out of the snow failed. The situation became really frightening when he also heard the wolves. He knew that the presence of the horse greatly increased the danger of an attack, and yet his sense of duty did not allow him to abandon the animal, and his pride prevented him from calling to us for help. In desperation he made one last effort to extricate the animal from the snow and this time, obviously sensing the seriousness of the situation, the horse decided to co-operate. Crouching on his hind-legs it pushed itself forward so vigorously that not only did it free itself but it also pulled Nooka with him. Safely back on the road they soon reached the Kazakh's hut and that nightmarish experience ended without further misfortune.

We all felt the Old Lady's death profoundly, but most of all our sympathies went to Maryla who was very deeply devoted to her mother. Now, even more than before, she concentrated on her little golden-haired son and it was very touching, even heart-breaking, to hear her teaching him new prayers and talking to him about his father whom he knew only from photographs. Mila took over the 'household duties' as dressmaking and embroidering had to stop. No woman was interested in new clothes in winter, besides which it was too cold and dark in the hut to sew. It was impossible to hold a needle with frozen fingers and in the dim light of a small kerosene lamp we could hardly recognise each other. Sometimes we did not even have enough kerosene to light the lamp and had to use a candle or stay in the dark. Winter seemed to drag on and on. The local people said it was the longest lasting winter in living memory. Just our luck! The snow had begun to fall at the end of September and now it was the beginning of April, but still the village lay under several feet of snow. We longed for spring, fresh air and the sun.

Then, quite unexpectedly, spring arrived, bringing us new problems. One morning we awoke to the sound of water

168

lapping under our floor and when we lifted the trap door leading to the cellar we found it was flooded. This was a very sad discovery as the potatoes which served as a basis of our diet were kept there. Now they were ruined, the water level was too high to attempt to salvage them and we feared it would overflow into our room at any moment. We could not understand where the water had come from as the snow in the street still looked impeccably white and solid. We could not exist without potatoes so I went into the village in the hope of finding someone willing to sell us some.

On my way there I inadvertently stepped off the road and one of my legs suddenly sank into the deep snow. I was not worried at first as I thought I could get it out as easily as it went in, but found I was trapped. This time the snow was not light and powdery as it had been during the Old Lady's funeral, but compact and wet. I was caught in it up to my knee and had to kneel on my other knee to retain my balance. I could feel the wet snow clinging to my leg but all efforts to free myself only made it worse. It was useless shouting for help as there was no hut nearby. My only hope was that someone might pass this way and release me.

My imprisoned leg was gradually getting wet as well as frozen and the knee on which I knelt was very cold and painful. I wondered how much longer I could remain like this without causing permanent damage. Would anyone at home notice my long absence and come to look for me? I knew very well that this was unlikely for at least a couple of hours. What would happen to me in the meantime? Now, stuck in my hole, I at last understood the reason for the water in our cellar: the snow was melting from below. The temperature of the air was still below freezing, but underneath the thaw had started. I did not know how much time passed since I had fallen into my trap, but it seemed like eternity and I began to panic. What if darkness fell – so small a spot so near the ground as I now was would be visible in daytime, but at night? And then I would not survive.

I did not want to die, but that decision was not left to me.

They say that death from freezing is pleasant and easy, but not in my case. I was aware of the situation and had time to reflect. I thought of my son. Poor child, how would he manage without me? I started to pray: 'Please God have pity on me and my child, don't let me die like this in this merciless country, where one cannot even have a normal burial.' I felt very sorry for both of us, tears began to fall and I felt utterly exhausted and, what was worse, sleepy. My thoughts were becoming confused, but I was still able to remember the words of prayers known to me and kept repeating them. My prayers must have reached the Almighty as I heard the squeaking of a sledge and, gathering my strength, called for help. It was the same kind Kazakh who had helped us with the Old Lady's burial. The predicament in which I found myself must have been quite common as he showed no surprise, but he quickly grabbed me under the arms and tried to pull me up. Unfortunately my foot could not dislodge the heavy snow on top of it and I was held down. I was afraid that too much pulling could break or damage my leg and soon we both realised that it could not be released without digging.

The Kazakh said he would get a spade and would bring his son to help him. I was terrified in case he was going to abandon me and beseeched him, perhaps unnecessarily, to come back. He did as promised and returned with his son. They started to dig me up so energetically that I was scared they might injure my leg. When they had finished, although I felt numb all over, my legs seemed all right, at least for the moment. Supported on both sides I got home. Although I did not bring back any potatoes, they were still pleased to see me, and I was given a very good rubbing all over with snow and then given hot tea with vodka in it. Now the story of my recent ordeal could be added to my more dramatic experiences; I seemed to get into trouble more often than any of the others. It was nothing short of a miracle that the whole episode ended for me without even a cold. (Other people, like our poor Armenian friend who after long hours of queuing got his toes frozen and subsequently had them amputated, were far less lucky.)

Ivan, Dounia and the Geese

Having tasted and survived traumatic experiences of the first weeks of spring we now watched its unmistakable progress with understandable joy. After the very hard, long winter which had brought our lives to a virtual standstill, it was pleasant to greet the sun which now not only shone but warmed as well. The days had lengthened considerably and now and then we could come out of the hut to take a deep breath and look at the world freely. In winter these delights, not appreciated in more moderate climates, were impossible because the cold air caught at our throats leaving us breathless, and white frost coated our eyelashes and gummed our eyelids preventing us from seeing properly. But spring brought its own problems. As the thaw began so the cellar filled with water, and the floor in the hut became so wet it was impossible to sleep on it. Janka complained of severe pains in her back which kept her awake and crying at night and, as she shared her bed with Mila, soon they were both completely worn out. We had to find a solution and, after a family council, decided that Nooka and I would move out temporarily so that they could use our beds. In addition Nooka had started to develop signs of rheumatism, so I was anxious to transfer him to a drier place. Happily such a possibility existed for us.

One of our summer customers who bought *kosynkas* and petticoats was called Dounia. She was one of the luckiest

171

women in the village as she still had her husband, Ivan, with her. He had a job in the tractor repair depot where I had tried but failed to get employment. With his military service behind him, he was highly valued in the workshop as a versatile handyman. Ivan and Dounia's hut was one of the best in the village because he used not only his exceptional skill in building it, but also materials taken from the workshop over which he presided. This was common knowledge and no one objected, for it was widely recognised that it was not the salary that mattered so much as the perks that went with the job. Everyone knew, for instance, that the *Kolhoz's* chairman abused his position shamelessly and that his family had supplies of food sufficient to last them several years. But this was a mixed blessing. In time, the punishment for thieving would be meted out to him when someone else replaced him, a foreseeable but unavoidable consequence of the job. Once offered, the appointment of chairman could not be refused because the punishment for refusal (or, as it was called lack of discipline or 'sabotage') was much more severe than that for theft.

Ivan's hut was far more spacious than Natasha's, although like hers, it consisted of a barn, kitchen and living-room. It was incomparably lighter and more cheerful inside, having more and larger windows. Only someone unusually prosperous could afford such luxury in Novo-Troitsk, for such a hut was much more difficult to heat. Dounia and Ivan seemed to manage very well. Dounia, her face disfigured by pock marks, was an excellent and thrifty housewife and when I visited her in the summer I had noticed how spotlessly clean the hut was and how well the mud floors were *polished*.

Ivan had one great advantage over the other 'well-to-do' villagers. He owed his position entirely to himself and not to Communist Party influence or other sources. He was under no obligation to anyone, and, more importantly, no one in the village was able to replace him in his job which relied entirely upon his personal skill. Probably because of that feeling of relative security in an altogether insecure country, his face,

172

which looked as if it was carved from a rough piece of wood by a very inept craftsman, wore a good-natured expression. He walked slowly with a characteristic heavy peasant's walk, swaying from side to side. Occasionally he would drop in for a chat on his way home from work and once, seeing how crowded we were, had suggested Henryk and I move into his house. To date I had always refused, but now the time had come when his invitation seemed welcome. The question was whether it was still open to us and whether Dounia would approve. In order to improve our chances, I decided to take a colourful scarf from my Pandora's box. This was a risk I had to take although I knew if my mission failed it would mean the loss of a kilo or so of precious butter from the free market.

I paid a visit on an exceptionally sparkling day, walking most of the way with my eyes shut blinded by the whiteness of the snow and the sun, relying on the feel of the hard road under my feet and glancing only from time to time to check that I was still on the right path. Ivan's hut was on the western outskirts of the village, some distance from the rest. When I thought I must be somewhere near I shaded my eyes and looked around. I was stunned; no hut was visible – just an expanse of white steppe. Was it possible I had lost my way? I looked back and saw the village where I expected it to be. So what had happened to Ivan's hut? Then I saw smoke coming from the ground, which, on closer inspection, turned out to come from their chimney which was now level with the road. The hut itself was down in a sort of courtyard surrounded on all sides by high walls of snow. To get into the courtyard you had to go down a ladder placed against one of the walls. On three sides the snow had been allowed to pile almost to roof level but the hut entrance and surrounding area were kept free of snow for about five metres. In this way the ingenious Ivan and his family spent the winter snugly protected from the nasty winds blowing in from the steppe. Doubtless it required constant hard work and vigilance from Ivan, Dounia and their teenage son,

173

Petka, to keep this white fortress in such an immaculate condition. I descended the ladder into the large white box and looked up at the cloudless blue sky.

I opened the door which as usual, led to the barn in which, apart from a cow and several chickens, Dounia kept three geese and a gander which raised a terrible din as soon as I entered. Petka came to see what had caused such an uproar and, although he did not show much enthusiasm at seeing me, nevertheless invited me inside. It was very warm and cosy and Dounia and Petka were just starting a meal of steaming potatoes smothered in goose fat. The delicious aroma made my mouth water and I could not help swallowing loudly. Petka's reluctance was well justified as he knew his mother would invite me to share their meal and that I would not have the decency to refuse.

Dounia accepted the scarf with just the correct degree of pleasure and dignity and, on hearing my request, gave her consent without hesitation. We agreed the terms of our tenancy and later that day transferred all that was necessary for our temporary stay on a small sledge we borrowed from Dounia. Henryk and I were allotted a bed in one corner of the room while Dounia and Ivan slept in the other. Petka's sleeping quarters were at the back of a large oven in the kitchen. I noticed straight away that the hut was very dry; no trace of humidity anywhere, which seemed almost incredible. For the first time in many months we were able to wash in a basin of warm water and undress for bed! By comparison with Natasha's hut, this was a palace. The mattress here was also filled with straw and placed on bare boards, but it was dry and did not smell of mould as had our straw one.

On the first night, overcome by all this luxury and afraid to stir in case of disturbing Nooka, I did not sleep too well, but towards morning I was kept awake by Dounia's and Ivan's animated conversation. I listened because I was worried in case it was caused by our presence, as it seemed to me that Dounia had agreed somewhat hastily to our move without first consulting Ivan. But the argument was about something

174

entirely different. In the dim light of their small kerosene lamp Ivan and Dounia were examining the inside of their night clothes. She complained that fleas were stopping her sleeping. Ivan tried to convince her that there were no fleas in their bed.

'There are fleas in this bed,' Dounia insisted, 'I couldn't sleep at all because they were biting me all night.'

'How is it that they did not bite me?'

'They must have, I can see plenty of flea marks on your shirt, but you sleep like a log.'

'And are there any marks on your shirt?' Dounia, after another look at her clothes, had to admit that there weren't any.

'How is it then,' asked Ivan, 'that fleas bite you and don't leave any marks, and with me they leave marks but do not bite?'

They both remained silent for a while and then Dounia, sounding as if she had made a momentous discovery, exclaimed, 'I know, fleas come to me to eat and to you to shit!'

The undeniable logic of that remark put an end to this unusual investigation and left me in stitches, so I quickly hid my face in the pillow to stifle my giggles. I only hoped that it was Ivan who was right, as the thought of fleas from which I had suffered so much before, filled me with horror. Luckily whatever it was that disturbed Dounia's sleep and left marks on Ivan's shirt, never worried us.

Dounia usually expressed her feelings crisply and somewhat crudely. If she wanted to show her dislike of someone, she would say, 'I wouldn't sit next to her to shit for anything in the world.' Could contempt be conveyed better than that? It made sense in Russia because people in the village often squatted next to each other in the field to relieve themselves.

On the whole we settled in at Ivan's without too much difficulty. We were warm, dry and clean but we greatly missed our dear friends as communications between us was temporarily interrupted because of the thaw. Owing to exceptionally heavy snowfalls during the winter and a late spring, with a sudden increase in temperature, the thaw was very rapid and

175

roads became treacherous. We still remembered my unpleasant experience and now often heard of people and
animals being trapped in the deep slushy snow and of the
difficulties experienced in pulling them out. Ivan's snow walls
were sinking fast and the ladder became unnecessary. He was
the only one who had to leave the hut to go to work and now
used steps which he cut in the remaining snow wall. When he
arrived home he was wet and his felt boots dripped with
water, so it was quite a task to get them dry for the following
morning. This was done in the oven and one night I was
awakened by a strong smell of burning; Dounia, in desperation, had put them in the oven too soon while the cinders still
glowed. Only the tops caught fire and burned but, had I not
awoken, we would have been in danger. It was fortunate that
during that critical period Dounia was able to help Nooka and
me with the necessary food so I did not have to risk going to
the village in search of it.

My memories of that time are strongly connected with
Ivan's geese. The feeling of relief at being accepted into his
household was marred by the thought of the geese in the barn.
The only way to the hut was through that barn and the birds'
deafening gaggling and menacing hissing terrified me.

Geese formed an essential part of Ivan's household. They
guarded the house and, what was more important, provided
food and additional income for the family, and I realised that
in order to remain in this house I had to overcome my fear of
them.

I well remember my encounter with geese on the first
morning after our move. On my way out to attend to a call of
nature. I opened the door to the barn very cautiously, trying
not to attract their attention. But it was a futile hope for there
was a terrific uproar and four pairs of eager eyes peered in my
direction. I ran outside as fast as I could but to my horror the
geese raced after me. I stood still and so did the geese, but as
soon as I moved, they did the same. Not being able to contain
my fear any longer I called Dounia for help. She rushed out of
the hut to see what was happening. 'The geese are going to

176

attack me!' I screamed. Dounia giggled, waved her hand contemptuously and saying, 'Go on, they won't harm you,' went back. Her attitude did nothing to reassure me. On the contrary, left alone with the hissing geese whose necks and large beaks stretched menacingly towards me, I forgot my intentions and, moving sideways and watching the geese out of the corner of my eyes, I fled back into the hut.

Finally, Dounia seeing my distress took pity on me. We went together behind the hut, always escorted by the geese, and only then did I understand the motives for their behaviour, which proved to be entirely peaceful. Not given enough proper food, they supplemented their needs by feeding on human excreta. In time my fear of the geese was conquered and was replaced by strong revulsion. From then on I looked at the bloated goose carcasses hanging on hooks in Ivan's barn, with quite different eyes. No more goose flesh or fat for us!

Nooka, however, who normally was not afraid of geese seemed to be seriously worried when he had to go outside in search of privacy. The poor boy used to say, 'It's all right for you, mother, but it is quite different for men,' and I could see his point as the greedy geese never waited until 'the food' fell on the ground, but caught it in mid air, and a mistake could easily happen.

Not long after we moved into Ivan's, I was brought into even closer contact with the geese so it was just as well that I was no longer afraid of them. One day Dounia placed three large baskets of eggs under our bed and installed the geese there for the incubation period, saying that our bed, being at the far end of the room and out of everybody's way, and having adequate space underneath, was the most suitable place. Not knowing what this entailed I cheerfully accepted the situation and subsequently acquired an intimate knowledge of these birds' habits.

The thing I noticed immediately, and initially admired, was their proverbial fastidiousness. They would go out several times a day in order not to soil their nests. While this was commendable during the day, at night it was exhausting to say the least. As the geese were nesting under our bed, the duties of being their attendant fell to me. I would scarcely have fallen asleep when one of them would announce with loud gaggling her desire to go out. Immediately the other two would join in the chorus but unfortunately they were never prepared to go out at the same time. Apart from the noise, there was a great commotion every time the goose went out or returned as it was not easy for such a large bird to move in the restricted space under our bed. Unwilling to leave my warm bed I would wait, hoping that Ivan or Dounia would get up. But they were either fast asleep, or, more likely, pretending to be so. Unable to stand the terrible fracas any longer, I would let the bird out of the room. While I held the door open waiting for the large clumsy creature on its short legs to cross the doorstep, I would become freezing cold and most anxious to get back to bed to warm up. Hardly had I got there than I had to get up again as the bird was gaggling at the outside door, impatient to return to her nest. Again, the other two would respond noisily, unable to resist the call of their friend. The same thing was repeated when the second and third goose decided to go out. In addition to all this, whenever one of them went out, the other two would be busy stealing her eggs by pulling them out of her nest with their beaks. Then a terrible noise and bustle would ensue when the returning goose noticed the theft.

Very soon I was utterly exhausted through lack of sleep and exasperated by the behaviour of my landlords whom I began to suspect of an ulterior motive in letting Nooka and me share their home. Natasha's hut with its frosty walls, the cold and humidity seemed now infinitely preferable to this 'luxury'. Nevertheless I knew I had to endure this unexpected torment. It was definitely much healthier for my son to stay here for the moment and, in any case, we could not possibly have returned to Natasha's hut while the thaw lasted. I could not revolt and refuse to be a goose doorkeeper for fear of being turned out, so I just counted the days before the goslings hatched.

At long last that day arrived. The mother geese returned to the barn to join the gander and Dounia hovered over the eggs, helping the goslings to hatch. As soon as they were out of the shells she put them in an enormous sieve which was placed in the warmest spot near the oven. She asked me to watch and help her, which I would have done anyhow out of curiosity, having nothing better to do, but the reason she wanted me there was because the previous day a large consignment of vodka had arrived in the shop and a party was to be held in the village. Being important members of the community, Dounia and Ivan could not possibly miss it. So off they went leaving me as nanny to the already hatched goslings and to help those as yet unborn, from their shells. Uncertain that Dounia's methods of extracting the little birds were right, I was very nervous despite Nooka's moral support. My involvement with the geese resulted in almost maternal feelings towards their goslings and the sight of those delightful fluffy little creatures almost compensated me for all those nights.

There was a 'femme fatale' among Dounia's geese. Everywhere she went she was accompanied by two ganders, while the other two had to be content with their own company. One of the ganders belonged to Dounia and the other to another household. He spent the whole winter with his own flock but as soon as spring came and Dounia's geese were out of the barn, he came to join them. The strange thing was that the two ganders never fought over their lady and the trio always kept close together, although slightly apart from the rest. Dounia had to chase the ardent admirer away at night, but he was back in the morning and once again the trio was inseparable. This strange affair had apparently been going on for some years.

There was also a female cat in the house, small, thin and bad tempered, quite unlike Natasha's cat, Vaska. As Nooka and I liked cats, we were pleased and although I never heard her purr or show any sign of affection towards anyone, I hoped that I would be able to befriend her during our stay. The most I achieved was when she let me stroke her in

179

exchange for a morsel of food. One day she was sitting on a bench in the kitchen and I bent over to stroke her. As soon as she realised I had no food with me she seemed cross and looked at me with peculiar intensity. Suddenly she stretched her paw and hit me in the eye. Her claw sank into my eyelid and stuck there so I had to hold her paw very tightly and twist it back to extricate it. The pain was severe and I could feel blood or tears running down my face and feared I had been badly injured. Only Nooka was at home, deeply shocked to see me in that condition. There was a terrible moment of tension before I finally managed to open my eye and examine the damage, but the eye was intact and I could see; only the eyelid near the eyebrow was punctured and bleeding. Luckily the thought of tetanus infection or other complications did not cross my mind, for there would have been no remedy anyway. For the next few weeks I paraded a swollen eye around which my skin gradually acquired different shades of black, blue and yellowish green. When I explained the reason for the bruises, the villagers found it hard to believe that such a small cat could inflict such injury with her tiny paws. The 'wicked cat' hid herself and did not reappear until the next day. Dounia wanted to punish her, but I thought I should take the blame for trying to impose an unwanted and unsought friendship upon her.

Life in Ivan's household usually started quite early in the morning, but Nooka and I tried to keep out of the way by staying in bed until Ivan had gone to work. While the geese were sitting these early hours were very valuable to me as I could snatch some sleep, safe in the knowledge that someone else was there to open the door for them. Ivan always shaved before leaving for work and I was amused to notice that, because no razors or blades could be bought, he used the blade from his carpenter's plane. There was also a great shortage of kitchen pots and pans. Natasha, who hardly ever cooked, was quite satisfied with her two cast iron ones, but Dounia, who frequently complained that she needed more, got very excited when the rumour spread through the village that enamel pots had been delivered to the shop. Energetic as usual, she was one of the first in the queue next morning and duly arrived home proudly carrying a chamber pot! Neither she nor any of the young women of the village had any idea of the purpose of this vessel and I was not going to be the one to enlighten her and spoil her pleasure. After all the pot, although too fragile to last long in the fierce heat of a Russian oven, was very pretty in her opinion and what's more it had a handle unlike the traditional cast iron pots, which could only be carried with long tongs.

While at Ivan's I occasionally had to borrow a saucepan from the Soborski's. I always tried to return it thoroughly cleaned with snow or earth, as soap was a luxury and detergent unknown. I was very surprised when Maryla once remarked, somewhat caustically, 'You know, saucepans not only have an inside but an outside as well.' That was a real revelation to me. I have never forgotten that reprimand and we had a good laugh when, years later during Maryla's stay in our house in London, I reminded her of it and was able to show that her remark had not been lost on me.

Finally, the last of the snow melted, the ground became dry again and the water in Natasha's cellar disappeared so Nooka and I could return. What a joy it was to be with our old friends again. The very first day after our return, Mila and I went for a short walk in the steppe. We had often done this the previous summer in the evenings after my return from the fields when it was too dark for her to do any sewing. This time it was an opportunity for us to share our thoughts and worries of the last few weeks. Our friendship grew stronger all the time, we understood each other perfectly and our conversations, often mingled with tears, did us both good. We could not talk so openly at home where we had to show a brave face to the others.

The steppe in spring was beautiful. The variety and brightness of the wild flowers was truly amazing. It must have looked the same the previous spring, but, stunned and shocked by the cruel and bewildering changes in our lives, I could see nothing but the hopeless monotony of the scenery and the neglect and poverty of the village. With the beauty of the country from which we had been uprooted, still in our minds we could not detect any attraction in that flat expanse. Besides, whatever attraction there might have been was too short-lived for us to notice; the grass and flowers were burned by the sun very soon after the steppe came to life. Now, after an incredibly long winter when all life came almost to a standstill, when its purpose was merely to survive, this rebirth of nature seemed like a miracle and the steppe revealed a charm and majesty I had not noticed before. Sometimes, overcome by sadness or depression, I went for walks in the steppe by myself. With the village far behind me, I looked into the far horizon where sky and earth seemed to meet and nothing, not a tree or a building spoiled that illusion. I imagined that if I walked long enough I could touch the sky and, perhaps because of that, I felt very close to God. Here no one but He could see me kneeling, my face uplifted to the sky, reproaching Him for abandoning us to our cruel fate and allowing the evil forces to inflict such suffering upon us; or, prostrated and in flood of tears, begging His forgiveness for my arrogance and lack of understanding of His will. After these sessions I always returned home with renewed strength to face the obstacles never absent from our life.

It was on one of these walks that I decided to escape and, because I believed the idea came from God I was confident that it would succeed. I was encouraged by the fact that I could speak Russian with a Moscow accent and no one would guess my Polish origin. Nooka had also learnt to speak it reasonably well and in any event it should not prove necessary for him to do much talking. We would have to dress like typical Russian citizens, I with a large shawl wrapped round my head and Nooka wearing a Russian cloth cap. Scruffy shoes, plimsolls or galoshes would also be needed and these I could buy second hand on the Troitsk market. But disguise and knowledge of the language were not enough to make travel possible. The papers issued to us in Novo-Troitsk authorised us to move only short distances within our own region and even our trips to nearby Troitsk were illegal, because it was outside the boundaries of Kazakhstan. My plan was to go through Troitsk to Chelyabinsk, a very important and busy railway junction lying on the Trans-Siberian railroad, and from there to Moscow. If we succeeded in getting to Chelyabinsk I hoped we could easily mingle with the crowd and by hook or by crook get on a train going in the right direction for us. I would have to trust our luck and very probably resort to bribery. On arrival in Moscow, I planned to contact a friendly foreign mission for help and, if that failed, to look for the families of my mother's old friends. As my mother and I had left Moscow only sixteen years previously, I felt confident that I would be able to trace at least some of them and that they would assist us in getting in touch with the appropriate authorities to whom I could apply for our release from exile. They might believe that we had been deported by mistake. All this might have seemed crazy but Russia is a very strange and unpredictable country where courage and cheek often pay dividends.

I still hesitated, weighing the pros and cons, chiefly because of Nooka. I had great misgivings about whether or not I had the right to expose him to such a risk. If my plan misfired and we were caught and found guilty of any crime, we could be separated or sent to the extreme north of the Asiatic Russia where conditions were far worse than in Novo-Troitsk. On the other hand, the thought of spending another winter in that village sent shivers down my spine. Nooka was already suffering from pains in his joints and back and a further stay in Natasha's cold humid hut could only bring a deterioration in his health. As our reserves of clothes dwindled and the women of Novo-Troitsk satisfied their needs for *kosynkas* and petticoats, we were becoming less of an attraction and I could not count upon Ivan's or any other Russian family offering us a dry corner in their home again. I was also convinced that Natasha would not want us in her hut after her husband returned from the army. We could not rely upon any help

183

from the authorities who had dumped us here. They were totally unconcerned about our fate, and did not even pay us for our hard work in the field. Altogether the picture looked very bleak. On balance I decided to go ahead with my plan and discuss it with Mila.

She thought it was dangerous but said she would have done exactly the same thing in my place, as sooner or later we would all die from cold and starvation and, who could know, I might even succeed and be able to help them to get out of Novo-Troitsk. She did not think that Leszek, who looked more and more transparent, would survive another winter or that Janka, whose pain was becoming unbearable, would improve in these conditions either. Watching the sufferings and deprivations of our children was the most painful of our experiences.

I had to act quickly as it was now the middle of June and our escape could take place only in summer. The most difficult part was to get a train ticket; even the natives could buy tickets only for very short distances, and for a longer journey it was necessary to have a specially written permit issued by a recognised authority before the ticket could be purchased. Such a permit was beyond my reach. Within this arrangement, which covered journeys of army and NKVD personnel and people sent on specific duty or transferred from one place of work to another, there was a category which allowed people to travel on holiday and for health reasons and although a permit was still required, I thought that here was a possible opening. We could pass as mother and son going to visit relatives in Moscow without raising the suspicions of fellow-passengers. I had heard that control on the trains was very lax, probably because it was considered that anyone who had boarded them not only had a ticket, but also the authority to travel. Our main problem was to get on the train. Thereafter things I thought would be easier.

The other problem was money. I relied partly on Mrs Semionova, the doctor's wife in Troitsk, to buy anything I still had to sell. There was not much left in my Pandora's box, but what there was, was very good. Two pairs of lovely shoes and a set of pure silk Viennese underwear, including a sumptuous negligée. I wanted a good price for them but, apart from Mrs Semionova, I did not think I would find any buyers willing and able to pay; certainly not in Novo-Troitsk and possibly not even in Troitsk market. There were also trinkets of little value, but very attractive and not found in the Soviet shops. My real treasure were two very beautiful diamond rings and other jewellery of considerable value which I kept in a large, heavy solid silver handbag. These I could not afford to let go cheaply as I needed every rouble I could get and I doubted whether even my prosperous and spendthrift Mrs Semionova could afford them. The thought occured to me that perhaps she could also advise me on how to obtain a ticket to Chelyabinsk, which I would say I wanted to visit out of curiosity.

I took a pair of shoes and a few items of clothing, but not the jewellery, and went to Troitsk by the first lorry whose driver agreed to carry me. My first thought on arrival was to call on the kind friend who had taken Halina and me under her wing when we were half frozen in the market. Full of joyous anticipation I knocked at her door and waited. After some time our friend opened the door, but was quite different from my recollection. Instead of a warm smile her face wore a cool, hostile expression.

'Please do not come here any more,' she shouted very loudly, 'I do not want to know you.' With that she slammed the door in my face. I felt more frozen than I had been on that terrible January day in the market. For a moment I stood rooted to the ground. Perhaps she had mistaken me for somebody else and any moment now would open the door and apologise. Something must have happened in the meantime to cause such a change in her.

I was still deeply shaken by my reception when I reached Mrs Semionova's house and rang her bell. What would await me here? If she rejected me, my plans would be seriously handicapped, if not thwarted completely. But she was all smiles and my spirits rose. She bought all my things and I mentioned casually that I would very much like to see Chelyabinsk and show it to my son as I had heard that it was a very interesting place. At the same time I expressed doubts about the possibility of getting a rail ticket. I told her that another reason for wanting to go there was to sell my jewellery which I hoped would be possible in such a large town. She reacted with great interest and made me promise to let her see what I had to sell before I went there in case she could afford to buy some of it. To my great surprise and joy she said that it would be within her husband's power to issue me with the necessary authorisation for a ticket to Chelyabinsk, as he often directed patients to the hospital there. It would have to be under the pretext of taking my child into hospital for special treatment not available in Troitsk. I had only to promise that I would not remain in Chelyabinsk for longer than a couple of days so as not to attract the attention of the NKVD, and to destroy her husband's letter as soon as we reached there. I understood her fears and, while uncertain that two days in Chelyabinsk would be enough for me to arrange the next stage of our journey, I was determined to keep my other promise and not to expose the doctor to the risk of losing his job, or worse. I also promised Mrs Semionova a present for her kindness.

In spite of the first upsetting incident, I was delighted with the result of my trip which was far more successful than I could have hoped. Mila was pleased too, but sad at the same time, and I found the thought of leaving them soon very painful. I had arranged with Mrs Semionova to go back in a few days' time with the remaining things which she wanted to buy, to show her my jewellery and collect the doctor's letter. I packed all my treasures in my little pigskin suitcase and left for the station. Before saying goodbye, Mila, who had come part of the way to the station with me, suddenly remarked, 'You see, you should not attach too much importance to your dreams as now you have a definite proof that they do not come true.' She was referring to a recent dream in which I was walking along the dusty road to Novo-Troitsk with a hunchback who said to me, 'You will go away from this village in October, not alone, but all together.' Mila was right; it was now June and I was ready to go away with Nooka. October seemed an absurd time in which to travel.

I was not very lucky this time and spent hours at the station before the train arrived. The station master and his wife had relatives staying with them so I could not wait there. The waiting and subsequent travelling was so much more exhausting because I had to keep a close watch on my suitcase for fear of being robbed. I began to be tormented by all sorts of doubts. Why, for instance, should the doctor, whom I had never met, agree to give me an incriminating letter? Wasn't his wife unduly rash in giving me such a promise? I was terribly tired when I finally reached the doctor's house so, when Mrs Semionova opened the door, I looked at her anxiously, but she seemed as relaxed and welcoming as before. Seeing how tired I was, she suggested I rest on a divan in her son's room. Although it was narrow and uncomfortable, before I knew it I was fast asleep.

I awoke feeling very refreshed and immediately looked at where I had left the suitcase. It was not there. I jumped up, thinking someone might have moved it but I could not see it anywhere. Then I thought perhaps Mrs Semionova had placed it in another room, so I called her and asked where it was. She appeared very surprised and said she had not been to my room since my arrival, but it was possible that someone had come in while she was out shopping. It could have been one of her son's friends who often popped in uninvited, and the woman downstairs might have let him in. As Mrs Semionova never locked her flat, anyone could have entered quite easily. She offered to go and ask the woman downstairs. By then I was in real despair. I had my most valuable possessions, in fact my whole fortune, in that suitcase. Its loss meant giving up hope of escaping from Kazakhstan. I felt certain that Mrs Semionova was lying and that she had stolen it. The woman from downstairs came and declared that she had not seen it and it was more than likely that someone had come in unnoticed and taken it away. The attitude of both women was hard and hostile. I suspected that they had entered into a conspiracy and that I would achieve nothing by pleading or threats. There was nothing else left to do but go to the militia post and report the loss.

When I told Mrs Semionova of my intention, she shrugged her shoulders and smiled contemptuously, certain that the militiamen would not side with a deported woman against the wife of a doctor who was head of the hospital. However, I was aware of the amazing contradictions and surprises in the Russian character. One never knew whether to expect indifference and cynicism or kindness and compassion in the face of misfortune. To me the loss of the suitcase was a real misfortune not only because it shattered my plans to escape, which, of course, I had to keep secret, but because its contents represented inestimable value if we had to remain in our village. I had to do everything I possibly could to recover it.

The outcome of my visit to the militia post depended very much upon the type of man in charge. He could be as hostile as the chairman of the *Kolhoz*, inoffensive as the NKVD man in Novo-Troitsk or as kind and compassionate as the doctor who had operated on Mila, or the station master and his wife who had helped us so many times when we were in need. A lot also depended upon my ability to gain confidence and arouse sympathy. I had not only to feel the great consequences of my loss, but also to convey it to others and this, I knew, would be difficult. Other people's misfortunes, or even a book, could easily move me to tears, but when it came to real life, I never could parade my misery.

Now, trying to relive the events of the last few hours, I worked myself into such a state of despair that when I reached the militia I was in tears and looked so distressed that the militiaman who received me helped me to a chair and brought me a glass of water before hearing my case. I was in luck; the man was obviously kind. I told him who I was and the circumstances, careful not to betray my suspicions, and explained as best I could what the loss meant to me and my son. He decided to come with me to the doctor's house to investigate and when we got there I saw that the appearance of the uniformed militiaman shook Mrs Semionova. She paled and very politely asked him in, at the same time giving me a very angry look. As soon as we were inside she said, 'Do you know this woman came here with the idea of escaping from Novo-Troitsk and that she should be arrested?'

He answered, 'The deported people are not my responsibility, that is the matter for the NKVD. I am here to maintain order. This woman has reported the loss of her suitcase from your house and I want to find out where it is.'

'Are you aware of the position my husband holds in this town?' She was trying to impress or frighten him, but this did not produce the effect she had anticipated.

'Yes,' he said, 'that is why I do not expect things to be stolen from anyone in this house. I am sure you do not want your husband to be dragged into this affair as it might do great damage to his career, but I may be forced to do it.'

Mrs Semionova's voice shook, but still she denied all knowledge of or connection with the suitcase.

The militiaman continued, 'Think well. Maybe your son or someone else put the suitcase in another place. This could easily have happened while you were out. Go and look for it.'

After a moment's hesitation Mrs Semionova left the room.

We sat in complete silence, he smoking a cigarette which he made out of shag tobacco, and I trying to steady my beating heart. So much depended upon the success of his tactics. He must have been pretty sure that she had engineered the theft and knew that she, or rather, her husband, had much to lose. Now he was showing her a way out, but would she take it? She must realise the risk I was taking if I decided to pursue the case further. What proof had I of her guilt? I listened with bated breath for any noise from downstairs and finally heard her coming back upstairs. The door opened, and there she stood, holding my suitcase.

189

With a forced smile she said, 'You were right. It was my friend from downstairs who took the suitcase; she thought it would be safer with her while this woman slept.' She put it on the floor and the militiaman told me to check its contents. Nothing was missing.

'So all is well. Good bye,' he said. I had nothing to say but felt that another miracle had happened. The militiaman and I left together.

In the street he shook hands with me and said, 'Go back to your child and don't be so careless in the future, you never know how things may end.' Tears of gratitude and relief filled my eyes. In the days of Stalin's rule there were many Russians banished to these remote parts of Russia because of their supposed 'unreliability'. These were the ones, like this militiaman and Mila's doctor, ready to show their compassion and offer help to outcasts like us.

I returned to Yemankino stunned by the turn of events, without the travel permit and with the hope of escape shattered. The shock caused by the loss of the suitcase and doubts about its recovery gradually receded, but I realised more than ever before how much I had risked in going to the militia. I still found it hard to believe my luck. I could so easily have landed in jail but here I was, still in so called 'free exile', intact suitcase in hand, and on my way home to our village, my son and dear friends. I could not wait to see them.

The joy of my friends that we were not going to part, at least for the time being, compensated for my thwarted plans. At heart, I had always doubted that I should seek my own way of escape and now that fate had ordained otherwise, I decided to share their exile till the end. But would I be able to hold faith with my decision? Mila and Maryla had inexhaustible reserves of submission and patience, things which I had always lacked.

A little while after my return Mila said, 'Do you remember your dream about the hunchback? He told you that we shall all leave in October.'

'Yes, indeed, that was what he said. But which year? He did not say. Perhaps in ten or twenty years time?'

'Never mind, we will wait until October.'

Strengthened by our new hope, because only hope could help preserve our sanity, we returned to our normal routine – day to day subsistence without starving and, as far as possible, without falling into deep depression. The saddest person was Maryla. Leszek was constantly ailing. He had a persistent tummy ache, probably caused by malnutrition. The Polish relatives kept sending semolina and dried fruit and we never missed the chance to buy a chicken to make him nourishing soup, but nothing seemed to improve his condition. He was losing weight, was very apathetic and grew weaker and weaker.

On the Road to Freedom

June 22nd 1941 started like any other day for us, but it
brought events which determined the future of Poland and
many other countries. On that day German troops crossed the
line which was supposed to divide the German zone of Poland
from the Russian. The non-aggression pact made between
Germany and Russia before the massacre of Poland, was now
broken by Hitler, who began a war against his 'friends'. We
got the news from the official Russian newspaper, the only one
printed in Kazakhstan. In Novo-Troitsk it caused an understandable stir and gave rise to all kinds of rumours and
speculations. We had an unending flow of other exiles in our
hut, wanting to discuss the events and share opinions. What
effect would this new war have upon our fate?

For centuries both Germany and Russia had been our
deadly enemies. One of them, seeking our destruction, had
brought us to the Kazakhstan steppes and now we might find
ourselves standing face to face with the other, no less sinister.
At that time we knew nothing of the atrocities committed by
the Germans in occupied Poland, but we had no illusions. We
could not decide which of the two evils was worse. The local
population, Russians as well as Kazakhs, seemed to have no
doubts. They had had enough of Stalin's rule of arrests,
deportations to the mines and concentration camps. Germany
brought hope of liberation from the Communist yoke and the
news of the outbreak of war was celebrated in the village with

undisguised pleasure, while vodka flowed freely. We had no doubts as to who would be the victor in this war if the people's reaction elsewhere in Russia were similar to this. We read the communiqués avidly and, although it was difficult to learn the truth about the strategic situation, it soon became apparent that, far from making better masters, the Germans would probably be worse than the Russians.

We read about Russian villages pillaged and burned by the Germans, about people executed on any pretext and about the persecution of anyone resisting the Draconian rule of the invaders. The mood of the people changed completely. Now the invader was feared and hated and patriotism revived. It was not a question of overthrowing the regime, hated by many people in Russia, but of defending their own country against the cruel enemy. In Novo-Troitsk, which was too far from the field of activities for the effects of war to be felt immediately, the temporary euphoria gave way to the usual apathy. There were some men of call-up age but, for the time being, they were left in their jobs which were essential for the normal functioning of village institutions. The women whose husbands had been taken away in previous years began to visit Mrs Kozlowska again hoping that she would be able to tell from the cards whether they would return; they thought that, sooner or later, the younger men would be called up and the older ones would be freed to take their place in the village community.

In the middle of August 1941, I received a summons to report to the local NKVD. Such a call never augured well, so we were all very worried. My first thought was that the doctor's wife had reported me out of revenge, or that my helpful militiaman considered it his duty, after all, to inform a higher authority of my intention to escape. It was quite probable, in order to save his skin, and in view of Mrs Semionova's allegations, he had had to do it. On my way to the NKVD post I tried to prepare myself for any eventuality. I knew that presence of mind could get one out of the most difficult situations. When I arrived I was so baffled by the reception I was

193

given that, for a moment, I was completely thrown. The NKVD man smiled, offered me a seat and addressed me by my first name and patronymic. Was this to sweeten the blow that was to come? I knew he was not a cruel man and that I could expect some sort of consideration from him. Nevertheless I was extremely apprehensive. But there came a most unexpected and wonderful news.

'Eugenia Pavlovna' he said solemnly, 'I called you here because I have a very important announcement to make. From now on all Polish deportees in the village are free. You can leave this place anytime. Poland is now our ally, and we shall fight our mutual enemy Germany together.' I covered my face with my hands to hide the emotion which that news had produced, and reflected for a moment on the situation. So now Germany was an enemy and we were friends!

I wanted to know more, but that was all he could tell me. The order had come from above with no further details.

Only much later, when we had left Russia, did we learn that our release was due to an agreement signed in London on 30th July 1941 by the representatives of the Polish Government in Exile and the Government of the USSR (General Sikorski and I. Maiski). The agreement contained two very important clauses: a) All changes made in the Polish territory by the treaty of 1939 between German and the Russian Governments were declared invalid; b) All Polish people deprived of freedom by the Russians, whether p.o.w. or any other, were to be released.

These clauses of the agreement were soon to be violated by the Russians, but in the meantime some of us succeeded in liberating ourselves, and Nooka and I and the remaining members of the Soborski family were among the lucky ones.

In our village, the reaction of the deportees to the news of the 'amnesty' varied greatly. It was obvious that some did not have the energy and enterprise even to comtemplate their departure. Many were afraid to embark upon a journey into the unknown, especially in view of the war raging in the west of Russia, while others were reluctant to leave their little patch of potatoes or beetroot, which they were growing for the winter and which was their only sure supply of food. There were others who advised patience in the belief that, sooner or later, the authorities would organise their departure. Having sounded the views of the village elders, I had no such illusions. They never had been really responsible for us and had no means or instructions to do anything now.

I remembered that after our arrival, when there was no food for our children we had asked how we were supposed to feed them, and they answered 'Teach them to eat grass,' although at that time there was none. With the so-called amnesty their attitude remained unchanged. Having seen the way in which the locals lived it was difficult to blame them; they too, were struggling constantly for survival, never sure what awaited them tomorrow. I tried to advise our people to get ready to go at once, especially as winter was not far away, but, apart from our little group, who shared the same views, no one seemed to agree. However, we were determined to leave and con-centrated all our efforts on preparations for our departure. At that time we had no idea where to go but were convinced that life in town, any town to start with, would be better and the prospects of getting away from Russia brighter than in this outlandish village where we were cut off from the rest of the world.

News of immense importance came from our friend the station master from Yemankino, who sent a message that, according to information he had received, trains with men released from concentration camps, who might be Polish, were passing through Magnai station about ten miles from us. They were going in a westerly direction, but he was unable to say where to. It was necessary to discover whether the men were really Poles and, if so, their destination. So, equipped with food and my friends' blessing, I went to Magnai.

Before very long a train arrived carrying Polish ex-prisoners and inmates from concentration and labour camps from different parts of Russia, but mostly from the extreme north of Siberia. It was a passenger train which I was able to board and travel to the next stop with them. The impression they made was shattering. What I saw was a collection of skeletons covered in rugs, their feet wrapped in newspaper or dirty cloth, kept in place with pieces of string, although many had nothing on their feet at all. There was not a normal looking face to be seen. They were either very thin, the colour and texture of yellow parchment, or bloated and shapeless like the face of a drowned man. Their eyes were sunken and either completely lifeless or glowing feverishly. They all looked old and shrivelled although some of them, at least, must have been young.

The sudden appearance of a Polish woman startled them. They could not understand how I happened to be on their train, but when I explained I was a deportee and lived in a nearby village, they came to life and started to bombard me with questions. Most of them knew that their families had been deported to Kazakhstan or Siberia and were avid for news. How had we managed to live and how had we been treated? I tried to reassure them that village life was not too bad, that we were quite well treated and there was no doubt that their families were alive and would soon join them. As I was wearing a Polish tweed suit and a good pair of shoes, someone asked me if all women were as well dressed. I felt that in some cases a lie was better than the truth. The cheer that greeted my answer was my reward. Their smiles revealed completely or partially toothless gums and, with obvious embarrassment, they explained that this was sometimes the result of avitaminosis, but mostly due to the treatment meted out to them by the NKVD officials during interrogations or by the guards in camps and prisons.

My turn to question them arrived. Had they ever met my or Mila's husbands? Where had they come from and where were they going? What did they know about the 'amnesty' and its consequences for us? To answer my questions they brought the 'professor', a shadow of a man who nonetheless must have been someone greatly respected and trusted. He was a university professor from Lvov and from him I heard for the first time the word *Buzuluk*. They were going there on the under-standing that it was the headquarters of the newly formed Polish Army and that it was situated in the Orenburg *oblast* of Russia. He was unable to tell me much more, but this was enough for me as I thought it would be where Polish women and children would find protection and guidance, and that it was where we should go. I was eager to return to our village at once and tell everyone what I had heard, but at the moment I was on the train going in the opposite direction, probably towards Chelyabinsk.

I had no idea whether it would stop in Troitsk or go straight to Chelyabinsk, the place of my dreams not so long ago. Ironically I now dreaded the thought of going there in case I became stranded, as the war had brought chaos to an already difficult transport system. While on the train I wanted to talk to as many people as possible so I went from one carriage to another, ignoring the protests of the female guard. After all she could not throw me out of the moving train and, in view of our newly acquired rights, she was uncertain how stern she should be with me. Everywhere I saw the same emaciated or swollen faces, the results of starvation. I learned also that apart from being cold and hungry, they were suffering from diarrhoea caused by rotten dried fish (*vobla*) which had been their staple diet in camps and prisons. Some of them could not get up from the bench, they were so weak. Nevertheless, the mood was one of elation, nothing mattered now that they were free and soon to join the ranks of an independent Polish Army. Apparently even those who had hated each other in captivity now forgot their animosities and helped one another by sharing bits of food, and in any other way they could.

I stopped in each carriage for a little and everywhere I met with the same reaction: bewilderment, followed by a flurry of excitement. I wanted to sit down in one of the cars, but an anxious voice cried, 'Please don't come too near us. We are dirty, our rags smell and are full of vermin and these benches are also infested.' The man who said this smiled apologetically and I saw with surprise that he still had his teeth. He spoke in a cultured voice and, despite his haggard appearance, there was an air of refinement about him.

In each carriage I asked about my husband and Mila's, but no one seemed to have heard or come across them. Of course, I realised that this transport was one of the first and that many more would follow. There were tens of thousands of Polish prisoners of war and other Polish men in labour camps or prisons in Russia. Regular army officers, members of the aristocracy, middle-class professional men, landowners and also soldiers, small tradesmen and peasants. People were arrested and deported indiscriminately to make room for Russian families who replaced the 'uncertain elements'.

The tragic impression that the sight of these people created made me wonder how it was possible to reduce normal human beings to such a pitiful condition in a comparatively short time. Yet I was told that these were the strongest and healthiest of the lot; many were so ill and weak that they had to be left behind and many more died before the 'amnesty' was declared. In which category of men could I expect my beloved Nik to be? One moment I felt optimistic, the next serious doubts crept back into my heart, and the dream of the cemetery was still at the back of my mind.

When the train stopped in Troitsk there were still many questions left unanswered on both sides, but I had to get off. This first meeting with my compatriots, miraculously delivered from slavery, was something I can never forget. We parted in the hope of meeting again in Buzuluk.

In spite of the long delays and the discomforts of the return journey, feelings of elation mixed with great sadness remained with me on my return to Novo-Troitsk. Utterly exhausted, I fell on my bed and was fast asleep before Mila and Maryla could help pull off my shoes and top clothing. They said later that I managed a faint smile and the nod, which they took as a sign that I was pleased with the result of my exploratory journey.

Buzuluk, this word we had never heard before, had a magical meaning. It became the promised land with which all

198

our hopes were associated. At last we knew where to head for and this gave an added urgency and reality to our preparations for departure. We tried to get as much money as possible by selling anything that the local people were willing to buy and, at the same time, reducing the bulk and weight of our luggage to a bare minimum.

Natasha denied herself and the children the more luxurious food, like butter and eggs, and slaughtered her chickens in order to secure things she knew would probably never come her way again. With regret I parted with one of my eiderdowns and Mila's great dilemma was whether or not to sell her sewing machine, it had been our great standby in hard times and perhaps it could still be useful in the future. Besides, there was no hope of getting a good price, as the local women had no idea how to use it, the art of sewing being completely foreign to them. In any case, they had exhausted their reserves of material and if, for example, a needle broke there was no hope of getting a replacement. In the end it was decided to take it and, if necessary, to abandon it later. A change of underwear, a minimum of bedding, one or two warm articles of clothing and, of course, a pair of shoes and *valenki* – felt boots – were all necessary. The rest of our luggage would be food, as much as we could muster, plus a minimum of cooking utensils. In the meantime we tried to eat well in order to gather strength and fatten ourselves before the journey.

We had to start from Magnai, the nearest stop for westbound trains. No one could foresee how long we would have to wait before being accepted on a train. It was now the end of September, the snow was beginning to fall and it was already quite cold. There was no question of camping outside the station even if we had been allowed to. All our plans might have been frustrated had it not been for our invaluable friend, the station master from Yemankino, who once again came to our rescue. He persuaded his colleague, the Magnai station master, to let a part of his hut to us. We were given the kitchen while the station master and his wife occupied the adjacent room. However, he reserved the right to use the kitchen whenever his wife needed it. It suited us as the more often the oven was used, the warmer the place would be. The great disadvantage was that the door from the kitchen led straight into the open because there was no barn. There was also a complete lack of privacy as the landlord and his wife and any visitors had to pass through the kitchen, and we often attracted spectators. By now we were quite used to having no privacy and, as we never undressed for bed anyway, it did not worry us unduly. In any case, we were compensated by the fact that we occupied an excellent strategic position for catching the train and this was more important than anything else.

Apart from our group, no one else decided to leave Novo-Troitsk, despite my newly acquired information. Before we left, people would come to have a chat or say goodbye, but it was obvious they thought us lunatics, diving into deep water filled with whirlpools without knowing how to swim. But nothing could deter us.

In our new quarters in Magnai the only place to sleep, apart from the back of the oven, was the floor. I missed my iron bed and *kelim*. I thought, too, that the cat Vaska, would have been most welcome to warm my feet. I had brought the *kelim* with me, but it was in tatters after the frost and humidity in Natasha's hut. I had carefully matched the individual pieces like a jigsaw puzzle as it dried in the summer and, while it could not be compared with the straw-filled mattress, it formed a good base and insulation between our bodies and the mud floor. The place behind the oven was assigned to Maryla and Leszek and Janka joined them there. The rest of us spread out on the floor as well as we could. Except for two benches there was no furniture in the kitchen, which was just as well as later we needed an additional space. We spent our days with nothing much to do but wait for the train. Only Mila was busy, sewing dresses for the station master's wife. Once again, the sewing machine proved its worth. The thought occurred to me that Mila's dresses here and in Novo-Troitsk, worn only during the very short summer, and even then only on

Sundays, might outlast the memory of the Poles whose visit would gradually fade into legend.

Although it was only the beginning of October, winter was already with us and we racked our brains what to do to prevent gusts of freezing air blowing into our kitchen each time the door was opened. If my *kelim* had only been in better condition we could have hung it over the doorway. As it was all we could do was keep the oven fire going in the belief that we would leave before our reserves of *kiziak* were exhausted. It was no good risking a cold or pneumonia and ruining our chances of departure.

One day Mila, recklessly adding *kiziak* to the fire, said, 'Do you remember your dream, it's October now and we should be out of here very soon, so why worry?'

Several trains passed through Magnai without stopping. They were mostly carrying Russian soldiers to the front, but every now and then a train with Polish ex-p.o.w.s stopped for a couple of minutes, not long enough to board it, but giving Halina and me the chance to distribute pieces of paper with Nik's and Frank's names, as well as the names and addresses of the families left in Novo-Troitsk. We hoped in that way to contribute to the uniting of separated families. We still did not know who was at the head of the organisation in Buzuluk, but the word was on everybody's lips. Buzuluk was their Mecca and they were on a pilgrimage to salvation.

Our landlord kept assuring us that 'our train' would come and we would have enough time to board it. What made him think that we did not know, but it helped sustain our morale. One day he rushed into the hut, breathless, saying that some men had got off a train and looked very ill and he thought they might be Polish. I doubted his words. Why on earth would Polish men stop at this Godforsaken station? But I went to see them. Only people returning from the hell of *katorga* a place of very cruel exile, could have looked as they did. There were four, half naked, bare-footed, dehumanised creatures in an even worse condition than the men I had met on the previous train. Only one could stand; the other three flopped down on

201

the frozen ground and stayed there, heads low on their chests, helpless and apathetic. The man who remained standing looked around slowly, trying to assess the situation. I watched him for a moment from our doorstep. I could well imagine the thoughts running through his head at the sight of this small gloomy railway station and a few mud huts.

I came nearer and greeted them in Polish, but they looked at me as if I were a ghost and did not answer. I repeated the greeting and this time they responded. They were Polish. I asked them why they had got off the train at this station, at which they smiled bitterly. It was not their choice, they were simply pushed off by the Russians who said that there was only room in the carriage for the men going to the front. I suggested they came inside to get warm. The station master, who was watching the scene, gave a few disapproving glances, but did not openly object. I could not blame him, for who would have liked such dirty tramps, covered in rugs, to be brought into their home? There was no need to ask Mila and Maryla for their permission as I knew what their answer would be and I just had enough time to whisper to the station master that we would recompense him for his kindness in allowing them to stay. The kitchen was warm and the men so tired that while we got busy peeling potatoes for soup, they all fell asleep sitting on the floor leaning against the wall. Then, just before the soup was ready, one of them pulled himself up and hurried to the door. We thought he must have had a nightmare and was running from an imaginary persecutor. A moment later he returned, holding his trousers with both hands. It transpired that all four of them suffered from diarrhoea, the terrible affliction of all inmates of prisons and concentration camps in Russia.

Our intention had been to give them temporary hospitality for perhaps a day, but in fact they stayed much longer. They were our compatriots and, in our eyes, elevated by their suffering and we were truly happy that we were there to help them. Nevertheless, at times we wondered what would happen when our food reserves became exhausted as, with

202

four extra mouths to feed, they were rapidly diminishing. We were rewarded by an improvement in their mental and physical condition during their twelve days' stay. The fact that they were still quite young helped; they were visibly gaining weight and energy and recovering their sense of humour and will to live.

Their presence had done us a lot of good as well. Instead of waiting passively for 'our train' to come, we were very busy baking bread each day and cleaning and patching their rugs. Their chilblained hands and feet were badly swollen and bleeding so one of the sheets was used for bandages and some sort of substitute for socks. When nature forced them to go outside, they wore wooden 'soles' made from vodka crates and tied to their feet by strips of material from the same sheet to protect them from the frost. A little later we were able to buy four pairs of *valenki* from our host and local inhabitants. The *valenki* were old but still in one piece and our men were delighted with them. The fact that they had to accept help from women who were already in a difficult situation embarrassed them very much, but we jokingly reassured them that we would get everything back with interest in Buzuluk. During their stay we spent much time listening to stories about their past lives in Poland and their terrible experiences in the labour camps in Russia, which made our own suffering seem insignificant.

Now more and more trains were passing through, some stopping quite a long time awaiting a signal to proceed. Most of the passengers were Russian, but occasionally we spotted Polish men. Our four protégés, at first too weak to continue their journey, recovered enough to push their way into one of the cars, but when we tried to do the same, we met with violent protests from the Russian passengers. Men were one thing, but women and children quite another and we were definitely not wanted. Our friends could do nothing to help us, but promised that as soon as they reached Buzuluk they would move heaven and earth to get us there.

With just the seven of us once more, our kitchen seemed the

height of luxury and at last we were able to have a good night's sleep, although that was not what we most wanted. Each morning we packed our bedding ready to leave, only to have to unpack again in the evening, as all our attempts to get into an overcrowded train failed. As there was no chance of all seven of us getting into the same car, the station master advised us to split into two groups. We could not accept his suggestion, such a separation might mean losing each other for ever because individual cars were often shunted into different tracks and attached to different trains. Besides, we did not even know if the trains were going anywhere near Buzuluk. Meanwhile the station master and his wife grew more and more impatient at our delay and we, more and more desperate. There were even moments when we contemplated returning to Novo-Troitsk in the hope that maybe the Russian or Polish authorities would finally arrange our repatriation. However, that, too, was a dismal prospect.

As so often happened before, when crisis loomed overhead, the answer to our problem was just round the corner. The next train which passed without stopping had carriages with 'Buzuluk' painted on them in large white letters. The station master said that these carriages going direct to Buzuluk were assigned exclusively to Poles. Now we trusted that we would be accepted and the prospect of temporary separation, in case we had to get into different cars, no longer dismayed us.

I often thought about the Russian woman who had befriended Halina and me in Troitsk. Her strange behaviour on my second visit did not obliterate the memory of her original kindness which I felt sure was as genuine as her outburst had been completely out of character. So when our departure from Magnai seemed almost a certainty I sent her a farewell note in the belief that the news of our liberation would please her. It took us all by surprise when, a few days later, she came by train carrying a basket of food. We embraced each other as if nothing had happened to cloud the wonderful relationship which had started on that incredibly cold January day. Later she explained that since our visit she had lived continuously in deadly fear that we might repeat our conversation to someone and thus endanger her and, most of all her son, so that when she saw me again, she wanted to show the neighbours that she had nothing to do with me. She said that she had felt like Judas Iscariot for denying all knowledge of me, but I could not hold it against her and was not surprised; after all, she knew nothing about us and spying and denunciation were widely practised and encouraged in the Soviet Union. Our poor, good benefactress. Her kindness had cost her a lot of nervous strain! I suppose our departure not only gave her reason to be happy for us, but freed her from further anxiety.

Her visit could not have come at a better time. Early next day, the 26th October, we were informed by the station master that a train to Buzuluk had been announced and was going to stop in Magnai. Terrified of missing our chance, we sat outside our hut hours before the train was due. In spite of the fact that we had been issued with the appropriate tickets, we were desperately worried that all or some of us might not be allowed onto the train. In order to increase our chances, we followed the station master's advice and split into three groups. Mila and Janka, then Maryla, Leszek and Halina and finally Nooka and me. We each had some dried bread, a tin of lard and a little sugar and this was now supplemented by a share of the food from our friend's basket. As it was only about one hundred kilometres to Buzuluk which should have taken less than a day, food was not a problem except for Leszek who needed frequent nourishment and whose ailing stomach could not tolerate heavy or cold food. He was so weak that we were very worried he would not survive the journey.

When eventually the train did arrive, nobody asked us for tickets, but several pairs of emaciated arms stretched out to pull Nooka and me aboard. With the doors being so high off the ground it was very difficult for anyone to get in without help. I looked out to see what had happened to our other two groups. They were no longer on the platform, so all was well. The car was so jam-packed with people that, before the train

205

moved, the door had to be closed and barred on the inside to prevent people from falling out. This was done by the passengers themselves and was the only real difference between this freight car and the one which had brought us to Kazakhstan: no armed guards to lock us in!

The congestion and stench inside were indescribable. I felt the pressure of bony bodies on all sides and, afraid that my Nooka would be in danger of suffocation, I pulled him tightly to myself to protect him at least on one side. It was a real sacrifice for those people to have taken us in under such conditions. As usual, there were only two small windows and it took some time before I could distinguish faces in the semi-darkness. As soon as the train started to move, people began to sing religious songs and I heard a few female voices, although the overwhelming majority of the passengers were men. There was such a squeeze that people fainted on their feet. To my horror I felt lice beginning to crawl over me and I knew that there was widespread epidemic of typhus in Russia which was carried by them.

After hours of travelling I felt faint from the stink and lack of air and terribly worried about Nooka. Someone was sick next to us and Nooka started to sob. Just then I heard a loud and obscene cursing in Russian. Startled, I tried to see where it came from and saw four bodies stretched comfortably on bunks. They were four young Russians, three in soldiers' greatcoats and caps with a red star, and the fourth in civilian clothing and a fur hat. I was flabbergasted. How and why were these Russians travelling in the car which had been assigned to Poles? I was sure that they should not have been there at all and yet they behaved as if the car belonged to them.

I asked our men to demand places on the bunk. They nodded in agreement but none of them had the nerve to do so. Only recently released from the slavery of labour camps, where they had been subjected to maltreatment and innumerable insults and humiliations, they were probably afraid of losing their newly acquired freedom and were uncertain of their rights. I asked the Russians to give up their places to the women and the very ill men.

They responded with jeers, 'Look at this Polish madam who must have maltreated and exploited her servants in the past. Now she expects us to be kind to these parasites who stay on their backsides eating our bread while we fight the Germans for them.'

I saw red. I grabbed the sobbing Nooka and, over the heads of the men standing next to me, pushed him towards the bunk. When the Russians tried to push him back I yelled on the top of my voice, 'If anyone of you touches my child, I'll smash his face with the buckle of my belt.' It was Nik's military belt which I wore on top of my coat and which I now took off. Only rage or despair could have made me do such a thing. While this was happening, the singing stopped and I could feel tension mounting. The mood of the crowd became menacing. Anything could happen.

To everyone's surprise the Russian in civilian clothes suddenly said, 'Get down comrades,' and the others picked up their bundles and slid down without a murmur, leaving Nooka on the bunk. I took a deep breath, wondering what would have happened if I had had to carry out my threat. Now the bunk was free for our people and the men nearest them rushed forward, but were stopped to let the women go first. About twenty people now occupied the space previously taken by four. Sixteen people less on the floor made quite a difference. It was decided that people would change every two hours so that as many as possible could have the chance to rest. The four Russians left the car at the next stop and did not reappear when the train started again. We wondered what had happened to them.

At last we could reach for our food and had enough to share with those on the bunk who had none. I keep a poignant reminder of that journey. My little pigskin suitcase. It still bears a deep scar as, pressed against the door, it was badly scratched at one of the stops. Although discoloured and deformed, it has a great sentimental value for me.

207

The singing resumed and sounded more vigorous than before. The unshaven gaunt faces seemed serene and calm as if the memory of the great misery and suffering of the past two years had been pushed aside to give place to new hope for the future.

After the night's journey we alighted at a stop and were surprised to meet the Russians who, we thought, had left the train altogether. They had spent the night on the platform of the guard's van and now looked very tired and frozen through. Seeing them in daylight I could not fail to notice the good looks and smart appearance of the man in civilian clothes. He had a kind of Caucasian, well fitted sheepskin coat, and a tall fur hat, called *papakha*, pulled slightly on one side of his head. He looked more like a Tsarist Guards officer than the modern Soviet man. When Nooka and I were returning to the car, he left his companions and came towards us. Not knowing what to expect after my outburst, I stiffened.

He raised his hand in a half salute and said, 'Madam, yesterday you were magnificent in your anger, just like a heroine in a romantic novel. I did not know that women like you still existed.' I wanted to go, but he stopped me. 'Please do not go away. Stay and listen to me. During the past night I have thought a great deal about you and the other people in the car. It was my first contact with foreigners and it was a kind of revelation to me. I had been watching people in the car for hours from my bunk and my impression was quite different from what I was brought up to believe and I must learn more while I can. Please let me travel the rest of the journey with you.'

I was stunned. That was the last thing I had expected to hear. 'It does not depend on me, I must ask the people in the car,' I replied. I told the others, who did not seem to mind.

'Let him come,' they said. 'The night in the cold has probably taught him some wisdom, but tell him if he starts offending us, we will throw him off the train.'

I felt there was no need to translate the whole of the message and the Russian joined us in the car. All the way to

Buzuluk he either talked about himself or asked questions. He said that, although he was a non-believer, he was deeply moved by the religious faith of the people, so clearly demonstrated in their singing. He was impressed and surprised by the friendliness and solidarity shown by men and women in the car towards each other, regardless of who they were. He soon realised that among them were soldiers of various ranks and civilians of different social standing.

Some of his questions seemed naive in the extreme, especially from a man who told us he held a university degree. Were the officers in capitalist countries cruel and did they hit soldiers with impunity for the slightest offence? Were workers extremely poor and badly exploited by their employers without the right of redress? Did the law courts discriminate between people of different social classes? Finally, he asked me to describe our regimental dances, reminding me very much of Alexei. If we could believe him, his encounter with Polish ex-prisoners had made a very strong impression on him. He had probably been quite satisfied with the world he lived in, but how would he feel from now on? However strange his behaviour so far, he surprised us even more when he said he would like to fight the Germans by joining the ranks of the Polish Army and asked to be introduced to the Polish C-in-C. The whole idea seemed so preposterous that no one believed he was serious and dismissed it lightly.

We knew that we were nearing Buzuluk and the excitement and tension became almost unbearable. Before the train came to a full stop the door was unbarred and slid open. An unbelievable and wonderful sight met our eyes. Men in the uniform of the Polish Army! Overcome by emotion and joy people started to jump out, but were soon stopped. The Soviet authorities had issued orders allowing only women and children to leave the train; all Polish men were to be diverted. Their reason given for this was the overcrowding of the Buzuluk camp. I was in a hurry to find the Soborski family, but the Russian passenger would not

209

leave my side, asking me to take him to the officer in charge. I looked round for help and, seeing a Polish lieutenant, handed the Russian over.

During the journey I had had only a glimpse of Mila, Maryla and the girls; our cars were quite far from each other and none of us dared leave them for longer than was absolutely necessary, fearing that the train would move off unexpectedly. We never knew whether it would stop for five minutes or an hour. Now we were reunited and I was very glad to see that Leszek had survived, apparently none the worse for the journey. Conditions in their cars had been much better than ours.

Passing the Polish lieutenant on our way to the truck which was to take us to the camp, I asked what had happened to the Russian and was told that his request had had to be refused as a Soviet citizen could not join the Polish Army. He had had to return to the train and I wondered what would happen to him in the end – doubtless his actions had not escaped the notice of his companions. Perhaps he would be sent into action at the first opportunity, distinguish himself in battle and die a glorious death. Just like a hero in a romantic novel! Still it would be a pity. He seemed such a nice man after all.

We were extremely lucky to have been on that particular train as it was the last one from which women and children were allowed to alight in Buzuluk. The later arrivals were turned away. Women and children arriving, like us, from the collective farms were sent to similar farms in the south of Asia where, at that time, even the native population was dying from famine and an epidemic of typhoid fever, the worst in the whole history of Russia. The fate of the men was even worse as they were redirected to the extreme north of Siberia and incarcerated again in labour camps. Very few people came out of these places alive.

On reaching the refugee camp in Buzuluk my first thought was to look for my husband. I asked the NCO escorting us whether anybody answering Nik's description was there. After a moment's hesitation he said that he thought there was an

210

officer of that name and rank in the camp. My heart jumped. Could it be true that I would find him there? I left our few belongings in Nooka's care on the bunk of the filthy, draughty and noisy barrack, and hurried to the camp's office where the register of occupants was kept, only to find that Nik was not recorded there. I was later told by the officer who gave me that information that I looked as if my life depended on his reply. He could not understand the reason for my extreme anxiety as only a couple of months had passed since the amnesty, and it was natural that time was needed before the p.o.w. camps could be disbanded. But he did not know of my dream about the row of graves, which had preyed on my mind even more since the realisation of my dream about the time of our departure from Novo-Troitsk. And then I recalled that one of the first people I had seen at the railway station in Buzuluk was a hunchback!

We tried to trace the four men whom we had taken under our wings in Magnai, but all our efforts were in vain. Although they had left before us, they never reached Buzuluk or any of the other Polish centres. Their train might have been sidetracked to give way to more important traffic. We were told that thousands of Poles released after the 'amnesty' were stranded for days or weeks at different stations, waiting for trains going in the right direction. In the extreme cold and without food and almost naked, thousands died. That was probably the tragic fate of our men.

The city of Buzuluk, situated in the Orenburg province, on the River Samara was founded in 1736 as a Russian fortress, and in 1941 became the headquarters of the Polish fighting force formed with Russia's agreement from former prisoners and deportees. This force was the beginning of the 2nd Corps of the Polish Army, which later distinguished itself in Tobruk and Monte Cassino.

In Buzuluk Nooka and I got separated from the rest of our small group. The two of us were allotted a place in a wooden building and the Soborskis in a brick one, more solidly built and therefore warmer, which was fortunate because of Leszek's fragile health. In the past, these buildings had been used as barracks for the local garrison.

In the first days after our arrival we had rain or sleet most of the time and the ground, which froze at night and slightly thawed during the day, soon turned into a horrible thick mud, made worse by people incessantly tramping through it. There were no beds in our barrack and people either slept on wooden planks, arranged in two tiers or on the bare floor. Being among the last arrivals we considered ourselves lucky to get a place on one of the bunks even though it was very near the outside door and felt the full blast of the wind every time the door was opened. Out of the people who shared our bunk I best remember two sisters both of them young and beautiful. They somehow managed to preserve their extremely elegant appearance and thus looked strangely out of place. On the bunk above us was a group of women, who turned out to be street walkers who had been rounded up and deported by the Russians. They used their own brand of very crude language, obviously enjoying the effect this had on the other women in the barrack, especially those who, like me, had children with them.

They lolled on the bunk with few clothes on, oblivious to the cold and in attitudes calculated to shock. Getting down from the bunk they tried to cause as much inconvenience as possible and, returning, they cleaned the mud from their shoes on the edge of our bunk, with obvious relish, and sent the rest of it down on our heads through the cracks between the boards. We soon noticed that in addition to dirt and particles of food we also received a quota of their lice. To prevent this we collected any pieces of material we could still find and, joining them together, formed a canopy over our heads.

We were issued with food three times a day. Tea and bread in the morning and soup, potatoes or cereals at midday and in the evening. There was no dining-room and, as food was distributed through a serving hatch opening into the yard, we had to queue for it outdoors, in the appalling weather. The cost of food was covered from the Polish funds deposited in

212

London. We also received a little pocket money from the same source. In Buzuluk we got our first taste of a typical refugee existence.

One of the saddest memories of Buzuluk camp was an epidemic of a particular virulent strain of Asiatic measles which invariably ended in pneumonia. It killed about eighty per cent of all little children there. By some miracle, Leszek escaped it.

At the beginning of November we were finally separated from the Soborski family who, together with other families with small children, were sent to the south of Kazakhstan to await evacuation from Russia. They were glad to leave, hoping that life in a warmer climate would be beneficial for Leszek's and Janka's health. As it turned out, the time spent there was to be the hardest of their exile due to famine and diseases.

Leszek died in the train on the way to the south, and Maryla had to hand his little body to strangers for burial at one of the stops. Those who witnessed the scene said that never in their lives had they seen such depth of despair on a human face and, even more tragically, not a sob or moan was heard. Such was Maryla!

Nooka and I were left to winter in Buzuluk. We lived through the frost which averaged −30°C and on occasions reached −50°. However without the strong wind and blizzards, which were normal in north Kazakhstan, it was much easier to bear.

In the hope of getting some kind of information about the p.o.w.s I went to the headquarters of the newly appointed C-in-C of the Polish Army, General W Anders. His office was situated outside the perimeter of the camp in a building which in the past must have belonged to a local bigwig and, although neglected, preserved traces of former elegance. There was a lot of activity in the building, and the sight of officers in Polish uniforms made my heart beat faster. Although still showing signs of their recent ordeal, they looked very different from the men I met on the train, yet it could not have been long since these same men exchanged their rags for uniforms.

I gave my name and the reason for my visit to one of the officers, and was received personally by General Anders. I had known him in Poland when he was the Commanding Officer of a cavalry regiment. It was ten years since I had last seen him. In the meantime, many tragedies had befallen us so it was a sad meeting. I learned that after the defeat of Poland by the Germans, he was captured by the Russians and kept in the notorious Lubyanka prison in Moscow. He must have recovered since as, in spite of a noticeable loss of weight and hair, he had not changed very much. He was a handsome man and his eyes retained some of their old sparkle.

The General received me in a most courteous and friendly manner, but in spite of that and of my pressing questions about the p.o.w.s he was strangely reluctant to give information, and I left his office with a very heavy heart.

What I did not know was that by then the fate of the Polish p.o.w.s was causing grave concern. It was known that there were altogether about 15,000 men in three camps, Kozelsk, Starobelsk and Ostashkov, but so far not one of them had reported in at any of the Polish recruiting centres. All official inquiries made by the British as well as Polish Governments in London were initially brushed-off by the Russians. Finally an explanation came. The p.o.w.s had been transferred to camps in the extreme north of Siberia and their evacuation had had to be postponed until the next spring, because of the severe winter conditions already existing when the news of the 'amnesty' arrived. Relying on that information the Polish Military Command organised expeditions to the various parts of Siberia, carrying supplies of food and medicines, but not a trace of the p.o.w. camps or of the individual men could be found.

On leaving General Anders' office I was met by the officer who had previously announced me to the General. He now stood by the door ready to escort me out. He was a Major, aged about 45. He had a long, aristocratic face and was tall

214

and lanky. While he walked by my side down the staircase, I felt his eyes fixed on me with puzzling intensity. Suddenly he put one hand on my shoulder to stop me from moving, and with the other hand carefully removed something from my temple. That something was a fat louse, which he then put on the nearest window sill and crushed with a box of matches without showing the slightest embarrassment. Seeing me blush, he gave me a reassuring almost paternal smile. That smile and the peculiar absurdity of the situation formed the beginning of my friendship with Major Strofski. He made me sit in a recess by the window and talk at length about Nooka and myself. When I described to him conditions in our barrack he insisted that we move out before one of us went down with typhus. I hesitated and, guessing that money might be one of the reasons for my hesitation, he produced his wallet, bursting at the seams with Soviet roubles.

'Look, I do not know what to do with these worthless pieces of paper. We are paid more than we need and there is nothing we can buy here except food on the black market. And how much can one spend on food, especially as we get our meals at the Officers' Mess? Please, let me help you. If you prefer, we can treat it as a loan.'

I said I would think it over and so I did, all through the night thus depriving myself of such little sleep as I could normally snatch. The proposition was most tempting particularly as since the Soborski's departure life in the camp seemed even worse than before, and there was nothing to keep us there. On the other hand, I had some scruples. It was no good pretending that I could borrow money with the hope of returning it, as there was very little left in my suitcase that I could sell on the black market in Buzuluk. The next morning, before I could reach any decision, a soldier came with a note from the Major, in which he said that he had spoken to two Russian women, teachers, who were willing to let me and my son live in their kitchen at a very low rent. He added that the kitchen was clean and warm, and that he would arrange for permission for the two of us to move out of the camp. I read the note to Nooka and the look in his eyes at the mention of a clean and warm room was enough to make me forget all my scruples.

We moved the same afternoon. The room was large, bright and spotlessly clean. There was a stove, which radiated delightful warmth, a bed that Nooka and I could share, and a table on which he could do his lessons. The owners occupied the adjacent room, the only access to which was through the kitchen, which they used for preparing their meals. This was a familiar situation and, after the life in the barracks, seemed the fulfilment of our dream for privacy. The only disadvantage was that the place was some distance from the camp and so by the time we brought the food from there, it was stone cold. However that problem was solved with the miraculous appearance not only of a primus but also of fuel for it.

Very soon we met other Polish people living outside the camp, and it was amazing how quickly a semblance of normal life was created with lectures, concerts and variety shows held in Polish Army headquarters. These were organised by a group of Polish actors who, happening to be on tour in Russia when the war started, were stranded there, and now flocked to Buzuluk to be under the protection of the Polish Army.

I remember particularly well our traditional Christmas celebrations in Buzuluk, but no words of mine could describe the feeling of elation and bewilderment at participating in the Midnight Mass and later sharing the Holy Wafer with our own free men and women. Many felt as if they had been resurrected from the dead.

I never forgot how much we owed to Major Strofski for changing our life in Buzuluk. His boundless devotion to us was something that I could not easily understand. It never wavered and was completely selfless. We both grew very fond of him, but there was nothing we could do in return for his kindness, and he never seemed to want or expect anything. He came to see us almost every day, accompanied me to social functions at the headquarters, if I wanted or, if not, stayed with Nooka reading books with him or playing cards or draughts. Almost every day he sent his batman with some food for us and for our landladies, who naturally adored him for it.

So it came as a terrible blow when, soon after Christmas, I was called to the office of the Camp Commander and told to stop seeing the Major. No explanation was given except that the demand had to be obeyed and treated as strictly confidential. I came back in a state of shock. What could the Major have done to deserve such treatment? I was under the impression that he was still working in the Headquarters and so could not have been guilty of any crime, and yet a deep shadow was cast on his character. At first I even suspected a simple male jealousy, but quickly dismissed it: there had not yet been enough time for our men to experience such basic feelings. There must have been a reason and ahead of me was the task of conveying the message to the Major without hurting his feelings too much. When the moment came I found the most trivial reason I could think of, my reputation. He pretended that he believed me. Only Nooka, not understanding my behaviour, gave me a painfully reproachful look.

It was only natural that we both missed the Major's company very much, but the crunch came when we both went down with a particularly nasty 'flu. We suffered from very high temperatures and a killing headache and sharing the same bed did not help. Nooka threw himself all over the bed and, exhausted by fever and lack of sleep, I became so shaky that getting up for a drink of water seemed too great an effort. Our landladies kept away from us probably from fear of catching an infection and I was gradually reaching the bottom of despair.

However before that was allowed to happen in came our Guardian-Angel bringing with him a doctor. At the sight of them I could hardly hold back my tears. We had been ill for several days and although our meals remained uncollected in the camp kitchen no one noticed our absence. The Major was our only real friend and I was determined not to push him

217

away now. By chance he met one of our landladies and learned from her about our illness. With the doctor's help and thanks to our strong constitutions we were gradually restored to health. The Major assigned his batman to look after us, and we were given innumerable cups of tea and, when we recovered enough to face food, chicken broth and other nourishing food. The Major, remembering our last conversation only seldom came to see how we were progressing. I became more and more determined to disregard the ban, as soon as I was well enough to return to normal life.

I had hardly got back on my feet when another summons came from the Commandant for me to report to his office. 'I understand Major Strofski is visiting you again. For your own and your child's good I am asking you to break your friendship with the Major. Otherwise we shall not be responsible for your safety.' That was all, but this time I could sense the seriousness of the situation, however incomprehensible it seemed. After that I never saw the Major again. He disappeared from Buzuluk, like so many others under Stalin's rule.

Winter in Buzuluk dragged on, but there was spring in our hearts as we knew that it would not be long before we left Russia for good. Our road to freedom was to run either through Persia or Afghanistan as the war closed all the other routes of escape.

Nooka and I left Buzuluk with a group of people going to Persia. The journey proceeded in stages and our next stopping place was in Yangiyul, a town in the Uzbekistan Soviet Republic. Situated in the middle of the Tashkent oasis, Yangiyul seemed like a paradise to people deprived of vitamins for long periods of time, and dreaming of a warmer climate. Here, at last, was an abundance of dried fruit and vegetables and the air was very mild. A rivulet running by the side of the camp was free of ice and the fruit trees looked beautiful covered with a profusion of delicately tinted blossom. Food in the camp was infinitely better than in

Buzuluk, especially as it could be washed down with quite good and cheap local wine. By selling our warm clothes which, I hoped, would not be needed any more, I was able to raise enough money to pay for private accommodation for the two of us and for any additional food we wanted. I had been asked to contribute to the information service and the educational activities of the camp, and that made life there much more purposeful and interesting. So much so that when the time came for the next stage of our journey, which was to take us to Krasnovodsk, the Russian port on the Caspian Sea, I debated whether to leave then or to wait until the next transport. After a short hesitation I decided to leave with the first group and, with that decision, probably saved both our lives.

We travelled to Krasnovodsk by train and from there an incredibly crammed boat took us to the Persian port of Pahlevi, where we had to undergo quarantine and be vaccinated and deloused. There were already many hundreds of Polish people in the camp and the dismal sight that most of them presented marred our joy at finding ourselves outside the Soviet borders. Victims of pellagra, a wasting disease caused by prolonged and severe malnutrition, they looked more like living ghosts than humans, and in the days that followed we witnessed many funeral processions. Especially tragic was the sight of the children affected by the same disease. Most of them were so-called orphans although, in fact, they were separated from their parents either at the time of deportation or later. Left to fend for themselves or shut in Soviet orphanages, they were rescued after the amnesty by Polish Delegates. For many of them that rescue came too late.

After the end of the quarantine period those of us that were fit to travel further were taken by truck to the refugee camp in Tehran. Of that journey I remember the breathtaking, springtime beauty of the narrow mountainous valleys, the hair raising speed and abandon of Persian drivers and the kindness and generosity of the Persian peasants, who came to the side of the road whenever we stopped, to greet us not only with warm smiles but with food and wine as well. But most of all I remember that wonderful, wonderful feeling of being free at last!

We arrived in Tehran in April 1942 and when the next group of people arrived from Yangiyul I learned that soon after my departure a warrant was issued for my arrest. It was signed by no less a person than Commissar Vyshinskiy, a deputy Foreign Minister and ex-Chief Public Prosecutor of the Soviet Union. No one knew what they wanted me for and no one could have saved me. The majority were of the opinion that the warrant was the result of my friendship with Major Strofski. I could never find out who Major Strofski was, what had happened to him and in what activities, if any, he was involved. For Nooka and me he could never be anything else but a very dear and noble friend.

While Nooka and I were comforted by the news of our narrow escape from grave danger, the other news was alarming and tragic. One of the worst was the discovery by the Germans advancing into Russia of the mass graves of the Polish p.o.w.s from Kozelsk massacred by the Russians in the Katyn forest. Not only was it a terrible blow to all of us, it had also far reaching repercussions for the Polish people who were still inside Russia. When the Polish Government in London demanded an independent inquiry into the murders, the Soviet Government not only refused but broke off diplomatic relations and stopped all further evacuation of Polish people from Russia. For them it was the labour camps and *kolkhozes* once again. All relief centres set up by the Polish Embassy for the distribution of medicine, food and uniforms were ordered to close, although their supplies came from England via Archangel in Russia and Ashabad in India, and not from Russia. Several of the delegates administering these centres were arrested. There were still 50,000 ill and starving children left in Russia but, in spite of intervention from the British and American ambassadors and requests from the International Red Cross who offered

220

to take upon themselves their welfare, they were refused permission to leave.

My husband's body was found in the mass grave among thousands of other Katyn victims.

Epilogue

Nooka and I were reunited with the four remaining members of the Soborski family – Mila, Maryla, Halina and Janka – in Tehran where they arrived, four months later, by a different route. Our joy at seeing them safe was marred only by the news of Leszek's death during the journey. The fact that he survived the lethal epidemic of measles in Buzuluk made his death more poignant. Like us, they were fortunate enough to get out of Russia before the release of Polish people was stopped. From Buzuluk they had gone to the Uzbekistan Soviet Republic in the South of Asia, where they suffered terribly only miraculously surviving starvation and an epidemic of typhus and typhoid fever, from which people were dying in their thousands.

Initially we all stayed in a refugee camp in Tehran, but soon we had to part again as the Soborskis were placed on the list of people to be repatriated from Persia to India. Nooka and I were to remain in Tehran as I was working at the Polish Headquarters as an editor of the Polish weekly *Zew*. However we did not stay at the camp for long as I got a new employment as a secretary and Russian translator at the British Military Headquarters. There was a great demand for people with a sound knowledge of Russian, as Persia, not actively involved in war, was divided into two military zones: the North was under the Russian and the South was under the British (and later American) Command. All correspondence

222

had to be in English and Russian. Persia in 1942 was a very important artery through which war supplies went to Russia, with Tehran as a venue for meetings between representatives of the Allied and Soviet Forces. As an interpreter I had frequent contact with high ranking Russian officers, which I did not relish, as it constantly reminded me of our recent ordeal and of the proximity of their country to Persia. So, at the first opportunity I applied for a transfer to India (according to my Siberian dream my fate anyway!).

In April 1944 Nooka and I left Tehran for a little town near the Persian Gulf. It was one of the hottest and most unpleasant places in the world with the river infested with Gavials (long snouted Asian crocodiles) and the surrounding country with German parachutists, who were kept in hiding and supported by their numerous Persian sympathisers. During the long wait for the ship to take us to India, I accepted a job as a secretary to the Head of a much overworked British Intelligence Service. Nooka instead of going to India was recruited by the Polish Junior Cadet Corps and transferred to their school in Palestine. So sadly we had to part.

On arrival in India I spent three agonising months in the heat and dust of a very primitive transit camp for Polish refugees in Karachi. Moving to Bombay meant to me a return to civilisation. I held two posts there one at the Polish Welfare Office and the other one at the Polish Consulate. From time to time I also contributed to our weekly newspaper *Polak w Indiach* (Pole in India). In 1945 I represented Poland (in exile) at the P.E.N. Conference in Jaipur, which was very exciting as apart from seeing that fascinating city, I had an opportunity of meeting many outstanding personalities, among others Pandit Nehru and his young daughter Indira.

I left India in December 1946, as that country's newly proclaimed independence brought fundamental changes into the life of the Polish community there. With the recognition by India of the new Polish Communist Government all existing Polish institutions were closed down and we had to consider the options open to us: either to return to Poland or to remain abroad settling in countries willing to accept us. We all realised that the present Poland was not the free and independent country of our dreams, but to all intents and purposes, a Soviet satellite. Soborski's house and nursery in Stanislavov, and our house in Wilno and Yaremche were now lost for ever as the Soviet Union had annexed the Eastern part of Poland. Our life was in ruins and we had to start rebuilding it from scratch. The Soborskis finally decided to go back to Poland, but I couldn't face subjecting my son and myself to the Soviet rule again. I opted to stay abroad. The main reason for the Soborskis decision was the fact that they had still many relatives in Poland, and news had also reached them that Maryla's husband was waiting for her there. After his escape to Romania he had been interned by the Romanians only to have the misfortune of being 'liberated' by the Russians, towards the end of the war. On his return to Poland he was given a good administrative job, but was soon accused of anti-Soviet activities in pre-war Poland, and sentenced to eight years imprisonment. Maryla, with the rest of the family, sat through an excrutiating show-trial to which he was subjected. The prison was a long way away from their home and Maryla, who was allowed to visit her husband once a week on Sundays for the whole of those eight years travelled by night train to see him the next day for just a few minutes and then travelled home again during the night to be at her office the following morning. When finally released, her husband was found to be suffering from an advanced form of cancer, and soon afterwards died in her arms. So poor Maryla suffered yet another tragedy in her life. As to Mila, she never discovered what happened to her husband except for the news that he had been in the POW camp at Ostashkov, from where no one had ever been known to come out alive.

Russia's 'compensation' for the seized Polish lands were the territories lying to the West from the pre-war borders and previously belonging to Germany, with the result that Poland now occupied a much smaller area than before the 1939 war.

In addition these new territories suffered very severe damage in the last stages of the war when the Germans fought fierce battles resisting the Russian advance westwards. Some towns like Wroclaw (previously Breslau) were almost razed to the ground and had to be completely rebuilt by the Poles after the war. On these uncleared battlefields the previous inhabitants of Eastern Poland, were resettled and after their return, the Soborski family, were sent there too. Nella and her family were also sent there. Both Mila and Maryla are now dead. Halina, Janka and Nella together with her family still live in Poland.

My first meeting with my son, after five years' separation, took place in Palestine. I left Bombay and secured a residential permit and a job in Lebanon at the Brazilian Legation in Beirut, in order to be as near him as possible. From Beirut, I was able to visit my son and we could spend a holiday together in Lebanon before parting again for a short time. He, with the Polish Junior Cadet Corps, was transferred to England in 1948 and I followed soon afterwards.

We now both live in London, he with his wife and two daughters and I with my English husband.

With England as our home came the final fulfilment of my prophetic dream: Kazakhstan –India – England.

The nightmarish experience of 13th April 1940 and the tragic consequences of the Soviet invasion can never be forgotten or forgiven. And the nagging thought remains: Will those responsible for these atrocious crimes pay for what they did or will the account remain unsettled for ever?